SAVVY INVESTING *for Women*

STRATEGIES FROM A SELF-MADE WALL STREET MILLIONAIRE

MARLENE JUPITER

Foreword by Elizabeth A. Tuttle, Senior Vice President and Treasurer of IT&T Corporation

Dear Abby,

Get started and make billions.

Best wishes,
Marlene Jupiter

PRENTICE HALL PRESS
Paramus, New Jersey 07652

Library of Congress Cataloging-in-Publication Data

Jupiter, Marlene.
  Savvy investing for women : strategies from a self-made Wall
Street millionaire / Marlene Jupiter.
      p. cm.
  Includes index.
  ISBN 0-7352-0003-3
    1. Investments—United States—Handbooks, manuals, etc. 2. Women—
United States—Finance, Personal—Handbooks, manuals, etc.
  I. Title.
  HG4527.J87 1998
  332.6—dc21   97-36471
                                             CIP

This publication is designed to provide accurate and authoritative information in
regard to the subject matter covered. It is sold with the understanding that the
publisher is not engaged in rendering legal, accounting, or other professional service.
If legal advice or other expert assistance is required, the services of a competent
professional person should be sought.

> —*From the Declaration of Principles jointly adopted by a Committee of the American*
> *Bar Association and a Committee of Publishers and Associations.*

Printed in the United States of America

10 9 8 7 6 5 4 3 2 1   *10 9 8 7 6 5 4 3 2 1*

ISBN 0-7352-0003-3   ISBN 0-7352-0080-7 PBK

ATTENTION: CORPORATIONS AND SCHOOLS

Prentice Hall Press books are available at quantity discounts with bulk purchase for
educational, business, or sales promotional use. For information, please write to:
Prentice Hall Press Special Sales, 240 Frisch Court, Paramus, New Jersey 07652.
Please supply: title of book, ISBN, quantity, how the book will be used, date needed.

 PRENTICE HALL PRESS
Paramus, NJ 07652
A Simon & Schuster Company

On the World Wide Web at http://www.phdirect.com

Prentice Hall International (UK) Limited, *London*
Prentice Hall of Australia Pty. Limited, *Sydney*
Prentice Hall Canada, Inc., *Toronto*
Prentice Hall Hispanoamericana, S.A., *Mexico*
Prentice Hall of India Private Limited, *New Delhi*
Prentice Hall of Japan, Inc., *Tokyo*
Simon & Schuster Asia Pte. Ltd., *Singapore*
Editora Prentice Hall do Brasil, Ltda., *Rio de Janeiro*

To my mother,
   for teaching me that I could travel the world through books.
To my father,
   for believing his little girl was as smart as any little boy.

ACKNOWLEDGMENTS

I thank all of the individuals who have added their expertise and time to this book: Ralph Acampora, Marcia Beck, Allan Berke, Jessica Bibliowicz, Jasmine Bilali, Jacqueline Cable, Greg Calejo, Lily Cates, Wilhelmina McEwan Combs, Jane Freeman, Fran Janis, Larry Gallus, Joe Knight, Nicole Kubin, Maren Lindstrom, Kim Purvis, Inge Reichenbach, Kurt Seidman, Art Spinner, and Alberto Vilar.

My dream has always been to be a writer. Many people have truly supported me through the highs and lows of trying to get published. They have given me spirit to keep trying. I sincerely thank all of you for keeping my dream alive: Salman Al Saud, Nancy Hall-Arno, Elizabeth Besen, Scott Bessent, Marwa Hammad-Bitar, Austin Burrell, Ludwig Dellova, Steven Eckhaus, Debbie Fiss, Leslie Klass Fridman, Hank Gioella, Carla Grillo, Janet Haimson, Melanie Hague, Lynne Hendel, Jay Hohmann, Claire Kinsella, Cynthia Medric, Janine Mejeur, Marilyn Modlin, Donald Ohlmeyer, Jr., Randye Ringler, Mort Rosenthal, Eleanor Eckhaus-Roth, Sana Sabbagh, Frank Scala, Gail Silberman, Elizabeth A. Tuttle, Steven Weber, Gordon Batinkoff-Winston, and Jane Wyeth.

There are three people who deserve special thanks, for they are truly an integral part of this book. Peter Tanous, for his direction and expertise, David Stine for his creative insight and assistance in shaping the manuscript, and my editor, Ellen Schneid Coleman, for her support and excellent editorial skills.

CONTENTS

Acknowledgments   *iv*

Foreword   *vii*

Introduction   *ix*

Chapter 1   Financial Basics Every Woman Needs to Know   *1*

Chapter 2   Don't Put All Your Eggs in One Basket   *19*

Chapter 3   Shopping for Stocks   *41*

Chapter 4   How to Pick Winners—and Avoid the Losers   *67*

Chapter 5   Who Needs Charts? You Do! A Beginner's Guide to Technical Analysis   *97*

Chapter 6   Safety First: "Worry-Free" Investment Tools   *119*

Chapter 7   Lending Your Money to the Big Boys: Buying Bonds   *137*

Chapter 8   Shopping Around for Mutual Funds   *159*

Chapter 9   Playing for Bigger Stakes: The High-Rollers Club   *193*

Chapter 10   Choosing an Investment Advisor   *219*

Chapter 11   Con Artists and How to Avoid Them   *235*

Chapter 12   Learning to Live with Risk: No Guts, No Wealth!
              249

Chapter 13   Your Money *and* Your Life   *261*

Chapter 14   How You Can Be Rich, Too!   *293*

Chapter 15   When You're Rich: Investing in Horses, Art, and
              Jewelry   *313*

Index   *331*

FOREWORD

Marlene Jupiter and I graduated from Cornell University in the late seventies. We did not become friends until we participated as members of an organization formed to enhance the role of women alumni, students, and faculty at our alma mater. By that time, we had both been working in the male-dominated world of Wall Street for over ten years, and had successfully managed to overcome similar obstacles while pursuing our respective careers.

As pioneers in a relatively new arena for women, Marlene and I feel strongly committed to enhancing the experience for the next generation. Furthermore, we believe women who have achieved a degree of financial success have the responsibility to share knowledge that will help others attain economic freedom. I was delighted to learn that Marlene was writing a book with these objectives in mind, and urged her to let me be among the first to read the completed manuscript. By the time an advance copy of *Savvy Investing for Women* finally landed on my desk, however, I had just survived a period of many months during which I'd been hopelessly inundated with financial models. The very last thing I wanted to peruse was a book on investments!

Much to my surprise, Marlene's book does not read like other financial handbooks. Instead, its messages are animated, filled with historical anecdotes, thought-provoking interviews, and personal stories. By explaining financial terms in a "user-friendly" format, Marlene makes the often intimidating world of Wall Street easy enough for any novice to understand. She takes her readers on a journey that begins with a discussion of basic economics, then transits easily through detailed explanations of some of the most exotic investments available in the marketplace.

I am reminded of a recent article by Scott Adams, creator of the Dilbert cartoon character, in the business section of *The New York Times*. Mr. Adams noted that his "only disappointment is with the professionals who are managing half his money. He manages the other half, and he is beating them hands down simply by investing in mutual funds with good track records and a few of Warren Buffett's favorite stocks."

The truth is that the knack of making prudent investments doesn't require a Ph.D. in Finance. All you really need is a good teacher with your best interest at heart, someone to explain the basic concepts in simple terms. Being financially astute is not as difficult as most of us are led to believe. Nor are well-educated consumers in the interest of most Wall Street salespersons who are compensated based on commissions rather than the quality of the investment advice offered.

By writing *Savvy Investment for Woman,* Marlene Jupiter has accomplished the all-but-impossible: She has actually infused the process of learning about investments and the mechanics of Wall Street with a sense of fun! Marlene has used her witty style, knowledge, and personal experience to create a financial book that reads like fiction. For example, she makes the analysis of a major corporation's financial statements as easy to comprehend as (literally) running a lemonade stand. Marlene proceeds to decipher the complexities of the mutual fund industry, and does so in a simple yet comprehensive chapter that's easy enough for a child to understand. She even turns the boring subject of cash management into a fascinating page-turner, by interweaving the story of how J. P. Morgan intervened to relieve the devastating bank panic of 1907 that nearly crippled the American economy.

Marlene not only gives us a working knowledge of financial instruments such as stocks, bonds, cash, emerging markets, hedge funds, venture capital, and private equity, but provides her readers with important legal advice relating to issues such as marriage, divorce, and inheritance. She also helps us understand the simple principles of saving for college tuition, purchasing a home, and planning for a comfortable retirement.

Importantly, Marlene encourages an increased sense of empowerment for women by relating a number of stories about dreamers who managed to crystallize their dreams into reality. As she so often reminds us, the present is the point of power. I wish each of you success in building the sort of financial world in which your fondest dreams can come true.

ELIZABETH A. TUTTLE

INTRODUCTION

Women control roughly 55% of America's wealth, yet they are tragically vulnerable when it comes to making important investment decisions. All it takes is one piece of bad advice to wipe out an investor's entire life savings in a matter of months, weeks, or perhaps *minutes*. The sad truth is that any woman brave enough to tread on Wall Street turf is much more likely to fall prey to a fast-talking broker than be counseled by a seasoned and ethical money manager. It's therefore imperative to thoroughly acquaint yourself with the wide assortment of financial instruments available in the marketplace *before* sitting down for an initial consultation. Let's face facts: Brokers work on a commission and/or bonus basis, and they all too often place their personal economic interests before yours.

Frankly, a female novice at investing puts herself at the mercy of nothing more than a well-dressed salesperson. An unscrupulous broker couldn't care less, for example, if the gas/oil partnership literally *goes up in flames* the very next business day after he invests your money in it. Why? Because his hefty commission check has already cleared at the bank.

Intelligent money management requires careful research and planning. If "knowledge is power," then *Savvy Investing for Women* empowers each of us women in what is still decidedly a man's world. Women are victimized by crooked automobile mechanics far more often than men are, and the same is true for women in their dealings with the male "mechanics" who control Wall Street. A broker may flash a million-dollar smile and pledge to put the very best financial vehicles to work for you, but is just as likely to "fix your wagon" in the worst possible way. Think about it: How did he pay for that million-dollar smile? Should you ever have the misfortune to come up against a Wall Street wheeler-dealer, this book will have taught you how to keep him from grinning at your expense.

While many ethical men (and women) on Wall Street can be trusted to offer sound advice, the Street also abounds with "grim reapers" in all-too-human form. Such real-life monsters regard women as the easiest of all prey, and have no qualms about selling us every share of the most worthless "lemons" on their computer screens. Rarely does a day go by without a first-time investor losing an entire fortune at the hands of such unscrupulous characters. Recently widowed women are particularly vulnerable during their time of bereavement. Would it surprise you to know that brokers in almost every city in the country read the daily obituaries, and then "go in for the kill" within hours of the funeral—all the while expressing seemingly *genuine* sympathy?

Most investors find it impossible to tell the "good guys" from the "bad guys." Wall Street's dress code doesn't require its cast of characters to wear white or black hats. (What a wonderful world that would be.) Not to worry: The subject of "Con Artists and How to Avoid Them" gets its own chapter in this book. These days, no woman can afford to take a life-or-death gamble with her financial security. Should any of you ever feel that you're being pressured into an investment, the chances are good that it's a *bad* investment. No matter what the slicker-than-slick salesperson tells you, there is no such thing as a "last chance to get rich quick." Promises of going from rags to riches, if believed, will almost invariably keep you in *rags*.

I can speak with authority about the plight of women in the world of investments because I have spent the past 19 years in the financial industry. During those 19 years, I have worked in a Wall Street trading room occupied by hundreds of men in three-piece suits, but precious few women. Sad to say, the male/female ratio of "registered reps" (legally authorized stockbrokers) on Wall Street has improved only slightly over the years. Ironically, my own career in the financial industry has centered primarily on the "hedge fund" market (among the riskiest of all investments), despite my lifelong tendency to be risk-averse with my own personal finances.

In fact, when asked to define the word *money,* I invariably respond, "vehicle of freedom." (And I have never been much of a gambler when it comes to freedom.) Yet I freely confess to having been extremely naive about how the financial industry operated when I first dared to invest my own money in the marketplace.

Looking back on those years with 20/20 hindsight, I now know that my initial conservatism prevented me from taking higher risks and reaping substantially greater rewards in the long run. Like most women, I had become so socialized to avoid any sort of risk-taking that it had become ingrained in my psychological framework.

The underlying problem is that, historically, women have been put at a disadvantage by being deprived of an adequate education in financial matters. We've been led to believe that "the man of the house" should take charge of both short-term and long-range financial planning. As we approach the twenty-first century, the time has clearly come for women to take on a more active role in investing. For a married couple, two minds are better than one when it comes to planning for a secure financial future. If you happen to be single, divorced, or widowed, such decisions are yours and yours alone to make.

Savvy Investing for Women helps you overcome the disadvantage of inadequate financial training. It enables you to understand all the financial tools at your disposal. It challenges you to decide which risk/reward ratio is best for you. And it empowers you to take appropriate action. Should your seemingly well-intentioned broker phone to pitch a stock that's "100% sure to be the next Microsoft," what should you do? If you do anything, please don't "bet the whole farm" on it. To put it bluntly, the chances are infinitely greater that your stock certificates will be worth no more than cheap wallpaper a year later.

What action should you take? Again, only *you* can answer that question. The key is to acquaint yourself thoroughly with the nuts and bolts of investing before sinking your hard-earned cash into *any* investment. Don't be smooth-talked. Understand the investment fully.

Regardless of your age, you really must start planning your financial future *now.* Why the urgency? The U.S. government daily proves itself less and less capable of ensuring the future social security and Medicare benefits for baby boomers like myself—and everyone else. We therefore must take full responsibility for our *own* financial fate. Both women and men must prepare to cope with what's sure to be a vast array of mind-boggling challenges as we enter the twenty-first century. One of the greatest challenges of all will obviously be financial: At this writing, the median income for a woman over the age of 65 in the United States is approximately

$9,000, while their male counterparts fare only slightly better. So start as small as you like in saving for your future, *but get started!* You will not only be on your way to a comfortable retirement, but you'll also be safeguarding the futures of your children, grandchildren, and loved ones.

Wouldn't it be wonderful if *you* could be assured of a comfortable lifestyle in retirement? You can. All it takes is proper financial planning as far in advance as possible. *Savvy Investing for Women* promises to get you off to the best possible start by teaching you the basic rules of the game in a simple and straightforward fashion. Each of us can be a winner at the investment game. But I'll warn you right now that the very *best* investments (like the elusive "next Microsoft") are inevitably offered to the "highest rollers" at the table long before individual investors—everyday folk like you and me—ever know about them. What you need to do is to put what you learn from these pages to good use. Here are some basic start-up rules:

- **Rule Number One:** *Each investor is different.* The style of investment you choose should fit your needs and expectations rather than satisfy the whim of your broker to buy another Mercedes Benz or six-bedroom house in the Hamptons. *Never* write a check for an investment without a thorough understanding of the investment. Should any salesperson (male or female) fail to provide all the information you require about an investment's risks and rewards, walk out of the office. For that matter, beware of the male broker who uses phrases smacking of sexism, such as, "Oh, you wouldn't understand the flow charts, but I only work with clients who give me their complete trust." *Slam the door behind you just as **hard** as you possibly can!*

- **Rule Number Two:** *To reap significant financial gain, you must accept some element of risk.* The higher the reward you shoot for, the greater the risk you must take. While playing it "safe" with financial assets may be appropriate for the more conservative among us, "safe" seldom leads to any real wealth. This poses a dilemma, to be sure, but you can find the right solution by carefully examining your own heart and mind—*not* by putting blind faith and trust in others to make investment decisions for you.

- **Rule Number Three:** *Only* you *can determine the balance between risk and reward that's right for* you. Once you know your own financial goals and level of risk tolerance, all that's left is to learn a few basic rules of the Wall Street "game" that make up the rest of this book. A thorough overview of the financial industry enables you to formulate the optimum risk/reward strategy to achieve whatever eventual monetary security you desire.

- **Rule Number Four:** *Every investor makes mistakes—myself included.* But you must *learn* from each negative experience. The "trial and error" process can be painful at times, both financially and psychologically. That's why first-time investors should seek the best "preventative medicine" on the shelf long before putting every dime in the bank at stake. My sincere hope is that *Savvy Investing for Women* is "just what the doctor ordered" and that you will learn how to become (and remain) financially healthy for the rest of your life.

Savvy Investing for Women will teach you everything you need to know about the current financial marketplace. You'll learn why some investments can often be "gold mines," while other apparent mother lodes of wealth are nothing more than "loaded minefields." Once you know how to tell the difference between the two, you're certain to prosper—while at the same time always getting a *good night's sleep!*

chapter 1

FINANCIAL BASICS EVERY WOMAN NEEDS TO KNOW

Workers in the financial industry have long referred to America's all-time greatest investment gurus as "the wizards of Wall Street." This distinguished group of the Street's most valuable players includes the likes of Cornelius Vanderbilt, J. P. Morgan, and Joseph Kennedy. These men were so extraordinarily rich and successful that they became household names the world over. What most people don't know, however, is that a remarkable nineteenth-century woman named Hetty Robinson Green also became a major force in the financial marketplace. Since the New York Stock Exchange was established in 1792, countless investment "wizards" have arisen, but only one bona fide "witch of Wall Street."

Lessons from America's First Female Investment Guru

By 1900, Hetty had amassed a fortune in excess of $100 million, a sum that would translate into well more than $1.5 billion in present-day currency. Regarded as the single richest woman on the planet, sadly she often used her incredible wealth to destroy her financial or personal enemies.

Hetty was born in 1834 in New Bedford, Massachusetts to Abby Slocum Howland and Edward Mott Robinson. Her maternal grandfather, Gideon Howland, was a self-made man who earned his fortune in the shipping and whaling industries. Howland became rich thanks to the great demand for whale oil, used to fuel nineteenth-century lanterns—the most modern source of light at the time.

Edward eventually took over the family business, but fate held something infinitely more exciting in store for Hetty than a career in whale blubber.

Had the elderly Mr. Howland not lost his sight, however, Hetty might never have developed an interest in investing. "Gramps" loved nothing more than to have his granddaughter read aloud from the daily newspaper. He particularly enjoyed staying abreast of all the financial news. The six-year-old immediately became fascinated with the world of economics, and the die was irrevocably cast. Hetty was destined to become a rich and powerful Wall Street player and say goodbye to the "blubber biz" for good.

Granted, Hetty had a healthy head start: when her father passed away in 1865, he left his 31-year-old daughter a cool $1 million in cash, as well as a trust fund from which she would receive interest on an additional $1 million. She immediately began to invest her inheritance with a view toward making her money work for her. The young heiress's initial investment strategies centered on a wide variety of real estate ventures, railroads, and lending funds. It's ironic that although during her era Hetty was one of the largest lenders to the burgeoning City of New York, she resided in Hoboken to avoid paying the Manhattan "wealth tax" of her day. Never a spendthrift, the eccentric millionairess managed to turn ordinary penny pinching into a high art.

Hetty's one and only marriage (in 1867) was to Edward H. Green, a millionaire in his own right. Green's talent for heavy speculation would lead to his eventual downfall; he somehow managed to "leverage" himself out of a fortune. But Green then made an even worse mistake. He used his wife's collateral to get a loan from the bank where she kept all her money, *without* bothering to ask her permission. The moment Hetty found out that her personal bankers, John J. Cisco and Son, had lent her money directly to Green, Hetty said goodbye to both bank *and* husband. Hetty immediately demanded full return of the sum in question and the bank, rather stupidly, refused her request. Mrs. Green promptly removed every cent she had in her accounts, which amounted to more than $25 million. (That equates to something like $375 million in today's dollars.) Needless to say, her husband went bankrupt in no time, as did John J. Cisco and Son.

The $25 million in cash and securities withdrawn from Cisco went straight into the vaults of Chemical National Bank in lower Manhattan, as did all of Hetty's personal belongings. The word *frugal* is perhaps a bit too kind when used to describe Mrs. Green. The fact is, Hetty conducted all her financial dealings for the next quarter century from a rent-free "office" of sorts near a particular staircase in Chemical's lobby, while squatting on the bank's rock-hard floor.

As she amassed more wealth by investing in stocks, municipal bonds, and real estate holdings, Hetty became increasingly unwilling to spend money on herself. In fact, she became what can only be described as a "billion-dollar bag lady." She let her clothes remain soiled and tattered, rather than pay the pittance it would have cost to have them cleaned, repaired, or (perish the thought) replaced. It gets worse: according to one reliable source, Hetty and her driver once spent an entire evening searching for two cents she'd managed to lose in the coach!

Yet let's give credit where it's due: the eccentric Mrs. Green possessed a number of highly commendable attributes that make for a truly great investor. Hetty wasn't merely good with numbers: she had an uncanny ability to analyze current events and trends. An expert at taking calculated financial risks, Hetty understood the Industrial Revolution and was willing to invest in America's future. She also had a great deal of patience, often using her money to back what looked to others like losing propositions.

When asked for advice on how to invest wisely, however, the world's wealthiest woman typically dismissed the question with a shrug. "There is no great secret to fortune making," insisted Hetty. "All you have to do is buy cheap and sell dear, act with thrift and shrewdness, and be persistent." (A bit too modestly stated, don't you agree?) In 1916, when she finally cashed in her chips at the age of 81, Hetty Robinson Green was one incredibly rich "witch."

I can't stress sufficiently the importance of following current trends in the marketplace. A great many parallels can be drawn between the Industrial Revolution of Hetty's era and the Information Revolution of today. The same methods that worked so well for Hetty in her day can work equally well for you in the here and now.

Technological advances in the computer industry over the past 25 years have completely changed the lives of each person on the face of the planet. Were Hetty Robinson Green in our midst today, she would no doubt be sitting on the floor of Chemical Bank, trading heavily in stocks such as Cisco Systems (no relation to her former bank), Intel, and Microsoft. Her "woman's intuition" would still be whispering advice about which direction America was heading, both philosophically and financially, and Hetty would be playing her hunches for all they were worth.

I don't recommend that you become some sort of "stock market junkie" or spend endless hours perusing annual reports (nor do I suggest that you live as frugally as Hetty did), but today's women simply *must* become educated in the fundamentals of making sound investments if we want to enjoy any sort of comfortable lifestyle, especially through our retirement years. It's really no more difficult than learning your ABCs. Very few of us will ever become as wealthy as Hetty, but once we know our ABCs we at least have a chance to achieve financial security.

My father has always been fond of saying, "A fool and his money are soon parted." Over the years, I've seen countless wise men (and women) accumulate great fortunes, only to turn into total "fools" and lose every cent in the end. In order to make money *and* keep it, the minimum requirement is a little homework.

Getting Down to Economic Basics

Always spend whatever time you need to understand a particular investment fully before you write a check and hand it to your broker or financial advisor. Don't believe everything you're told, even if you think the salesperson has your best interest at heart. It's essential to get a firm grip on a few basic principles of economics *before* you start investing, and that's how this book can help you.

I literally fell asleep in high school economics because the material wasn't presented in an interesting fashion. At a recent high school reunion, a former classmate reminded me that Mr. Irgang (our economics teacher) had to bang his chalk or blackboard pointer on my desk just to wake me up. "Who cares about something called *the marginal propensity to consume?*" I thought to myself. None of that nonsense interested me, so I switched to a major in science when I arrived at Cornell University. However tortuous I would eventually find organic chemistry lab, I figured that at least I was learning something *real*.

Had my high school teacher been able to explain such a "far-out" economics principle in terms of how it affects our everyday lives, I might have stayed awake. (Mr. Irgang's *marginal propensity to consume* would have been much more interesting had he explained how it ties in with the market fluctuation of stocks and bonds.) Poor Mr. Irgang never learned to keep me awake in the economics classroom, however. His parting words are scrawled in familiar style under his photo in my high school yearbook: *"Hang in there, baby!"* So what are the essentials of economics that you need to know?

A KEY FACTOR: INTEREST RATE

Let's get started with our basics. First is what's known as the *interest rate*. Each of us is already familiar (or should be familiar) with how much interest we pay on the all-too-convenient credit cards we tote around in our pocketbooks. The prevailing interest rate in a particular country (such as the United States) serves as the number one factor that affects the entire economy. In fact, the prevailing interest rate directly affects consumer behavior, influences subsequent shareholder behavior, and serves as the primary screen companies use to determine their capitalization as they devise research and development strategies for the future.

The interest rate that prevails on any given day when the opening bell rings on Wall Street serves to orchestrate that day's economic events, both nationally and internationally. Currencies like stocks trade in a global marketplace. The United States' interest rate affects the value of all other currencies and hence all other markets. Wall Street professionals are paid millions of dollars a year just to predict interest rates, and those who are best at it are known in the trade as Fed watchers. These men (and women) are paid megabucks just for making educated guesses as to how the U.S. government is likely to regulate the economy. In its simplest terms, the government only has two main regulatory tools at its disposal: (1) fiscal policy, and (2) monetary policy.

Fiscal policy is controlled by the president and Congress, who decide on a day-to-day basis how to spend taxpayers' money and how much of it to spend. Congress and the president may, for example, vote to spend millions (or billions) to create jobs by funding federally mandated construction projects. Conversely, they could decide to withhold spending. Such decisions affect all of us—directly or indirectly.

Monetary policy is steered by the Federal Reserve System, which operates independently of both the president and Congress—in theory, at least. The Federal Reserve meets on a regular basis and sets the short-term interest rate known as the discount rate. In the real world, however, the autonomy and objectivity of the Federal Reserve are limited because the Fed's chairman is appointed by the president and confirmed by the Senate. (We have yet to see a chair-*woman* of the Federal Reserve, but that day may eventually arrive.) However, once appointed and confirmed, the chairperson of the Federal Reserve can't be removed before the end of a six-year term, except as the result of improper behavior. Because the *absolute integrity* of the chairman of the Federal Reserve is essential to the welfare of the entire country, this regulation protects the Fed from political pressures, at least to some degree.

The interest rate of the country is crucial because it affects most large consumer purchases, particularly houses and cars. It determines whether corporations will be able to borrow and expand. It affects earnings, since interest expense is a cost of doing business for most companies. It influences the value of all other nations' currencies and is a major determinant whether money will flow into bonds or stocks.

The key to a nation's overall welfare always lies in its economy. The ultimate job of the Federal Reserve is to ensure the highest level of economic growth possible without allowing inflation to rise above 3% per annum (as measured by the Department of Labor's Consumer Price Index). This index tracks a "fixed basket of goods" that the average consumer can be expected to purchase on a regular basis.

BAROMETER OF THE NATION'S WEALTH:
THE GROSS DOMESTIC PRODUCT

You now know why the prevailing interest rate is so important.

The *gross national product* (GNP) is a measure of what America produces, both domestically and on foreign soil. Although economists still monitor the GNP, they also track the *gross domestic product* (GDP), which takes into consideration only what is produced within America's borders. The GDP is the barometer by which economists measure the nation's wealth at any given time.

Let's take a look at the formula for the *gross domestic product,* broken down for you the way I wish Mr. Irgang had done it. What follows is no more difficult than basic math, so *"hang in there, baby!"*

$$GDP = C + I + G + (X - M)$$

Simply translated,
*Gross domestic product = Consumption + Investments +
Government spending + Difference between exports and imports*

In the foregoing equation, C stands for consumption, that is, the total amount of money that American consumers collectively spend on goods and services. (The fact may surprise you, but what you spend at the local shopping mall actually *does* affect the GDP, as well as the economy of the United States as a whole.) The total dollar figure for consumption represents roughly 50 to 60% of the GDP, and can be broken down into the following categories:

- *Durable goods* are items expected to last three years or more. Your family car and dining room furniture are durable goods, as is your personal computer—although technological advances may make your PC obsolete long before the three years run out.

- *Nondurable goods,* on the other hand, are items expected to last *less* than three years. These products include items such as food, clothing, soap, perfume, toys and so forth.

- *Services* currently represent more than 50% of the consumption sector. With each passing day, America is becoming a more service-based economy. How much money do you spend each year for medical, vision and dental care? What about that huge sum you just forked over for some high-priced plumber to fix the backyard septic tank? Many of us spend small fortunes on the services of manicurists and hair stylists, not to mention lawyers and tax accountants.

Getting back to the GDP equation, the *I* stands for investments. This category includes all investments made by the nation's businesses (both great and small). This category includes such costly items as airplanes, manufacturing plants, and the materials needed to create anything from Barbie dolls to microchips.

In the GDP mix, *G* stands for government spending and represents approximately 17% of our total gross domestic product. As much as we like to complain about the way big government spends our hard-earned tax dollars, these expenditures include such useful items as road and highway repair, public schools, and social security entitlements. This sector of the GDP also includes the vast sums of money spent by the major bureaus such as the IRS, the FBI, the CIA and NASA, as well as the interest payments on our $5 trillion (and counting) national debt.

X stands for exports and *M* stands for imports in the GDP formula. Since 1970, when total U.S. imports (items we *buy* from abroad) have been subtracted from total exports (what we *sell* abroad), the resulting figure has been increasingly negative. We've consistently imported more from international ports than other nations have imported from us, and that's certainly not in America's best interest. (I'm still waiting for Mr. Irgang to explain how we got into that particular kettle of fish or, better yet, how we can get out of it.)

Here's a list of some of the major goods we *export*:

Agricultural products such as corn and wheat; machinery (for example, tractors made by Caterpillar, Inc. or Deere & Co.)

Automobiles manufactured by companies such as General Motors, Ford, and Chrysler

Computers and related products, including the various wares of IBM, Compaq, Intel, Microsoft, Hewlett-Packard, Texas Instruments, and Motorola

Airplanes, especially those made by Boeing and McDonnell-Douglas

Entertainment-related exports such as those of Disney, Viacom, Time-Warner, ITT Sheraton (even the Hiltons)

Scientific instruments (those of particularly high quality) such as Fischer Scientific International

America's two largest trading partners at the moment are Japan and Canada. We depend on these and other countries around the globe to provide us with a wide variety of *imports*, including the following:

Oil (especially from our friends at the Organization of Petroleum Exporting Countries, commonly known as OPEC)

Automobiles (mostly from Japan and Germany)

Computer chips (largely from the Pacific Rim)

Personal computers (often with Japanese brand names such as NEC and Toshiba)

Anyone who understands the equation GDP = C + I + G + (X − M) can solve it simply by plugging in the right numbers. Economists compare the current GDP to that of the previous year, and analyze the results accordingly:

An annual increase in the GDP of 5% or more is considered high growth.

An increase of 3.4 to 5% is thought of as moderate growth.

A gain of 2 to 3.3% is low.

Two consecutive quarters of decline in the GDP spell trouble in the form of a recession. The GDP is an indispensable barometer of the nation's financial well-being, which is why it's constantly monitored by both financial and political analysts.

TAKE STOCK IN YOUR FUTURE: THE STOCK MARKET

A leading indicator of our nation's economic health is the stock market; that is, the basic business of buying and selling the future earnings potential of firms listed on the New York and American Stock Exchanges and traded in the over-the-counter market. Those who work on Wall Street are in the business of "buying the future" by trading the future earnings of others. The Street's major analysts project what they think the GDP and other economic indicators (such as the S&P 500 Index) will be six months down the line. (Quite a few "suits" on the Street are paid seven-figure salaries to do this.) These forecasts are constantly revised, of course, as the economy gains or loses steam, but decisions to purchase particular stocks are influenced by predictions of general economic trends. Brokerage analysts who predict a significant increase in the GDP, for example, encourage colleagues to buy stocks that promise high earnings potential.

The S&P 500 is a market index of 500 U.S. stocks selected by one of the nation's premier credit rating agencies, Standard & Poor's. The index is composed of 500 widely held stocks. It tracks industrial, financial, transportation, and utility companies. If what follows is the first chart you've ever tackled in your life, don't sweat it! Economic charts and graphs are much more user-friendly than you think. You'll soon learn how to read stock market indices on your own. In fact, you may enjoy teaching your kids or grandkids what those columns of tiny symbols and numbers actually signify.

SUMMARY OF STOCK MARKET RETURNS FROM 1950–1989*

Following Year's Real Growth in the GNP	Number of Years	Standard & Poor's Return	Adjusted for Inflation
5.2 or more (high)	10	22.5%	19.9%
3.4% to 5.1% (moderate)	10	16.5%	12.9%
2% to 3.3% (low)	10	11.7%	7.9%
Anything less (very low)	10	2.3%	−5.0%

*Source: J. Franklin Sharp, Sharp Seminars, CFA Preparation E24-1.

It's obvious that the stock market and the national economy are not just directly related, but positively correlated. Investors buy stocks for the future earnings of a company. When the economy is doing well, the earnings of the companies go up and stocks will go up in anticipation of the higher earnings. Actually, the stock price increases before the economy, since people are buying the future earnings. The stock market is usually an early indicator of the direction of the economy.

While there are no guarantees in life, over the years stocks have been quite a rewarding investment for the average long-term investor. The *best* ten-year period for the stock market to date was launched in 1948, not long after World War II, when stocks provided an average annual return of 20.1%. Conversely, the *worst* ten-year period in stock market history (1928–1938) resulted in an average annual return of −.9%. From 1926 through 1992 the stock market produced an average annual return of 10.3% after taking into account capital appreciation and dividends, whereas the rate of interest on money produced an annual average return of 3%. If history is an indicator for the future, you'll get double to triple the "bang for your buck" by interesting in the stock market.

The most important lessons to be learned from this section of the book are these: (1) a growing economy generates a growth in earnings; and (2) a steady growth in earnings usually creates a healthy stock market.

INFLATION: THE "GREEN-EYED MONSTER"

Unfortunately, the element of growth itself has its drawbacks at times. When an economy grows too quickly, a tenacious "monster" with an all-too-familiar face is bound to make its presence felt. This proverbial monster goes by the name of *inflation,* and is extremely difficult to control. Whenever too much money chases too few goods, prices go up at the local gas station and grocery store. Suddenly, the "green" in your pocketbook becomes worth less with each passing day.

The principle is the same one that applies when you find yourself surrounded by more women than men in a social setting. If you're single and looking for a date at a party where only five men are present, it's tragic when another 49 women (each with the very same thought) compete for the attention of those five men. What most of us would consider a case of ridiculously bad luck, economists refer to as an *abnormal distribution.* A normal distribution, on the other hand, would be girl-boy-girl-boy-girl-boy— the way life should be.

Oddly enough, each of the five available men in the room might be left altogether dateless were there a normal distribution of 50/50 in the room. Frankly, the five men who showed up at the party all look and act a bit boring. Put the same five bores in this abnormal distribution, however, and the odds are better than 15 to 1 that each will find a date. The fact that the men in attendance are perceived as a limited (yet highly desirable) quantity makes each appear more dashing, charming, and intelligent than he would seem were there a normal distribution. And each of the five men will at least be noticed, if not directly approached, by women who otherwise wouldn't have given him a second glance.

The formula is virtually the same, whether applied to matters of the heart or one's personal finances:

A High Ratio of Women to Men = Higher Desirability Factor for the Men
Too Many Dollars Chasing Too Few Goods = Higher Prices for the Goods

(The smartest of the 50 women attending the social gathering I described would leave the party alone, rather than settle for another "loser," and wait to be invited to a party with 50 or more men from whom to choose.)

HOW THE FEDERAL RESERVE BANK PULLS THE STRINGS

Maintaining a healthy balance between a growing economy and an economy that's growing out of control is extremely important. The cost of basic human needs such as food and shelter cannot be allowed to skyrocket until general unrest results. For example, just prior to Hitler's rise to power in Germany, inflation there was completely out of control. I remember a photo in one of my high school history books of a man pushing a wheelbarrow filled to the brim with deutsche marks, yet it was barely enough for him to buy a single loaf of bread.

Earlier in the chapter, I mentioned the extremely difficult role that the chairman of the Federal Reserve plays in the nation's economy. His most important job is to make sure that America's "excesses" of economic growth today don't leave us with a gigantic "hangover" of inflation tomorrow morning. The Federal Reserve must use monetary policy as a tool to stimulate growth when the economy is sluggish or to slow down growth when inflation rears its head.

Whenever our nation's economy appears weak or sluggish, there are two major ways by which the government can give it a much-needed booster shot:

1. A change in *fiscal policy,* such as when Congress passes a bill to create work projects (for example, highway construction) in order to stimulate growth via government spending.

2. A change in *monetary policy,* as a means of controlling short-term interest rates. When the economy is weak, the Federal Reserve lowers the discount rate—the interest charge at which the Reserve is willing to lend funds to member banks. You may think that a change in monetary policy has nothing to do with you as an individual, but nothing could be further from the truth. Each fluctuation of the discount rate makes it either easier or harder to borrow money from your local lending institutions. Since 1929, the discount rate has been as low as .5% and as high as 14%.

Note that the interest charge on $10,000 borrowed at 14% is $1,400, while the interest on the same principal amount at .5% is only $50. That's why what the Federal Reserve ultimately decides to do in terms of monetary policy really does make a difference to our pocketbooks.

Each time the Fed lowers its lending rates, the savings "trickle down" to virtually everyone in the nation. A low discount rate economy provides an excellent opportunity for the purchase of big ticket items. Housing and automobile sales tend to rise, and corporations borrow more money to expand, creating more jobs for people like you and me. Corporate borrowing costs are lower, which normally reduce a firm's expenses, at the same time that sales are increasing. This in turn creates a healthier stock market, and those with money in the bank at low interest rates are more prone to take a chance on the stock market.

When the economy starts growing too quickly, however, the Federal Reserve increases the discount rate before inflation sets in. Many of us, at least temporarily, put off buying the car or home we had in mind, until the interest rate becomes more attractive. The average consumer is tempted to keep his or her money in the bank whenever interest rates are higher. Why "gamble" with your savings, if you're able to earn as much as 8–10% on money that's fully insured by the U.S. government? Taking a risk on the stock market becomes less attractive, considering that shareholders earn roughly 10% per year on average.

Key rates can be found in your daily newspaper's financial section.

The rates for a three- to six-month Treasury bill give you an idea what your money is worth in the short term. Purchase of a Treasury bill represents a loan to the government. In this case, the term *three- to six-month* refers to the date of maturity, that is, the term of the loan and the Treasury bill rate represents the amount of interest that the government is willing to pay for the use of your funds.

The real key to remember is that consumer investments are invariably tied into interest rates. A low-interest-rate environment creates economic growth, whereas high interest rates serve to "put the brakes" on the national economy so as to frighten away that green-eyed monster, inflation.

Get a Piece of the Action: Invest

The stock market is one of the most excitingly intricate puzzles on earth, and no two days of trading are ever the same. There's always something completely new to be learned and filed away to share with others.

The stock market involves a concept much greater than the vast amount of money that changes hands between opening and closing bells each day. You're buying the future earnings of a firm each time you invest in its stock. Should you happen to own stock in Coca-Cola, you'll share the profits from each can sold the world over, even the one you treat yourself to. If you prefer to buy a piece of the action in a fashion concern such as Liz Claiborne, you can watch your investment grow with every outfit that's sold. You even have the same shareholder voting rights enjoyed by the big fish in the Wall Street pond (although you'll probably have considerably fewer votes to cast). Still, you might actually enjoy attending "your" company's next shareholder meeting—so, go for it.

Which industry trends have you personally noticed of late? Perhaps you're a Microsoft fan and liked the comments Bill Gates made the other day on television. If your dream for the future is a good match with his, then buying a small piece of Microsoft serves a philosophical goal that the two of you share. Naturally, you also get a financial "kickback" (via stock appreciation) for every Microsoft product sold from then on. The stock market enables you to invest in just about anything and everything that appeals to you personally, from McDonald's Golden Arches to Compaq's Presario. Perhaps you already know of a firm that's been producing reliable products for many years; by becoming a shareholder, you can tell its management what a satisfied customer you are.

After taking the kids to the latest Disney movie for the umpteenth time, you may realize what a hit it's likely to be on video when it's released in six to nine months. Why not go with your gut instinct and buy at least a small share of Disney's "dream," and at the same time rack up some sizable stock dividends for yourself?

One of the most common misconceptions about the stock market is that it's a form of legalized gambling. Nothing could be further from the truth. Those who take time to learn the rules of the game *before* sitting down at the table are always going to be the real winners. The losers are those who get suckered into a seemingly harmless hand of blackjack, for example, then wake up to find that they've been financially slaughtered.

Another common misconception is that buying and selling stocks is exclusively for the very rich to participate in. *Au contraire!* Anyone and everyone can invest. In any event, "playing the stock market" is much too important to think of as a "game." Anyone who invests in the various wares sold on Wall Street should proceed carefully. Before spending any money the careful investor must

- Understand which part of the economic cycle we are presently experiencing

- Know the growth rates of key industries, and observe how these industries behave at diverse parts of the economic cycle

- Become fully acquainted with the company's present financial position and whether or not the management team has been doing a good job.

As an investor, you'll need to be on the lookout for any new competitive forces that may enter the picture and affect the size of your profits as a shareholder. Given the right set of circumstances, what once looked like a safe bet can easily become a risky proposition.

There's Murphy's law to worry about, as well. Suppose a firm in which you're heavily invested is forced to discontinue its most successful product line and recall a few million units. A previously undetected flaw that causes a single consumer injury can turn your "dream investment" into a nightmare.

If you are not yet sufficiently stressed out about playing the stock market, here are a few more worries to consider.

- *The foreign exchange* vis-à-vis corporate profits

- *Unforeseen disasters* (the sort that only God Almighty can foresee), the calamitous nature and complete unpredictability of which fairly necessitate the inclusion of an act-of-God clause somewhere amidst the fine print of most contracts.

- *Financial fraud,* because for all you know the company's seemingly respectable CEO may be dipping a hand into the corporate "cookie jar," leaving the firm's shareholders with nothing but "crumbs" at the end of the day.

- *General mismanagement,* because the CEO or other decision makers may be doing the firm more damage simply by "falling asleep at the switch" than they could by helping themselves to a few "corporate cookies."

These concerns are more than enough to keep any intelligent investor tossing and turning in bed at night. So if you'd still like to think of the stock market as a gamble, be my guest. At any rate, for many people the stock market is far more addictive than dropping silver dollars into one-armed bandits in Las Vegas or Atlantic City. Whether you're a worker on Wall Street or an individual investor, from the outset you risk becoming addicted to the market.

Knowledge is power, however; and you're well on the way to learning the basics every woman needs to survive (even thrive) financially. Don't "slam on the brakes" now by putting down this book, because the information you need about investments gets easier to understand from this point on.

chapter 2

DON'T PUT ALL YOUR EGGS IN ONE BASKET

Do you recall my personal definition of money? For me, it's nothing less than a *vehicle of freedom*—something too precious to put a price tag on. To quote from our grammar school history books, "Give me liberty, or give me death!"

Lessons from History: Freedom from Debt

As Patrick Henry would tell us if he were alive today, America's freedom came anything but "free." A whole lot of folk in our historical past paid a dear price for the civil liberties and freedom we enjoy today.

You're probably carrying a few of our forefathers' faces in your pocket, even as you read these words. The visages of Washington and Lincoln are those we see most often—sad to say! But the next time you spot a $10 bill in your wallet, stop for a moment and take a good, hard look at it. Check out the fellow pictured on its face, then ask yourself if you even know his name. Yet, it's unlikely that *any* of America's legal tender would be worth the paper on which it's printed were it not for the courage, wisdom, and bull-headed determination of the remarkable Alexander Hamilton.

Hamilton never became president of these United States, as did the better-known personages on our legal tender: Washington, Lincoln, Jackson, and Grant. Most Americans know less about Hamilton than about the other "face cards" in our wallets—which is a shame, because Hamilton was arguably the wildest "joker" in the pack. I for one think it's high time to sing the praises of a man to whom we're all indebted for literally saving America from bankruptcy: Were it not for Hamilton's noble and tenacious spirit, this country of ours would no doubt have "gone bust" before it had a chance to open up its first checking account. More than 200 years later we would be mourning a "stillbirth" on the Fourth of July rather than celebrating the nation's birth.

Let's "time-warp" back through the pages of history to the roots of the American Revolution. Freedom always has a price tag, and the new United States of America (all 13 of them) had to borrow heavily to win their war against Great Britain. This nation came into the world owing roughly $50 million to various foreign entities and private individuals who believed in our cause. (Can you imagine what that sum would equal in present-day currency?) The war had been won, the new brotherhood of states no longer had taxation without representation, but it had to pay off its gargantuan debts or face dissolution. To make matters worse, it lacked the most fundamental power of government itself—a system by which to collect taxes from the new nation's citizenry. (Those days will never come again!)

In 1789 our Commander-in-Chief, George Washington, chose Alexander Hamilton as the country's first secretary of the newly created Department of the Treasury. The Treasury's cupboards were completely bare.

Enter Alexander Hamilton. The first major (if not overwhelming) task facing Hamilton as secretary of the Treasury was to save the new nation from bankruptcy and prevent default on the multi-million dollar debt. With all the vigor he could muster, Hamilton argued that America must honor its war debts by repaying all investors (both foreign and domestic) in full. How else could we hope to become a prosperous nation, one respected on a global basis? By demanding that the United States always keep its word, Hamilton literally created history.

The American Revolution had been financed by the issuance of public bonds not much different from the ones isssued today. Those bonds were backed by the Continental Congress, not by the newly formed U.S. government (although in reality the two entities were pretty much one and the same). Once the Revolution had been won, most of the bonds that had been issued were considered worthless. The global consensus was that America's war debts would be impossible to pay off. Speculators capitalized on the ensuing panic by buying the bonds at rock-bottom prices, as the original owners unloaded them for pennies on the dollar. (A principle to keep in mind is that *uncertainty creates risk*. Many lenders become frightened in bad times and opt to recoup a small portion of their initial investment rather than risk losing the entire amount.) The sale of the bonds to speculators created an ethical dilemma for founding fathers such as James Madison, who argued that for the U.S. government to pay off these new speculators would anger those who'd been patriotic enough to finance the Revolution to begin with, and that we should honor only those bonds that were still held by the original purchasers. Hamilton refused to back down from what he knew was the only course of action that would ensure America's future. He contended that defaulting on any of the bonds would discourage foreign parties from investing additional funds in the new nation and argued that America needed to establish a good credit rating, just as individuals do.

To put it in the simplest terms possible, America urgently needed to "refinance its mortgage," and here's how Hamilton pulled it off: the government successfully raised more cash by issuing a new series of 30-year bonds at 6% interest, which sold well thanks to Hamilton's pledge that the United States would always stand by its debts.

I relay this story for two reasons: Primarily, to illustrate that if a nation can default on its debt, any corporation can fail, as well as any country. If a corporation fails, it will not be able to pay its obligations and will face dissolution. It is important never to hold your financial fate to one source, no matter how sound you feel it is at the moment. Secondly, the credibility of the nation's financial system is the root that must be strong in order for all economic activity and investment to prosper. The nation's financial system is the number one determinant of all market risk.

Risks and Rewards

An anonymous rich-and-successful TV producer once told writer Gail Sheehy, "I worry that I will wake up as a bag lady when I'm old" (reported by Sheehy in *Money* magazine). Sheehy found herself agreeing with her friend, then wondering if more of their peers felt as they did. After expressing this "paranoia" to other friends, among them author Gloria Steinem and film maker Nora Ephron, Sheehy discovered that similar fears were shared by other women as well.

Movie producer Sherry Lansing (*First Wives' Club, Fatal Attraction*), who excels in one of the most competitive and riskiest businesses ever, confessed to downright risk aversion when it comes to her personal finances. Lansing keeps virtually all of her sizable fortune in Treasury bills or their cash equivalents. *Some folk just don't like risking their life savings.* In fact, many people, especially those who survived the Great Depression, can only rest easy at night knowing that their retirement nest eggs are safely 'neath their "risk-free" mattresses.

For those folks and Ms. Lansing, T-bills may be the answer. They offer what's known as a "risk-free rate"—that is, the percentage the U.S. government is willing to pay you for borrowing your hard-earned cash. These investments are as close to risk free as you can get, since the U.S. Treasury has yet to default. Another safe bet is a savings account. The FDIC (Federal Deposit Insurance Company) insures individual savings at most banks up to $100,000 in the event that a crisis triggers a run on the banks. Except for two very real worries, namely, quirks of Congress and that green-eyed monster inflation, savings accounts are just about as risk free as you can get.

But those who play it absolutely safe will never gain optimum rewards in terms of investments. Most of us can live with at least a bit more risk than that required to put our money in a savings account forever, or to invest it all in T-bills.

VOLATILITY: THE UPS AND DOWNS OF INVESTMENTS

We who work on Wall Street refer to *risk* as "volatility." *Volatility* is a measure of how much a portfolio of stocks (or just a single stock) is likely to fluctuate in value over time.

Here's an amusing way to explain the concept: Imagine for the moment that each of your colleagues at the workplace is a "stock." That's not so far-fetched, because companies are actually no more than conglomerates of people with individual ideas, ethics, and work habits. Perhaps there's already a boss characterized by you and your chums at the office as volatile, because of the outrageous changes in mood he or she displays.

In America, we make career choices according to the nature of our talents and personalities, yet each office environment can be its own "melting pot" of idiosyncrasies. So, pretend with me for a moment that each of your friends and work associates is a stock, and assign a "volatility rating" between 1 and 100 to each of them. I'll give you an example, using two of my own friends named Maureen and Chuck.

MAUREEN

Accountant, 20+ years with her present firm. Dedicated, hard-working, never misses a day of work, and always right on time. Socks a little portion of her weekly paycheck into a mutual fund via payroll deductions, so she'll be sure to have a nice nest egg on retirement.

Volatility Rating: 15

CHUCK

Actor, often out of work when the show he's rehearsed for three months closes off Broadway in a single night. Whenever he has money (even if he's just cashed an unemployment check), Chuck splurges on dinner with a friend at a posh New York restaurant. He's never had anything more than a checking account in his life.

Volatility Rating: 75

It's easy to see why Maureen is a "steady Eddie" with a low volatility rating, since she knows with relative certainty how much she'll be earning (and accruing) five to ten years down the line. She rates a 15 on the volatility scorecard, because she's unlikely to change her habits over the course of her working life. On the other hand, Maureen doesn't warrant a rating of 1, since there's a degree of uncertainty in her life as well. What if the major firm for which she works is dramatically challenged by new competition or a sudden change in technology? What if personnel are suddenly downsized, beginning with those who'd been with the company the longest? (Hey, it *could* happen—and does happen just about every day.) Barring such a fateful corporate blow, however, my friend Maureen is a "steady Eddie" who knows she'll have about $250,000 in net assets within the next 20 years or so.

Chuck's a "ready Freddy" with a volatility factor of 75, since he lives from paycheck to paycheck. Like most of his own artistically-minded friends—writers, dancers, and assorted Thespian waiters and waitresses—Chuck takes tremendous risks by pursuing a career in which there's so much competition. He usually waits tables or tends bar between acting "gigs." He might be homeless five years from now, or an overnight sensation who makes millions a year. Who knows? My highly volatile friend may soon be enjoying an elegant lifestyle in a Laguna bungalow with a private beach—or own a palatial mansion in Beverly Hills!

Before you assign points for volatility to each of your friends, stop to consider why a "ready Freddy" always gets a higher score in terms of risk. The irony is that Chuck might actually be the next Kevin Costner, with a *Dances with Wolves* up his sleeve. Should he ever hit the big time, he'll make more money than Maureen and I combined (and have an Academy Award to decorate the mantelpiece, to boot)!

Which outlook on life, or volatility level, is best? The answer lies in *diversification*. Life wouldn't be nearly so interesting if all of our friends were the same—all doctors, for example, or lawyers. I enjoy the company of my friend Chuck, because he's a "ready Freddy" always out for an adventure or good time. On the other hand, Maureen's "steady-Eddie-ness" is calming and reassuring. She's an invaluable source of good sound counsel and advice, as reliable as they come. And the beauty of diversification is that I can enjoy a rewarding friendship with *both* Maureen and Chuck. I simply won't put all of my eggs in one basket.

DIVERSIFICATION: CUSHION THE SAVINGS

Choosing stocks or other investments can be almost like choosing a wide assortment of friends. I can tolerate the emotional ups and downs of my actor friend Chuck, and don't even mind lending him a few bucks every now and then. My steady friend Maureen adds something else very special to my life. My choice of friends shows diversification, and I employ the same philosophy in the financial marketplace. At any given time, my own personal portfolio may include various utility and industrial stocks (for steadiness), mixed in with a few technology and biotechnology stocks for the sheer excitement of it. Who knows, the next firm I invest in may really *be* the next Microsoft! The stock you choose to invest in could be that of a medical company destined to discover the cure for breast cancer, in which case your personal investment may do all women on the planet a great deal of good! .

You might choose a company with a hot new retailing concept, such as Starbucks, and enjoy adding to the company's coffer with each cup of coffee. Diversification is fantastic, isn't it? I can handle the ups and downs of my erratic actor and writer friends (because they're so damn interesting), while at the same time enjoy the company of my more reliable and less eccentric accountant, lawyer, and broker chums. I simply put the same philosophy to use in terms of stocks.

I try to make my financial life tolerable in terms of risk, and interesting at the same time. We simply can't keep all our eggs in one basket, because if the basket breaks we're each out a nice breakfast. Our primary goal is to have all the proper investment tools firmly in place. Then we have a diversified portfolio of investments on which to rely.

Hedge Your Bets: Create a Diversified Portfolio

I usually read the newspaper while I'm on the treadmill at the gym, but Michael, who works out there on a regular basis, never fails to distract me and make me laugh. Most of the club's members think of him as the resident comedian. Michael and I soon became friends, and one day he confided to me that he'd just inherited a thousand shares of General Motors. What should he do with that investment, he wondered. Should he cash in, or let it all ride on GM?

Since he asked my opinion, I told Michael about the concept of diversification. I convinced him that it's better to be half right than all wrong about an investment. He agreed and decided to sell 500 shares (50%) of his GM stock and use the money to diversify his holdings. Michael made me proud by actually doing his financial homework and, after thorough research, he decided to buy the following:

100 shares of Coca-Cola

100 shares of Gillette

100 shares of McDonald's

100 shares of Intel

Six months later, General Motors had gone down 4 points, which meant that Michael's entire stock assets would have gone down by 4 points had he not sold off the 500 shares in order to diversify his holdings. As it stands, Michael lost $4 on each of the 500 GM shares in his portfolio, for a net loss of $2,000. (Should he immediately sell out rather than hope for a future price increase?) But look what happened to the other stocks he purchased with the money from the GM stock he decided to unload:

- Intel rose by 43 points. That's an increase in value of $4,300 on Michael's investment in only six months, given that each of his 100 shares is now worth $43 more.

- Gillette is also up, by 12 points. Those shares are worth $1,200 more now than they were six months ago when Michael bought them.

- Coca-Cola is up by 11 points, for a net gain of $1,100.

- McDonald's played "steady-Eddie" and remained unchanged.

Just as I've never believed in having only one friend, I don't believe in owning only one stock. Yet, given the foregoing scenario you would not necessarily sell your remaining shares of General Motors and put the money into Intel. Remember, it's all about diversification, which demands that you be balanced with your investments. At different points in the economic cycle, certain industries rise and fall in reaction to a wide range of factors. It's no surprise that Murphy's law ("whatever can go wrong, will go wrong") works on Wall Street: chances are you'll sell those

500 GM shares when they hit rock bottom, while those who didn't panic will watch the stock take a sudden upswing the very next day.

KNOWING YOUR OPTIONS

The fact is, life really *is* a gamble. The best we can do is hedge our bets through diversification. The average investor does this by spreading out investments among these three main asset classes:

1. *Cash reserves:* These include Treasury bills, money market funds, savings accounts, and certificates of deposit. (Don't worry about these in detail now; Chapter 6 is devoted entirely to such "worry-free" investment tools.)

2. *Bonds:* These interest-bearing debt obligations are issued by federal, state, or local government. The latter two types are called municipal bonds. A variety of corporate bonds is also issued each year. Unlike bonds issued by the federal government, municipals and corporates carry credit risk as well as interest-rate risk (the details are in Chapter 7).

3. *Common stocks:* These investment vehicles offer the greatest chance of reward, but we pay for that chance in terms of risk. As you've already learned, the higher the risk, the greater is the chance of reward. You also know that stocks represent ownership in the future earnings of a corporation.

Should you invest some of your assets in common stocks, you will have two sources of potential financial gain: (1) dividends, and (2) capital appreciation. Older, more stable firms normally pay out some of their earnings in the form of dividends. They may dole out 12 cents per share, for example, by means of a corporate check that appears in each shareholder's mailbox on a quarterly basis. What we call "capital appreciation" simply means that the stock you own has increased to a higher price per share. If you sell a stock that has appreciated, the price you receive per share will be higher than what you paid originally.

Over the past 70 years, common stocks have offered investors the very best "bang for their buck." Here's how stocks compared to U.S. Treasury bills and bonds during 68 of those fiscal years:

Average Annual Returns (1926-1994)

Cash reserves (U.S. T-bills)	3.0%
Bonds (long-term Treasury bonds)	4.8%
Common stocks (S&P 500 Index)	10.2%

Would you rather have had your money in Treasury bills, or in the stock market? The next table shows just the 30-year period from 1964 to 1994. What would $10,000 have been worth to the typical investor in each of the three major asset categories?

Average Annual Returns (1964-1994)

Cash ($10,000)	$ 69,240
Bonds ($10,000)	$ 75,200
Stocks ($10,000)	$171,940

Source: Vanguard Investment Planner.

That same $10,000 works for you over a period of 30 years, proving there's no way to lose by *saving* money! So put a little something aside from each paycheck, no matter where you sink the investment. Suppose you've never had anything more than a checking or savings account. If $10,000 can make $171,940 over 30 years in the stock market, isn't it high time you deal yourself into the game? The only thing holding you back is your personal level of risk tolerance, a decision that is yours alone. Above all, make sure that you are happy and comfortable with whatever investment strategy you choose.

This very last chart in this chapter shows the rate of growth that $10,000 would have had over a 67-year period (1925–1992).

Asset Class	Nominal Rate	Real Dollars
Cash reserves	$ 114,000	$ 14,400
Long-term bonds	237,100	30,000
Common stocks	7,273,800	918,000

Source: Bogle on Mutual Funds, p. 28.

"Real" dollars are what the middle column figures (nominal rate) translate into, after factoring in the effects of inflation. The average inflation rate in the U.S. (as measured by the Consumer Price Index) is roughly 2.9%. A Treasury bill that earns an average rate of about 3% would barely break even with inflation. The stock market has historically provided much better returns.

You may be thinking, "Hey, if it's so ridiculously easy to make money on paper, why hasn't everyone with $10,000 to play the market become filthy rich?" That's a very good question; one that deserves a good answer, or three or four.

1. For those who play with relatively small sums of money (and the "big boys" think of $10,000 as child's play), truly diversified mutual funds have only recently been introduced to the marketplace. You see, the actual picking of stocks is the most difficult part of investing: it's pretty much like handicapping a horse. But a good mutual fund does all that nasty "homework" so its investors don't have to. The mutual fund industry didn't begin to flourish until the seventies, then during the eighties and nineties, mutual funds became the investment vehicle of choice. Only recently has it become possible for the average investor to put his or her money into what we call the "broad market," as opposed to a mere handful of specific stocks.

2. Information about the stock market has never been so instantaneously accessible—via investment newsletters and the Internet, just for a start. The small-time or novice investor can also tune in to CNBC via cable television, and follow the market that way.

3. And this one is a "biggie" that should be scrawled on our "mental walls" in as large a script size as possible: *Past results don't always guarantee future performance!*

4. Finally, suppose the short-term outlook for the common stock you've chosen suddenly looks horrendous. For whatever reason, whether psychological or financial, you simply can't weather the storm. So you bail out in order to save the already diminished assets you have, then kick yourself when the price floats upwards the very next day.

This scenario raises the subject of *systematic risk* (also known as market risk). A wise man I once knew on Wall Street finally convinced me that "perception is 90% of reality."

Wall Street Whims: From Panic to Euphoria

When I started working on the Street, I couldn't understand why each stock wasn't independently priced and autonomous. Why did everything seem to move in sync with the Dow Jones Average? After all, I came to Wall Street fresh from Cornell's College of Human Ecology—with a major in nutritional sciences, no less. To me, as a budding scientist, everything in life was either black or white. (I learned a lot about the gray areas soon after I became secretary to a few Wall Street superstars.)

The world of economics didn't always operate in clear-cut areas of black and white, and (even more disconcerting) the "gray team" often won the game. This sudden revelation led me to reconsider my training in the sciences in a new light. Economics is one of the so-called social sciences, to be sure, but even in the physical sciences, we learned the concept that an observer's biases can affect the outcome of an experiment. In other words, all prophecies are self-fulfilling.

As in life, everything in the stock market revolves around expectations. Why do most of us on Wall Street worry about every move we make? We know that things are not always what they seem. What looks good on paper (in terms of a company's profitability) might actually conceal the activities of a sticky-fingered CEO who is just playing around with the numbers. A host of other factors, such as the direction of the company itself, global influences on the economy, domestic strife, and even the president's love life, may affect the stock price of any company.

For example, market valuations are based on the future expectation of earnings. The usual way to measure such expectations is through what we call a price/earnings ratio. Simply stated, if a stock earns $10 in fiscal year 1996, and it's trading at $100 per share, it has a P/E ratio of 10. On the other hand, if we believe it will earn as much as $14 in 1997, we hope (or expect) the stock will be valued at $140 per share in 1997.

Before adopting this formula as a benchmark, however, a few more *caveats* are in order:

- The expected earnings of a company are based on nothing more than predictions, not much more reliable than those of your local weather forecaster. Anything unexpected can affect the final outcome. And the unexpected happens all the time!

- The price/earnings ratio for an individual common stock can fluctuate with overall market conditions.

For example, the overall price/earnings ratio of the S&P 500 Index has fluctuated between 7 and 23 over the years. Whatever most of us feel is the market's fair price from year to year is affected by so many different factors that the actual figure boils down to a matter of sheer perception. An apt analogy to the price/earnings ratio might be the sort of dollar-per-square-foot ratio by which real estate is evaluated, except that the latter is far more concrete.

The average P/E ratio of the S&P 500 Index is approximately 14. In September of 1996, the S&P 500 was trading at a P/E ratio of 19. Does this mean that stocks are overvalued simply because the P/E ratio was suddenly above average? Let's say that earnings are expected to grow by 8% per annum, and we're in an extended bull market due to a high demand for American products. (That's when the mass consciousness on Wall Street generally turns optimistic.) Also assume that the national economy is rolling along beautifully without our green-eyed monster friend, so that little or no inflation is plaguing the economy.

As good as things may be at present, who's to say that things won't turn completely sour at the same time next year? Alternatively, who's to say that next year (1) we won't have even higher expectations in terms of earnings, and (2) the market won't be trading at a higher P/E ratio? The notion that perception is everything sounds terrific until one day "everything" turns topsy-turvy, and the mass consciousness of the market goes from total optimism to the sort of fatalism that borders on nihilism.

Those of us who work on the Street, along with everyone who dabbled in the stock market a decade ago, will never forget the incredible stock market crash of October 19, 1987. The Dow Jones Industrial Average had dropped a whopping 508 points in a single day. The stock market had dropped by 20%, and it really did seem that the American economy was bankrupt.

The day had been an extremely long one. I was having a drink (or two) at Harry's Bar after the market shut down that fateful Black Monday, and my good friend Kurt, a broker at Smith Barney, was matching me drink for drink. Kurt was as astonished as I at the day's turn of events. The bar was packed with a great many journalists, reporters, and television cameramen, asking the Wall Street patrons at the bar exactly what had happened that day and, more importantly, *why* it had happened.

Were we suddenly the world's experts on the subject? I certainly didn't think so; the crash had been as much of a shock to us as to anyone else. I declined to offer an opinion for the media or the world to hear, although others at the bar blamed the crash on everything from a comment made by the Secretary of the Treasury James Baker to our absolute proximity to an Armageddon of Biblical proportions! Yet the next day it seemed to me that the nation's entire viewing audience had focused on me, silently sitting and minding my own business, sipping a glass of my favorite white wine. You wouldn't believe how many calls I received from friends and acquaintances congratulating me on my network television debut and on having taken the biggest stock market crash since the twenties in such casual, wine-sipping stride!

The moral of this story isn't hard to figure out, at least in retrospect: The stock market had experienced disaster that day. Many of my colleagues and friends thought the entire world was coming to an end. In the long run, however, the market not only recovered, it *tripled* in value over the course of the next nine years, bringing us to a little Q & A:

Q: Can the stock market ever crash again?

A: Sure, it can. And at virtually any moment.

Q: Can the market rise to new heights?

A: Of course! As these words were being keyed into my computer, the stock market broke through the ceiling of 7,000 for the first time in history—less than ten years after the great stock market crash of '87.

Q: If the market does crash again, will it recover?

A: Not necessarily, but the history of our country indicates a general movement forward with a good rate of economic growth—which tends to indicate fairly good odds over the long haul. For most of us, that factor outweighs any "crash and burn" theory.

Systematic risk is the risk that a change in perceptions about the overall financial system will affect the overall market. It isn't necessarily logical. Keep in mind that what colors our perception is more often various shades of gray than dyed-in-the-wool blacks and whites.

In the years following World War II, the worst bear market (a pessimistic era marked by a general downward spiral) occurred in the two-year span between 1973 and 1974. In this brief period alone, the value of even the most diversified portfolio fell about 40%. Assuming that whatever dividends were distributed at the time were reinvested, it still took roughly four years for owners of common stock to recover those substantial two-year losses.

Turning back the clock a bit further, if you had invested in the stock market prior to the granddaddy of all crashes back in 1929 it would have taken only about eight years to see your initial investment return to its original value. (And eight years wasn't too long to wait out the effects of the worst stock market crash in history, for those who had diversified their assets properly.) The bottom line is that systematic risk is very real, and few people in the world know how to "time" the market just right. Should you be unable to weather the storm of an elongated recession, you will likely make the mistake of selling each stock in your portfolio at the lowest possible dip on the charts.

To counter this all-too-human tendency, you need to *know yourself* as well as possible, and to design an investment plan you can live with from year to year. Should the stock market crash again, you can't just claim that your broker was responsible for your financial misfortune. You alone must decide the appropriate risk-tolerance level for your unique personality and circumstances. The "buck" stops with you!

Aside from an unavoidable amount of market risk, a number of other factors should be considered when it comes to making investments. Here's where that green-eyed friend of ours creeps into the picture again: virtually all assets are exposed to some degree of inflation risk.

Historically speaking, inflation has an average increase of 3.1% each year as measured by the Consumer Price Index (CPI). One dollar today will probably buy only 97 cents worth of goods next year. Many other countries fare much worse when it comes to inflation: in a country with an inflation rate of 14%, for example, $1 would buy only 84 cents worth of goods at the same time next year.

Variables we've already touched upon include the following:

1. Systematic risk, also known as market risk

2. Inflation risk

3. Interest-rate risk

4. Credit risk

The latter two are explored in full detail during the discussion of bonds in Chapter 7. Beyond these four types of risks, which reflect factors acting on the economy as a whole, is something we call *nonsystematic* or *diversifiable* risk. Nonsystematic risk applies to particular segments or sectors of the economy, and can be broken down further into two categories: individual stock risk and industry risk.

Nothing Is Forever: The Lessons of Tulip Mania

"Manias" occur from time to time in all sorts of commodities: stocks, real estate, art, oil, silver and gold, autographs, junk bonds, comic books, baseball cards, and so forth. Yet, I'll bet you've never heard about the *tulip mania* that became the rage throughout Western

Europe in 1559. This implausible tulip scenario kept escalating until it caused a financial crisis that shook Holland to its very core. It began when a man named Conrad Gesner saw his first tulip at the estate of Counsellor Harwart, a well-known collector of exotic flowers. Harwart had acquired the flower from a dealer in Constantinople, Turkey, where it was relatively common.

Gesner found the tulip a thing of wondrous beauty and he began to spread the word about this rarest of all exotic plants. Suddenly, owning a tulip was the ultimate symbol of wealth! Before long, rich individuals from all over Europe (especially Holland and Germany) felt the overwhelming urge to "keep up with the Harwarts" by adding tulips to their own gardens. From 1600 to 1634 the price of tulips climbed, as owning the flower became an absolute must for any man or woman of wealth. By 1635, the entire Dutch population had become so obsessed with owning tulips that even the poorest citizens caught the fever and invested their entire life savings in the imported bulbs.

Tulips began to be offered formally on the stock exchanges in Amsterdam, Rotterdam, and Haarlem; they actually replaced gold, silver, and diamonds as the soundest investment one could make. All over Europe, people forfeited both houses and land just to own tulip bulbs, in the expectation of doubling their money in a matter of months, and "tulip mania" continued to escalate.

What happened to the tulip industry reminds me of the Hans Christian Andersen story, "The Emperor's New Clothes." A few bright minds suddenly woke up and realized that tulip bulbs weren't worth their extravagant price. Although the tulip is a beautiful flower, it is decidedly inedible, and certainly not worth starving oneself for.

As soon as the wealthiest tulip investors in Europe stopped bidding up the prices, the rest of the populace started to get wise as well. Prices fell so dramatically that a panic was set off among traders. Dealers and ordinary citizens soon went bankrupt; Holland's richest merchants became beggars. Government officials desperately sought some remedy, but no effort on anyone's part could reverse the simple change of heart that had taken place virtually overnight. Again, perception is 90% of reality. It took decades for the Dutch economy to make a full recovery.

WHY INDUSTRIES (BOTH GREAT AND SMALL) CAN EASILY FALL APART

Companies aren't tulips, but even successful companies don't last forever. Remember that each individual company is just a conglomerate of people who make decisions within a specific industry. Virtually anything can happen, which is another reason never to "bet the whole farm" on one individual stock. Diversifying is best, because slow and steady wins the race in the end.

So many vastly different things can go wrong in terms of any individual stock that it would take an entire book just to enumerate them. Suffice it to say that Pan Am was one of the largest airlines in existence from the sixties until the mid-eighties, then it went bankrupt almost overnight. Suppose all your life savings were tied up in Pan Am stock at that time. *You* would have gone belly up with them!

An example of industry risk: Hetty Green's prosperous family whale oil business was eventually undermined by Thomas Alva Edison's invention of the electric light bulb, which soon replaced nineteenth-century lanterns.

At present, a vast revolution is occurring in communications. For example, how will the Internet affect the price of long distance phone calls in the future? Thanks to the Internet, I can now communicate with friends all over the globe for the price of a local hookup. Instead of paying exorbitant long distance rates from New York to China or Egypt, I can e-mail my friends and even attach newspaper articles that might interest them. (Soon I'll be able to "zap" photographs their way via e-mail, as well.) Can you imagine how nervous AT&T must be getting?

The dramatic technological changes we've seen in our own lifetimes make one stop and think. Where would the Wells Fargo Wagon have been, historically speaking, had Wells Fargo never gone into banking? Along the same lines:

▶ Who could have envisioned something called a biotechnology industry a mere 20 years ago?

▶ What if, in the future, we're able to harness solar energy to the point that America could offer clean air for everyone, and for all time? How would such a change in technology affect the powerful and super-rich oil companies of our present era?

- Who would have dreamed of cable television a mere 20 years ago?

- How many of us would anticipated the Internet a mere 10 years ago?

- When did the concept of a discount broker come into being? How will the emergence of this new industry-within-an-industry affect the full-service brokers of today? For that matter, how will the general breakdown of banking laws affect brokerage houses of the future?

- When was the last time you actually used a typewriter, rather than a computer keyboard? Wang introduced the very first computerized word processor in 1976, at the whopping retail cost of $30,000. Soon after, the market abounded with word processors that cost a good deal less than the average typewriter. Ten years later, the emergence of Microsoft Word for individual PCs (personal computers) has entirely revolutionized the word processing business.

- Have you thrown out or given away your entire collection of vinyl records in favor of CDs? The first CD players and CDs were introduced by Phillips and Sony back in 1978. Can you imagine what that did to the vinyl industry? What about all the companies that used to reap huge profits making record players, which were suddenly made obsolete?

As Bob Dylan said, "The times, they are a-changin'!" By the year 2000, many believe that a personal home computer will hold just as much information as your local public library. Think of the technological opportunities we've come to enjoy in recent years: I've already confessed that I'm an e-mail addict, but I also "surf the net" like a kid in a candy store. Naturally, I look up everything of interest to me in my CD-Rom Encyclopedia. Should I ever get bored with that, I opt either for a guided tour of the Cornell campus (if I'm homesick for my alma mater) or shop around for new and exotic vacation sites. Some days I just like to "sift n' surf" through various mainstream magazines, and other times I prefer to take an "armchair visit" to Washington via the White House Web Site. That's *http://www.whitehouse.gov/*, by the way, for those of you who'd like to tell the president what's on your mind!

AN OVERVIEW OF INDUSTRIAL LIFE CYCLES

Like people, industries have recognizable life cycles with major stages:

▶ The first stage is *early development,* when we see a new industry emerge with its own unique potential and risk. (Biotechnology firms, especially those engaged in genetic experimentation to create new medicines, are an excellent example of this category.) The company in which you invest may be the first in a particular marketplace, but always remember that other firms will "follow the money" once your company introduces a highly profitable product. Look what happened to Henry Ford, for example: between 1900 and 1908, more than 500 automobile companies followed his lead. Whenever the possibility of great wealth presents itself, rest assured there will be many contenders for those earnings.

▶ The second stage of growth is *rapid expansion.* This occurs when a relatively small number of companies comprise a fairly large percent of an industry's overall volume. Other contenders will enter the marketplace, and your profit margins will be squeezed a bit, but you'll usually experience some degree of growth.

▶ The third and final stage of growth is the *mature phase,* that is, when age-old industries experience slow growth and output tends to level off. What we call "replacement demand" never really grows or declines significantly.

At any point in this life cycle, your company's product can pull a disappearing act the moment another firm builds something cheaper or more efficient to take its place. That's show biz, as they say, and an extremely good reason for never putting all of your proverbial eggs in one basket. Since perception is everything, diversification is the *only* viable insurance policy—and that's an important lesson for each of us to learn. No industry is safe from eradication. Can you imagine what would happen to the automobile industry if we could say, "Beam me up, Scottie!" and be transported wherever we wished? Layoffs would occur from Tokyo to Detroit!

Recap

To close out this chapter, let's review the top six reasons why individual stocks experience risk:

1. Competition within the industry

2. A new industry arises that infiltrates an already established one

3. Financial misjudgments, because companies (just like individuals) tend to borrow beyond their means

4. Product liability

5. Financial chicanery

6. Overall bad business judgment

I don't know about you, but I like to get a good night's sleep—each and every night. That's why I've learned through the years to take only risks that are well calculated. I think the most prudent way to invest is to position yourself with a diversified pool of assets. Always understand *each* risk that you take, but hedge your bets so that you're ready to roll with the punches no matter what financial or industry climate prevails.

Over the course of the next few chapters, we explore in detail each of the asset classes I've named in this chapter. You'll soon be able to choose intelligently those you can live with. And, just as important, you'll become acquainted with the sort of poor investments you can live *without*!

chapter 3

SHOPPING FOR STOCKS

Would you find it hard to believe that the powerful Wall Street industry we know today was birthed just a bit more than 200 years ago in
the shade of a buttonwood tree? In 1609, our present financial district
first "took root" (pun intended) in a Dutch trading post known as
New Amsterdam, located at the base of Manhattan. The original "Wall
Street" can best be described as a dirt path near a makeshift wall of
brush and mud. The wall itself was extremely important: It kept the
cows in and the Indians out—an odd thing to contemplate as we
approach the twenty-first century. But isn't it refreshing to consider
that what's now the financial center of the entire world was named
after nothing more than a slipshod wall made of sticks and dirt?

America's First Exclusive Men's Club: Wall Street

In 1791, only two years after Washington took office, Alexander
Hamilton established America's very first bank. Aptly enough, he
named it The Bank of the United States. Shares were offered for
public sale, and the securities market was born. Investors indicated
interest in buying or selling stocks at various gatherings in coffeehouses or through offerings that appeared in newspaper ads. Almost
immediately after The Bank of the United States was founded, a
wide variety of new banks and insurance companies were formed,
with shares also offered to the public.

THE NEW YORK STOCK EXCHANGE

Soon the time came to establish a central meeting place for the
booming new financial industry. Leading merchants organized a

central noontime auction at 22 Wall Street on behalf of customers who would leave with professional auctioneers stocks for sale (or bids to purchase other stocks). Naturally, something known as a *commission* came into play with each transaction.

This *modus operandi* wasn't quite exclusive enough for the original band of traders, however. Other businessmen soon began to eavesdrop on the auctions, then tried to cut themselves in on the action. After each noontime trade was completed, these outsiders would offer the same securities at reduced rates. Growing anxious over an impending loss of control, the resident Wall Street leaders convened on March 21, 1792 at a new and improved auction center at Corre's Hotel. On May 17 of the same year, a group of 24 men signed a covenant agreeing to trade only among themselves and to maintain fixed commission rates. It's hard to believe, but those 24 men of 200-plus years ago were the original members of what's now known as the New York Stock Exchange. This all-male "club" of sorts met under the buttonwood tree located at 68 Wall.

The old boy network grew and later moved into the Tortine Coffee House, a short walk down the same street. A formal constitution was created in 1817, and membership suddenly had its price. The right to sit in at the daily auction (the equivalent of owning a seat on the New York Stock Exchange today) went for $400. Compare that figure to those of more recent times, in which a single seat on the New York Stock Exchange has sold for more than $1 million! Once the coffers of the exchange were filled with this new income, the traders moved out of the coffeehouses forever. Of course, everyone had to bring his own coffee to the new meeting place which was completed in 1903. This location, at 20 Broad Street, is where the New York Stock Exchange is still headquartered today.

THE AMERICAN STOCK EXCHANGE

On the opposite side of Trinity Church stands another securities trading place, now called the American Stock Exchange. Its present-day nickname is still "The Curb," however, since this alternate exchange began as various traders began to shout out bids and offers on the corner curb of William and Beaver. These men bought and sold more speculative (that is, riskier) issues than those traded on the New York Stock Exchange, which is still generally the case.

In time there were so many "curbstone brokers" that they moved from the original curb to various spots along Broad Street. They continued to conduct their business outdoors, however, with certain stocks traded at designated lampposts. Thus began the custom of trading stocks in a maze of specialized booths, the method employed to this day by traders on both the New York and American Stock Exchanges. By 1921, however, these curbstone auctioneers had grown tired of being street peddlers—particularly in inclement weather. So they moved into their present-day headquarters directly behind Trinity Church. Only recently (in 1953) was the name of this group of traders legally changed from the New York Curb Exchange to the American Stock Exchange.

THE OVER-THE-COUNTER MARKET

So far we have described the beginnings of the New York Stock Exchange and the American Stock Exchange, but securities are also traded in what's known as the over-the-counter market (OTC). This "market" is basically just one huge computerized system of trading stocks. Talk about no frills! Those who trade on the OTC market have no physical premises to occupy; trading occurs via a state-of-the-art electronic marketplace. Perhaps you've heard the over-the-counter market referred to by its more official name, NASDAQ, which stands for National Association of Securities Dealers Automated Quotation System. Stocks traded here are bound to be even more speculative than issues traded on the New York or American exchanges, because OTC listing requirements are less stringent than those of the other exchanges.

Most of today's leading technology companies, for example, Microsoft, Intel, Oracle, Applied Materials, Dell Computer, and Cisco Systems (to name a just few) are traded over the counter. Perhaps, as we enter the twenty-first century. all markets—from stocks to raw commodities—will become completely computer driven. Following in the footsteps of Hetty Robinson Green, we should consider investing at least some of our savings in what appears to be the major trend of our own era.

How to Buy a Stock— and Where

In no time at all, you'll know everything you need to know about buying a stock on each of the three exchanges—and I promise that it won't be that difficult. One rule of thumb for all three market-places is that publicly traded stocks are bought and sold in "round lots" of 100 shares. Smaller trades (between 1 and 99 shares) are known as "odd lots," whether the actual number of shares is odd or even.

Suppose—just *suppose*—you find a Grand Prize sweepstakes notification in your mailbox. Sure, it's happened a zillion times before, but this time it's for real: You actually *are* a winner! What you're holding in your hands is an honest-to-goodness check for a tax-free $25,000, with your name on it. My heartiest congratulations, but don't rush out and spend it all. For the first time in your life, you have a sizable head start when it comes to devising a plan for achieving the retirement lifestyle of your dreams!

You already know how little interest you'll get for your money in a savings account when compared with other investments (at least at this writing), so why not finally take the plunge into the stock market? But first, let's go through a "dress rehearsal" on paper and "buy" one stock listed on each of the three different exchanges.

Even if you've never bothered to thumb through stock market tables in your daily paper, it's never too late to start. No matter if all those columns of figures in the financial section look like Greek to you at first, I promise you'll soon master the language. (If our old friend Hetty Green found the daily financial reports fascinating at the age of six, they can't be all *that* difficult to read and compre-hend.) The first step is to pick up any newspaper that features stock market listings. I read *The Wall Street Journal* and *The New York Times* every day, but if you're a novice you won't need such sophis-ticated dailies right away.

The *Journal* is, however, an excellent source of information on trends in the marketplace. Until recently, it was the only daily busi-ness paper in the United States. Its most direct competitor, *Investor's Business Daily,* was launched in 1984 by a man of foresight named

William O'Neil. The *Daily* publishes a considerable amount of technical information useful for those who monitor trends.

Our objective is to buy three different stocks with that $25,000 of yours, choosing one from each of the three exchanges. So let's get started, shall we?

STOCK PICK #1: DISNEY

When you open a major newspaper or an investment daily, you will find three listings—one for each of the three markets. The New York Stock Exchange trades stocks of more established firms such as General Motors, International Business Machines (commonly known as IBM), Merck & Co., Xerox, AT&T, General Electric, and so forth. Roughly 1,500 different stocks are listed each day on the New York Stock Exchange; 750 on the American; and more than 6,000 over the counter. The qualifications for a stock to be traded on what we call "The Big Board" of the New York Stock Exchange are considerably more restrictive than those for the other two markets.

Let's choose Disney as our first stock, because everyone on the planet is familiar with this firm. Perhaps your own kids watch The Disney Channel on cable TV, bringing back memories of the hours you spent in front of the black-and-white screen as a card-carrying member of The Mouseketeer Club.

The listing in the financial section of your paper for Disney on the New York Stock Exchange on October 19, 1996 looked something like this:

52-week High	Low	Stock	Div	Yld%	P/E	Sales 100s	High	Low	Last	Change
69-7/8	53-1/4	Disney	.44	.7	27	10104	65	64-1/2	65	+1/8

Within a year, the entire system of price quotations will switch to decimals. Until that day arrives, however, the majority of stocks will continue to trade at one-eighth intervals. Let's assume that Disney traded from 64 to 65 in one-eighth increments on the day in question. Here's how to calculate how much you'll have to pay for a round lot of Disney:

64	— 100 shares × $64.000 = $ 6,400.00		
64-1/8	— 100 shares × $64.125 = $ 6,412.50		
64-1/4	— 100 shares × $64.250 = $ 6,425.00		
64-3/8	— 100 shares × $64.375 = $ 6,437.50		
64-1/2	— 100 shares × $64.500 = $ 6,450.00		
64-5/8	— 100 shares × $64.625 = $ 6,462.50		
64-3/4	— 100 shares × $64.750 = $ 6,475.00		
64-7/8	— 100 shares × $64.875 = $ 6,487.50		
65	— 100 shares × $65.000 = $ 6,500.00		

If an investor buys 100 shares at $64 and the stock's value increases by one point (whether in the course of a day, month, or year), the investor will make $100 on the original investment of $6,400. But let's agree that you won't try to sell *your* shares of Disney right away for the sake of a quick buck. Instead, hold on to the stock in the expectation of Disney's increased "future earnings" over the long term.

Here's what the information in the listing signifies:

1. The *price* of the stock is reflected in the *52-week high and low,* indicating that Disney has traded from 53-1/4 to 69-7/8 over the course of the past 52 weeks. This means that, for each 100 shares owned by shareholders, the stock's value has fluctuated between a low price of $5,325.00 and a high of $6,987.50.

2. We also know that its *dividend* has been "44" (or 44 cents per share) over the course of the past four quarters. In round numbers, that means that for every 100 shares owned, Disney has dispersed a check for $44 to the shareholder—a check that you as a Disney owner can endorse and deposit in your bank account.

3. The *yield percentage* is computed by using the information appearing in Disney's listing for the day in question, as follows:

Dividend = $44.00 on 100 shares of stock
Last price of stock: 65
Cost of 100 shares = $6,500
$44 divided by $6,500 = 0.68%
    (0.68% is rounded to the nearest tenth, becoming 0.7%)

4. The *price/earnings ratio* represents the ratio of the price of the stock to its earnings per share over the past year. The P/E ratio of 27 for Disney comes from working out a relatively simple algebraic equation: 27 = price (in this case 65) divided by X (earnings over the past year). Therefore, $X = 65$ divided by 27 = $2.41 per share.

5. The sales column refers to the volume (in hundreds) of Disney shares traded during the day in question. Simply take the "10,104" figure that's provided and multiply it by 100. This tells you that 1,010,400 shares were traded on October 18, 1996. A dramatic increase in trading volume during the course of a single day can alert you to the fact that something extraordinary is happening with the stock. Those with inquiring minds will certainly try to figure out what all the fuss is about.

6. The *high* column shows the highest price for the day, in this case 65.

7. The *low* column shows the lowest price for the day, 64-1/2.

8. *Last* refers to the final trading price of 65.

9. The *change* column indicates the difference between the last trade of the day (65) and the previous day's final price (64-7/8), which is equal to +1/8.

Now that we know how to read a stock market chart (bearing in mind that Disney has a long track record of expansion in all media), it's time to take the exercise one step further by pretending to buy 100 shares. Here's how to proceed:

Step One: Call a Broker You Can Trust. If you don't already have a broker in whom you have every confidence, do not pass "GO" (much less fork over $100 or more) until you've read Chapter 11 on the subject of "Con Artists and How to Avoid Them." Assuming you do have a broker you can trust, however, it's time to phone and place either (1) a limit order, which specifies an exact price at which you're willing to buy Disney; or (2) a market order, which authorizes your broker to buy Disney at the prevailing rate.

Step Two: Relax; It's Your Broker's Serve. Rest easy for a moment, because the ball is now in your broker's court. He or she will call up Disney on a computer screen, and see the stock's name accompanied by a quote of 64-3/4 to 65. The broker will also note that the size of the market is presently "10,000 by 15,000." The 10,000 is a bid, while the 15,000 is an offer—and both are being placed in a designated booth on the floor of the New York Stock Exchange. A bid is where someone is willing to pay and an offer is where someone is willing to sell. Would you believe it? There's actually a person we call a *specialist* who oversees all bids and offers in Disney. Brokers flock around this Disney specialist shouting out bids and offers, as well as orders they've received by computer. In our case, there are 10,000 shares bid for at 64-3/4, and 15,000 shares are being offered at 65.

If you've already discussed your spending parameters (the top price you want to pay for Disney) in advance, your broker doesn't absolutely need to phone you at this point—but he or she normally will let you know what the computer screen shows. Your broker will usually place a market order on your behalf to be filled somewhere between 64-3/4 and 65. One alternative is to lower the bid, taking a chance that you'll get lucky and be able to purchase the stock at a lower price. But if you place a limit order, the stock can run away from you, which means you may never again be able to own Disney at the price of 64-3/4 or 65 per share.

If you're resolute in your decision to buy Disney, even at 66 or 67, a market order is your best bet. But if you don't want to "chase the stock" (another term used on Wall Street) and wish to buy it only at what you believe to be a reasonable price of 64-3/4, you can exercise one final option: to enter a good-until-canceled order for 64-3/4. (Devout *Star Trek* fan that I am, I picture a good-until-canceled order as hovering somewhere in space until I choose to "zap" it out.)

Back to planet earth: Let's suppose you specify a firm price of 64-7/8, a reasonable limit order given the current day's trading. Your broker waits for a seller to offer to unload 100 shares of Disney at that exact figure. One of two things can happen next: either a new seller may walk into the booth, or the seller at 65 may get nervous and sell his or her stock at 64-7/8. (See what an exciting minimelodrama each trading scenario can turn into?) The good news is that you get lucky; a new seller may walk up to the specialist in the booth with 100 shares of Disney at the price you bid. You're now the proud owner of the best "Mickey Mouse stock" on the market!

But what do you have to show for your purchase? Will you have something to put on display next to the pair of mouse ears you've finally unearthed in your attic or basement? I hate to break the news to you, but you will probably never see the actual Disney stock certificate. If it's any consolation, however, you *will* receive a computerized statement known as a *confirmation*.

Step Three: Check Out Your Confirmation. Your broker will normally take a moment to phone with the news that you've successfully purchased 100 shares of Disney at 64-7/8. You can also look forward to receiving a written notice that specifies both the purchase price of Disney and the commission charge you've just paid for the transaction. All confirmations look something like this:

Name of Brokerage Firm
Address of Brokerage Firm
CONFIRMATION
Your Name
Your Account Number

You bought 100 shares at a price of 64-7/8
DISNEY (Name of Company)

Gross Amount:	$6,487.50
Commission:	$ 75.00
Total:	$6,562.50

Trade Date: 10/18/96
Market: New York Stock Exchange
Cusip # (Computerized Tracking System):
Settlement Date: 10/22/96
Type of Account (Cash or Margin):

The confirmation is fairly self-explanatory, except for the final two items. The *settlement date* is the day on which the money that's just been exchanged should be in the appropriate broker's hands. It's always the trade date plus three business days. In this instance, it would be 10/22/96, so that's what appears on your Disney confirmation. The type of account refers to your method of payment—

that is, whether you bought Disney with 100% cash or purchased the stock on margin. With a margin account, you pay only 50%, and borrow the rest from your broker.

One final note: Always check each detail printed on your trade confirmations! As with everything else in life, mistakes happen from time to time—both the human and computer variety. As with an error in your checking account, it's easier to correct a problem sooner than later.

As an added bonus, you will see the 100 shares of Disney you now own reflected on a monthly brokerage statement mailed out at the end of each month. Such statements update you on the positions and value of your entire brokerage account, so they serve as a monthly "health checkup" on Disney and the other two stocks in which you're about to invest.

That's really all there is to it! Now that I've walked you through buying Disney on the New York Stock Exchange, it's time to spend some more of that $25,000 windfall. This time, let's diversify by investing in one of the most remarkable technology firms around and make our trade over the counter.

STOCK PICK #2: INTEL

By taking a plunge into the Information Age with Intel, you'll be following in Hetty Green's footsteps of keeping up with current market trends. However, with all the information stocks from which to choose, why pick Intel? Perhaps you were just as amazed as I was by how well an office or home computer works, thanks to its Intel-manufactured Pentium processor. (After all, that's the real "brains" in your PC, and Intel's goods are strictly state of the art.) Let's take it for granted that you've either researched Intel on your own, or have received from your broker detailed answers to each of the questions you've posed concerning the company's financials. You should also be sure that you're financially and psychologically able to handle the volatility of the stock—as always, an extremely important factor. (At the conclusion of Chapter 5 is an extensive list of questions to ask your broker about any particular stock.)

Once you've made your decision, open the newspaper to the over-the-counter listings. Here's what you would have seen on October 19, 1996, once you've located Intel:

52-Week		Stock	Div	Yld %	P/E	Sales	High	Low	Last	Change
High	Low					100s				
114-1/4	49-13/16	Intel	20	.2	24	77822	110-3/4	109-1/4	110	−3/4

You decide to put in a bid for 100 shares at the price of 110, which means that you're prepared to part with $11,000 plus a commission charge. (As you know, we call this a *limit order,* and you run a risk of being unable to buy the stock at that exact price.) Once you place the order with your broker, he or she phones or electronically places it with the over-the-counter trading desk.

A dealer will either "fill us" (it sounds dumb, but that's the phrase we use) from his or her inventory, or contact another dealer who is making a market in Intel. Here's where the mini-melodrama begins to take place. Even if the transaction is completely accomplished via computer, the excitement of working on Wall Street becomes addictive to most of us who work there. (As a history buff, I find it fun to use my imagination and pretend that the same trade is being made near a mud-thatch wall under the original buttonwood tree of yore. The process itself hasn't changed much.)

Getting back to our Intel trade, we learn that quite a few dealers are in the picture at the moment. The difference between the bid and offer is usually tight, meaning there will only be a one-eighth spread in the price. For some over-the-counter securities, the spread is wider because the stock doesn't have many active dealers. When a particular stock isn't seeing much trading action on a given day, the spread may be as much as a point or more.

Assuming that all goes well with your bid to buy 100 shares of Intel, congratulations are once again in order. You have been "filled" (if you'll pardon the expression) at 110, thereby adding Intel to your investment portfolio.

Never forget that the name of the game is diversification. Once you've learned that lesson (as did my friend Michael from the health club) you'll never again "put all your eggs in one basket." So, let's diversify even further, shall we? For our final trade, let's buy 100 shares of a company in a fairly new industry.

STOCK PICK #3: CABLEVISION SYSTEMS CORP.

For the purpose of this exercise, we wanted to "play" all three markets, so I've selected a stock that trades on the American Stock Exchange (located at 86 Trinity Place). You decide to buy a cable company.

You decide to buy 100 shares at 34, and this time it'll be a breeze. Buying a stock on the American Stock Exchange is just like trading on the New York Stock Exchange, so you've already got the knack. But do take a moment to go through the process in your head, beginning with the initial phone call or visit to your broker. You may find it fun when buying a stock to "creatively visualize" all the hectic activity on the exchange floor. Imagine the sort of dealer hysterics that your own whim to buy Disney, Intel or Cablevision Systems may have caused!

I'll trust you to go through steps one through three on your own and buy 100 shares of our final stock pick. You now own a *portfolio* (anything more than one stock), and can congratulate yourself for being so diversified. Your end-of-the-month position in all three stocks will soon be yours to review in an easy-to-read statement from your brokerage firm.

One final word of advice in the good housekeeping department: invest a few cents in a manila file folder or two, and make sure to file each confirmation you receive just as soon as you've verified all the printed information. Keep this file in a safe place, as you will eventually need to locate the "confirms" for tax purposes. Knowing the original purchase price of the stock is essential when the time comes to sell it, so you or your accountant can calculate your capital gain or capital loss. Each of these terms is defined in the brief tax section included in Chapter 13.

I learned the importance of neatness in recordkeeping the hard way, so don't make the same mistakes I did. I can't tell you how many hours I used to waste searching for an important piece of paper that had been carelessly misplaced or discarded into the garbage pail. By filing each confirmation and brokerage statement the same day you receive it, you'll save loads of time in the long run.

It's a given that Uncle Sam will want what's coming to him on April 15th every year. If you engage in a substantial number of transactions, it's not a bad idea to have your tax advisor or accountant

automatically copied with each confirmation and brokerage statement you receive. In a worst case scenario, your broker should also
have a backup in his files.

Remember our original premise that you won a tax-free $25,000?
Now that you've purchased a total of three stocks, it's time to calculate how much you've spent so far. Let's see if there's anything left:

100 shares of Disney	$ 6,487.50
Commission:	75.00
100 shares of Intel	$11,000.00
Commission:	100.00
100 shares of Cablevision	$ 3,400.00
Commission:	50.00
TOTAL:	$21,112.50

This means that $3,887.50 of the original $25,000 remains. You
may wish to invest the extra money in a money market mutual fund
that will earn substantially more interest than it would sitting in a
savings account. Or you could congratulate yourself on having
made what looks like three great stock picks, and think of the rest
of your windfall as "mad money." Why not live it up a little by treat-
ing yourself to that luxurious coat or dining room set you've always
wanted? Money is a *vehicle of freedom,* remember? And you're free
to spend it any way you choose!

Keeping Up with the (Dow) Joneses

Charles Dow and Edward Jones were the two financial visionaries
who created *The Wall Street Journal* back in 1889. Their accom-
plishments didn't begin and end there, however: Mr. Dow is credit-
ed with the original concept for what became known as the Dow
Jones Industrial Average. (I sometimes wonder what would have
happened if Jones had come up with the idea instead: Would we be
referring to it as the *Jones Dow?*)

More than 100 years later, the Dow Jones Industrial Average is
still the most followed financial index in the world—and it's really

nothing more than a mathematical calculation incorporating certain stocks as a microcosm (for lack of a better word) of the entire market. When the idea first occurred to Dow in 1884, he chose a total of 12 stocks on which to base his industrial average. Nowadays, the Dow Jones Industrial Average is composed of 30 major stocks:

A T & T	Eastman Kodak	Merck & Co.
Allied Signal	Exxon	Minnesota Mining and Manufacturing
Alcoa	General Electric	J. P. Morgan
American Express	General Motors	Philip Morris
Boeing	Goodyear	Procter and Gamble
Caterpillar	Hewlett-Packard	Sears
Chevron	IBM	Travelers
Coca-Cola	International Paper	Union Carbide
Disney	Johnson & Johnson	United Technology
DuPont	McDonald's	Wal-Mart

Which of these would you guess has been on the list longest? Incredibly enough, General Electric (then known as Edison General Electric) was one of the original 12 stocks.

Unless you're already a savvy market watcher, you may be surprised to learn that there are actually *three* Dow Jones averages to follow: Industrial, Transportation, and Utilities. The Dow Jones Utilities Average correlates to the bond market, but what we on Wall Street refer to as *Dow Theory* encompasses only the Industrials and the Transports.

Although the Industrial Average is most indicative of the economy's health, keeping an eye on the Dow Jones transportation picks is important also. This latter average reflects the financial well-being of the firms that transport all those industrial products from manufacturers to consumers. To choose a random example, suppose Coca-Cola is producing more than ever in the firm's history, but the firms that transport all those cans and bottles to your local grocery store are doing poorly. See what I mean? The concern is all about moving the goods to market.

Dow theory postulates that in order to have a truly healthy stock market, both the Industrials and the Transports should keep hitting new highs together. The Dow Jones Transportation Average was originally known as the Dow Jones Railroad Average—not surpris-

ingly, since it predated the airline industry. Nowadays, it's composed of the following 20 transportation firms: ·

American Airlines	Caliber Systems	UAL Corp.
Airborne Freight	Delta Airlines	Union Pacific
Alaska Air	Federal Express	US Airways
APL Ltd.	Illinois Central	US Freight
Burlington Northern SF	Norfolk Southern	XTRA
CNF Transport	Ryder Systems	Yellow Corp.
CSX Corp.	Southwest Airlines	

Many brokers and investors also keep a close eye on the Dow
Jones Utilities as an indicator of the general direction of the bond
market. The reason is simple: a substantial number of investors buy
utilities because they normally have a high-dividend yield and are
thought to be relatively stable, safe investments. The yields provided by these stocks have proven to be a reliable source of income
over the course of America's history, which is why utilities are considered a reasonable alternative to investing in the bond market.
The following 15 stocks make up the Dow Jones Utilities Average:

America Electric Power	Edison International	Public Service Enterprise
Columbia Gas Systems	Enron	Southern Co.
Consolidated Edison	Houston Industries, Inc.	Texas Utilities
Consolidated Natural Gas	PG&E	Unicom
Duke Power	Peco Energy	Williams Cos.

Add all three averages together and stir, and the result is The
Dow Jones Composite. This heady index mix isn't enough to satisfy the most discriminating market watchers, however, so read on!

Watching Other Indices

Standard & Poor's 500 Index is carefully monitored by most professional portfolio managers on Wall Street because the S&P accounts
for about 85% of the market dollar value of *all* stocks listed on the
New York Stock Exchange. It's a *capitalization-weighted index*, that

is, the higher the market value of a company, the greater is its influence on the index.

Only the very best portfolio managers consistently beat the market—the truly gifted virtuosos at the Wall Street game. A few of the best (such as Peter Lynch, Michael Price, and George Soros) might be compared to a brilliant conductor of a symphony orchestra. Now that mutual funds have become widely available to the general public, more of us are able to harness the genius of these Wall Street "maestros" in acquiring a substantial amount of wealth.

There are mutual funds that replicate the S&P 500 Index. The difference between investing in an S&P Index fund versus an actively managed mutual fund is discussed in detail in Chapter 8, but what follows is the S&P 500 Index as of June 1997. The top 40 stocks are accompanied by their member weighting percentages, but keep in mind that it takes all 500 stocks in the index to total 100%.

General Electric	3.150%	Mobil	.822%
Coca-Cola	2.567%	Citicorp	.818%
Exxon	2.292%	Hewlett-Packard	.804%
Microsoft	2.273%	SBC Communications	.798%
Intel	1.803%	Gillette	.781%
Merck & Co.	1.713%	Abbott Labs	.764%
Royal Dutch Petroleum	1.590%	Fannie Mae	.752%
Philip Morris	1.566%	American Home Products	.740%
Procter & Gamble	1.431%	Chevron	.717%
IBM	1.241%	NationsBank	.711%
Johnson & Johnson	1.241%	Bellsouth	.682%
Bristol-Myer Squibb	1.133%	Ford Motor	.673%
Wal-Mart	1.091%	Amoco	.673%
Pfizer	1.039%	BankAmerica	.672%
American International Group	1.001%	GTE	.660%
DuPont	.941%	Chase Manhattan	.654%
AT&T	.889%	Cisco Systems	.649%
Pepsico	.876%	General Motors	.642%
Disney	.831%	Lucent Technologies	.631%
Eli Lilly	.828%	Boeing	.614%

Most companies are consumer driven, which is why ordinary folk like you and me account for the bulk of our gross domestic product. This point may hit home when you add up how many of the top 40 S&P firms you and your family do business with.

To review what we've covered so far, you now know what makes up the Dow Jones Composite (the Industrials, Transports, and Utilities), as well as the S&P 500 Index. But hold onto your hats, there's more:

1. *The NASDAQ Composite* measures the general activity of the over-the-counter market.

2. *The NDX 100* is composed of the most widely followed over-the-counter stocks. Approximately 30% of this index is made up of Intel and Microsoft.

3. *The Russell Index* is a broad index of many smaller-capitalized companies.

You'd be surprised at how many registered reps on Wall Street don't have any real grasp of the Dow Jones Industrial Average, let alone what makes up the rest of the Dow Jones Composite, the S&P 500, NASDAQ Composite, NDX 100 or Russell indexes. The most novice investor reading this book right now knows probably more about these indices than do most brokers!

Choosing a Broker and a Brokerage House

Many types of brokerage houses are available to choose from, and making an intelligent choice before you fork over your first commission dollar is imperative. The major retail brokers (also known as *full-service houses*) will assign a registered representative to serve you as an individual investor. In return, you can expect to pay a higher commission rate for his or her services. A full-service broker is able to trade in stocks, bonds, mutual funds, money market funds, and international stocks. He or she can even sell you shares of partnerships in real estate, oil, "plain vanilla" Treasury bills, or commercial deposits.

The major brokerage houses are Merrill Lynch, Bear Stearns, Paine Webber, Salomon Brothers, Smith Barney, Morgan Stanley–Dean Witter, First Boston, and Goldman Sachs. You pay (often dearly) for the services of brokers at any of these firms, but you'll always have someone you can phone or visit for research and investment advice. Most of the time, these brokers are willing to go out of their way for you, because their pay is tied to commissions. Don't forget that you are your broker's boss in a very real sense, because you're paying for what should be top-rate service!

Any first-time investor should go with a broker who comes well recommended by someone she trusts, so ask your friends or acquaintances for names of qualified brokers. Be leery of any registered representative who doesn't come highly recommended, as most care only about the size of their commission checks. (They make most of their income by pushing all the junk on their computer screens, rather than by selling high-quality stocks.)

If none of your friends or family has a good recommendation for you, why not visit an office of Merrill Lynch or Smith Barney and conduct broker interviews on your own? Never settle for someone with less than a proven track record and with whom you have a good personal rapport. (This book will help you ascertain how much real working knowledge a prospective broker has!) You may even be able to go solo by using a discount brokerage firm. If your only interest is investing in mutual funds, you can find all the information and advice you need in Chapter 8.

I always say that it's worth spending a little extra in terms of commissions in exchange for quality service and peace of mind. You need to find someone who's not only ethical and competent, but who will keep a watchful eye on all your stock and bond positions. You can then take a "breather" from reading the stock market quotes every day. (Think of any such time off as a paid vacation.) Investors normally enjoy more peace of mind with a full-service brokerage house for two reasons:

1. Assuming the broker is honest and of good character, he or she won't permit any of your funds to be disbursed without your authorization through verbal or written confirmation. It will therefore be difficult (if not impossible) for somebody to get into your account or make unauthorized trades.

2. All brokerage firms are insured for up to $500,000 in securities by the Securities Investors Protection Corporation. However, no more than $100,000 can be comprised of cash held dormant in your account awaiting reinvestment. Large firms offer additional coverage (up to roughly $50 million) through various insurance companies.

If you're not one of the fortunate investors with $50 million at play in the market, all of it thoroughly insured by a major brokerage firm, there's a final *caveat emptor*: like any individual investor who makes bad business decisions, *your broker can go bankrupt, too!*

Drexel Burnham, one of the larger full-service brokerage firms, went bankrupt in the late eighties. Countless "small shops" have likewise gone "bust" over the years. Most investors choose to keep their security portfolios in *street name,* which means that their brokerage firm represents them as a custody agent. You may opt to have securities registered in your own name instead (which would probably entail keeping them in a vault somewhere), but that would be a colossal waste of time and energy for most of us. If your brokerage firm goes bankrupt and your stocks are in street name, you must recoup your funds from SIPC and any insurance company covering the firm.

If you're absolutely certain that you're dealing with a financially sound brokerage firm of good reputation, you won't have to worry about the safekeeping of your portfolio. That's good news indeed. In fact, after nearly two decades of trading on Wall Street, I can probably count on the fingers of one hand the number of times I've personally seen a stock certificate. Like all Wall Streeters, I have my own personal broker keep track of my investment portfolio for me.

The bottom line is that it's completely impractical *not* to use a brokerage firm, so be sure you make the right choice from the very start of your investment career. In the next section of this chapter, we analyze what makes a typical brokerage firm tick.

Playing in the Major League: How Full-Service Houses Operate

Most full-service houses have two primary components, the brokerage unit and the investment banking division.

THE BROKERAGE UNIT

This unit is comprised of two sections: institutional sales and retail sales.

Institutional Sales. The division that handles institutional sales employs salespeople able to trade with mutual funds, hedge funds, pension funds, and with various other investment advisors. Many readers are already familiar with pension funds because their employers include them as part of an employee benefits package. For those readers not so fortunate, a pension fund or 401(k) permits you (and/or your company) to make contributions through payroll deductions in order to ensure a retirement nest egg once your working career has ended. Members of the institutional sales division sell equity as well as bonds. It is split into two units, equity sales and fixed income. If you happen to be a large institutional account, you will have quite a few folk working on your behalf—including a research salesperson, a block position trader, an over-the-counter trader, and a derivatives salesperson. If a portion of your diversified portfolio is composed of bonds, in most cases you will have additional advisors who cover government bonds, corporate bonds, municipal bonds, high-yield bonds, and derivatives. The term *high-yield bonds* refers to what were commonly known as "junk bonds," while most *derivatives* are leveraged bets on the direction of the market.

Retail Sales. In this section of a brokerage firm, your own personal broker hangs his or her hat and coat each morning. This is perhaps the only part of any full-service organization that you'll ever see personally. Most brokers with any of the major houses deal in *all* the investment tools available in the marketplace. There's really not much difference between such a broker and the manager of your local supermarket, because each has countless thousands of products on the shelves with which to tempt you. (By the way, we who work on Wall Street actually refer to those things a broker sells you as *products.*) Your personal broker is a generalist, not a specialist. He or she is a registered rep who can place orders on your behalf for stocks, mutual funds, and fixed income. (*Fixed income* always refers to bonds of one type or another, including municipal bonds, corporate bonds, and government bonds.)

THE INVESTMENT BANKING DIVISION

The investment banking division is where you'll find the "big boys" (and the occasional "big girls") on Wall Street, the real deal makers who make the global economy tick. These men and women generally earn annual incomes ranging from $500,000 to $10 million or more, and wield enormous power. Not surprisingly, many have enormous egos to match. Investment bankers deal with corporate giants, and often handle major negotiations with foreign governments and municipalities. What makes a full-service brokerage house tick? Money—and lots of it! And that's where the investment banker comes in, eager to offer service with a smile. The deal makers in the investment banking division make it the most profitable area of the firm. Investment bankers specialize in raising capital for business. One of their primary functions is to introduce a company to the marketplace, permitting it to be traded on one of the three stock exchanges.

Those who knock on an investment banker's door are invariably business folk who need more capital in order to expand. Various financing alternatives can be explored, such as taking on long-term debt via private or public transaction, but most companies want to "go public" by offering stock to regular investors like you and me (although we'll normally be at the bottom of the pecking order when there's a truly good deal in the offing). Huge institutional investors such as Fidelity or T. Rowe Price generate a lot more in commissions for the underwriters than we small-fry who want to buy into an initial public offering. Unless you're a very active trader or a major account (and therefore a big source of commissions), be extremely cautious when someone pitches such an offering to you. Chances are that the salesperson is trying to unload less-than-spectacular merchandise that none of the "big boys" want for themselves. Face facts: If *they* don't want it, *you* certainly don't want it!

Investment bankers underwrite the issue of new stocks by buying the entire issue (all the shares being offered) in order to resell them to the general public at a specific price. An investment banker often invites others to join a syndicate that collectively tries to rope in other dealers to help sell the offering. Before the firm goes public, however, it is legally obliged to make a full financial disclosure in a registration statement to be filed with the Securities and Exchange Commission—which then becomes a prospectus that can be shown to potential investors. The prospectus is referred to as a *red herring* until the stock actually goes on the market, and by no means represents an *endorsement* from the Securities and Exchange

Commission. The prospectus simply indicates that the company has adequately disclosed its financials in accordance with government-mandated securities laws.

SELLING THE PRODUCT

You now know that the investment banking division is the "product generator" and the brokerage unit is the "distribution channel" that sells it. The former division normally racks up most of the profit for the brokerage firm—but rest assured that everyone gets a piece of the action, including the hundreds of men and women employed in the research department. The financial analysts study the many stocks in each industry group and recommend what they believe to be the most attractive stocks to the brokerage unit. Financial analysts also help the investment bankers evaluate a company that's being packaged as an IPO.

Theoretically, financial analysts should provide a totally objective opinion of the companies they research. Their yearly bonus checks (often in the millions) are tied into the profits earned by the investment banking unit, however, and this fact creates an obvious conflict of interest. Once a company goes public, a less-than-ethical analyst will keep raving about the firm, even if doing so involves telling outright lies. The size of an analyst's bonus check may be contingent on telling such untruths, and sadly, many ethical analysts find themselves on the bread lines after being replaced by those without integrity who continue to thrive and prosper.

Any intelligent salesperson in the brokerage unit knows which financial analysts are downright corrupt. An ethical broker therefore disregards the opinions offered by those motivated by sheer greed, and goes by the advice offered by the "good guys" in the research department. On the other hand, unethical brokers have no qualms about handing you stacks of research material that glorify what they know full well to be the worst garbage available in the marketplace!

Ask any potential broker point-blank whether such unethical behavior occurs in the financial industry. If the broker answers no, then find another broker. The banking division of a brokerage firm cares only about selling a deal, and usually asks its analysts to tout the product. In many cases, a secondary offering (the sale of additional shares of stock) is made after six months go by. On many occasions, after the secondary has been sold successfully, the price of the stock drops drastically. An occasional good deal may present itself, but it's far better to be cynical than optimistic about getting involved with IPOs.

Taking a Chance on the Minors: How Small Houses Operate

You may not have a veritable army of financial analysts and investment bankers working for (or *against*) you if you decide to go with a smaller firm. Yet, for those who want to save on commission rates, a number of alternatives to full-service houses are available, for example, regional brokerages, discount brokerages, and on-line services.

REGIONAL BROKERAGES

Regional houses may be advantageous to some investors, because they specialize in companies based in their particular neck of the woods. Two of the better-known regional houses are Alex Brown (based in Baltimore) and Dain Bosworth (of Minneapolis), but the list goes on and on. Perhaps the state in which you live has a regional firm of its own you should investigate.

DISCOUNT BROKERAGES

You can also use what's known as a *discount firm*. In many respects it's the difference between flying first-class and coach, but if you know what you're doing in the marketplace you may not need to pay full commissions. A few of the most notable are Charles Schwab, Quick & Reilly, Muriel Siebert, Fidelity, Waterhouse Financial, and American Express Direct. Another advantage of dealing with discount brokers is that they won't constantly phone you and try to create transactions. Think of it as shopping in a self-service department store, rather than being pressured by a salesperson who insists that you look great in a suit that doesn't suit you at all. Your savings through a discount brokerage can actually amount to 50% or more, as evidenced by the following comparison of commission rates recently drawn up by Quick & Reilly:

Commissions	100 shares @ $10	500 shares @ $15	1000 shares @ $20
Merrill Lynch	$50.00	$174.00	$374.00
Smith Barney	$50.00	$150.00	$400.00
Charles Schwab	$47.00	$101.50	$144.00
Fidelity	$46.50	$101.50	$143.50
Quick & Reilly	$37.50	$ 77.75	$109.00

ON-LINE SHOPPING

Thanks to the incredible Information Age in which we live, you can now buy stocks on-line. All you need is a computer, a modem connected to a phone jack in your house, and an internet hookup (amazing, isn't it?). In time, this trend may put countless high-paid brokers out of business. This method of trading is strictly "no frills," but it comes with an unbeatable commission rate. You won't have an army of researchers to do your homework for you, however. So don't try this until you've become totally confident in your ability to make the right market decisions on your own. According to a recent survey by *Barron's,* the highest-rated on-line services were offered by the following firms: Lombard Institutional Brokerage, Waterhouse Securities, E*Trade Securities, Accutrade, American Express, Muriel Siebert, Quick & Reilly, and Wall Street Electronica.

FEMALE INVESTMENT ADVISORS/WOMEN-RUN INVESTMENT FIRMS

Last but not least, consider giving your investment business to a female entrepreneur. If you happen to be a woman in a male-dominated industry, you know from personal experience what it's like to stare up at an impenetrable "glass ceiling." Have you stood by in disbelief as men with much less experience and expertise have been promoted ahead of you and male colleagues with similar job duties make considerably more money for less work? It's true that Wall Street isn't the exclusively "all-male club" it used to be. Yet even today, with the exception of Muriel Siebert (who operates a brokerage firm based in New York), virtually all brokerage firms are run by men. If you can find a female broker you can trust, and who is as good (or better) than a male broker at managing your money, then why not give her your business?

With regard to this option, I can't resist sharing another piece of American history. Permit me to introduce you to Victoria Woodhull (the very first woman to run for the office of President of the United States) who, along with a sister named Tennessee, bravely flew in the face of nineteenth-century convention and opened the first all-female brokerage firm!

The Woodhulls were intimate friends of Cornelius Vanderbilt, one of the most renowned "wizards of Wall Street." Although by no means a feminist, Vanderbilt knew full well that Victoria and Tennessee had both the brains and determination to succeed on Wall Street. To the utter amazement of the entire financial industry, the Woodhulls put together a firm called "She Brokers," and soon amassed a fortune.

Commissions Are the Name of the Brokerage Game

The wealthier a female investor is, the more she needs to worry about being taken for every cent she has. Her broker puts a substantial amount of money in his own personal bank account every time a trade is made.

By the time you've finished reading this book you'll know how to "gird your loins" and protect yourselves against the bad guys. But I want you to face the fact that countless men (and women) on Wall Street have become grim reapers and should be avoided like the plague. I want to acquaint you with the all-too-common practice of *churning,* which is illegal, but very hard to prove. That's when a broker talks you into buying and selling as many stocks (or other financial instruments) as possible, in order to rake in a fortune via commissions. Brokers who churn accounts are certainly not operating in their clients' best interests, as much as they convincingly pretend to. Brokers aren't paid according to how well they handle their clients' money, but rather according to a ratio based on the number and size of the transactions they complete. The simple fact is, the more commissions your broker charges you, the more he or she gets paid.

Once you've turned the final page of this book, you can never say you weren't fully warned. What is the overriding rationale for these grim reapers? They simply think that if their clients are stupid enough to have fallen for the bull they're handing them, the damn fools *deserve* to be taken for all they're worth.

HOW TO PICK WINNERS— AND AVOID THE LOSERS

Should you be fortunate enough to have children, I hope you start teaching them the value of money at an early age. Remember the story of Hetty Green and how she read the daily financials to her blind grandfather? Like Hetty, perhaps your six-year-old will glean enough market savoir-faire eventually to become the single richest person on the planet.

Lessons from a Lemonade Stand

I can't say I started reading *The Wall Street Journal* at such an early age, but I'm eternally grateful that my father taught me a thing or two about money not long after I'd "graduated" from kindergarten. With the help of my mom (who stirred up pitchers of lemonade while I manned my makeshift booth outside), I literally started my own business. The location I chose was the corner of 90th Street and Northern Boulevard in Jackson Heights, Queens, a few steps outside our apartment building.

Perhaps a great many readers of this book learned the value of hard work and enterprise in much the same way—whether peddling cookies for the Girl Scouts or delivering newspapers. But in my case it was a long, hot summer (made to order for selling lemonade) that prompted my first enterprise. My father told me right from the start that the goal of selling my product to thirsty customers on the street was to make some sort of profit. In retrospect, I'm certain that's the first time I ever heard the word. What he meant was that all the nickels and dimes I took in had better eventually add up to more than it cost my mom to purchase the raw ingredients. (Happily, I didn't have to pay her for all the labor in the kitchen.)

The story of my lemonade stand may at first glance appear to be nothing more than a sentimental trip down memory lane, yet the basics of starting up a $50-million business to be publicly traded on Wall Street are virtually identical. It cost my mom less than $5 to subsidize my first entrepreneurial effort, but the lesson I learned was how to make sufficient profit to ensure a good return on all the time and effort I put into the venture.

Was my lemonade stand a success, you ask? Well, I didn't earn enough to buy my own condo and become independently wealthy, but I do recall making enough to buy the Barbie Doll Dream House I'd spotted at the local toy store. (I had been yearning for it since the spring, and couldn't bear the thought of waiting until my birthday rolled around in October.) I loved being able to treat my beloved Barbie to the "home" of her dreams much sooner than expected, but more important by far was the lesson I had learned about the value of good, hard work.

In order to maximize my earnings, I even learned how to diversify my business by adding Kool-Aid to the mix just in case any of my potential customers had an aversion to lemons. Still, the business was seasonal, so as soon as the weather turned cool it was time to pack it all in.

They didn't teach the value of making money in the classrooms of PS 149 in my day, sad to say—just regular stuff like reading, writing, and arithmetic. Yet, the financial lessons my parents taught me that summer were every bit as valuable in the long run. That's why I stress that if you have kids of your own, it's never too early to prepare them for the "real world." How else will they become well versed in what it takes to make a living and put a bit of money aside as adults?

Although I don't yet have any children of my own, for the rest of this chapter I'm going to pretend that I'm the proud mother of a six-year-old named Lisa. She doesn't know it yet, but I'm about to stake her to a little start-up money for her first business—and I'll even stir all that lemonade mix into ice water, same as my mother did thirty years ago.

In retrospect, however, I wish my parents had suggested that I diversify my business even further by selling something to eat at my own childhood stand. So the first thing that Lisa and I plan to do is shop for the raw ingredients for cookies, as well as lemonade; and we'll be sure to keep a precise record of what each item costs at the local market. For the sake of this exercise, here's what we end up buying:

Plastic cups and napkins	$ .75
One frozen container of lemonade	.89
One package of cookie mix	3.19
Total Cost:	$4.83

After reading the labels, Lisa and I know that our package of cookie mix should make a total of 17 cookies. We can likewise count on our container of frozen concentrate to stir up 8 mouth-watering glasses of lemonade. The next step is to carefully plot out on paper how much we should charge for each product we sell, in order to make the whole enterprise worthwhile.

According to our calculations, if we charge 50 cents per cookie and 50 cents per glass of lemonade, we'll make a "gross income" of $8.50 for the former and $4.00 for the latter. That's a total of $12.50, which is not bad considering that it only cost $4.83 for supplies. We assume, of course, that our stand will be a smashing success, or that we at least manage to sell one full batch of cookies and pitcher of lemonade before it all turns stale. Lisa's new business (with a simple yet catchy name) would then proudly be able to issue an income statement that looks like this:

LISA'S LEMONADE & COOKIE STAND

Total sales	$12.50		
Costs of goods sold			$4.83
Total costs			$4.83
Gross profit (before taxes)	$ 7.67		
Federal, state & city taxes		$3.60	
Net income	$ 4.07		

The foregoing assumes that Lisa will be taxed at a typical corporate rate of 47%, so we have to plan on a tax bite of $3.60. (My

"daughter" and I arrive at that figure by multiplying 0.47 by $7.67.)
We adults know full well how much in taxes is taken out of our pay-
checks each week, so it's only cheating our kids if we don't tell it
like it is right from the start. The good news is that Lisa can still
make a handsome profit, even after she "pays the piper" at the
going corporate rate.

Were we professional financial analysts, Lisa and I would be
looking at a couple of key ratios. We might even begin to extrapolate Lisa's future earnings on the basis of this draft income statement,
in which case we would come up with the following equation:

$$\text{Lisa's Gross Profit Margin} = \text{Ratio of Profit to Sales}$$
$$= \text{Ratio of \$7.67 to \$12.50}$$
$$= 61.3\%$$

Let's face it: 61% is a rather high *gross profit margin* compared
with that of most businesses. (I wish that more stocks in my own
Wall Street portfolio did as well!) But we're nonetheless optimistic
at maintaining a profit margin at this level, because Lisa has little in
the way of "overhead" (expenses) and there doesn't seem to be any
direct competition in the neighborhood at present.

Another financial ratio we'll need to understand is Lisa's *operating profit margin.* That's the term used to describe what's left of our
profit after all costs have been deducted. Gross profit takes into
account only the costs of manufacturing the product. Lisa has no
costs other than the $4.83 we spent at the supermarket, so her gross
profit margin will be precisely equal to her operating profit margin.

In the foregoing scenario, Lisa's income is equal to her operating profit, and therefore her operating profit margin will be the
same as her *pretax profit margin.* I'm afraid we'll have to take out
our pocket calculator one last time to examine her lemonade business from the standpoint of Lisa's *net profit margin,* however. That's
the amount we can "take down to the bottom line" (as we say on
Wall Street), once Uncle Sam takes a dig into our pocketbooks! In
my pretend daughter's case, this percentage is calculated as follows:

$$\text{Lisa's Net Profit Margin} = \text{Ratio of Net Income to Total Sales}$$
$$= \text{Ratio of \$ 4.07 to \$ 12.50}$$
$$= 32.56\%$$

So far, Lisa and I have constructed her enterprise only on paper,
in order to make sure in advance that she stands a good chance of

making a profit. But the whole scheme looks so financially mouth-watering that Lisa asks me whether it's possible somehow to double her potential income. (Looks like my fictional offspring has already caught the entrepreneurial bug big time!) I suggest that she consider expanding her cookie and lemonade business by setting up a second stand a few blocks away, thus broadening her territory. It's a given that she won't be able to man both business locations at the same time, so Lisa decides to hire her best friend Christine to run the additional operation. She promises to pay her new employee a total of $2.00 should she be able to sell the first batch of cookies and pitcher of lemonade we give her. (The only thing that bothers me about this plan is that Christine's mom gets to sun herself in the backyard hammock while I do all the work!)

But before she actually phones to hire her friend, Lisa confides her concern that Christine may not be quite the crackerjack salesperson that Lisa knows herself to be. I suggest Lisa "hedge her bet" by taking out a local newspaper ad. The additional cost will amount to $3.00, but Lisa agrees that this expense will be more than offset should her business manage to sell twice as much product. Just to be certain we're making the right decision, we go back to the drawing board and plot out Lisa's new and improved plan on paper:

34 cookies @ 50 cents	=	$17.00
16 glasses of lemonade @ 50 cents	=	8.00
Total sales:		$25.00
2 sets of plastic cups and napkins	=	$ 1.50
2 packages of cookie mix	=	6.38
2 containers of lemonade	=	1.78
Total cost of goods sold:		$ 9.66

Lisa now needs to factor in the costs of expanding her territory. In financial circles, we refer to such line items as "Selling, General, and Administrative Costs."

Christine's wages	$2.00
Newspaper advertisement	3.00
Additional costs:	$5.00

If all goes according to plan, total sales will be $25.00, and total costs should equal $14.66. Let's pretend that the first day the kids open up shop is an absolute scorcher, with lots of thirsty (and hungry) passersby. Happily, Lisa's Lemonade and Cookie Stand is a resounding success, and everything works out just as planned. Naturally, as with all start-up enterprises, there were some elements of risk. For example, a single downpour might have totally screwed up the bottom line—or even wiped Lisa's business out altogether, resulting in a loss of the $14.66 she'd invested.

A rainy day isn't the only disaster that may have occurred, however. Lisa had been smart enough to choose someone she knew well as her first employee. What if the classmate she'd selected to manage the other booth had dipped a hand into the till? With more or less the same catastrophic results, a less principled employee might have been unable to resist the temptation to eat and drink up every nickel of Lisa's profits!

As noted earlier, however, Lisa's Lemonade and Cookie Stand is a success. For the sake of simplicity, let's suppose that Lisa and Christine want to call it quits after the first day. The pair of entrepreneurs pack their duffel bags and head off to summer camp, delighted to have some extra money on deposit in the camp canteen with which to buy sodas and candy. They enjoy a great summer but, since the new school year begins just as soon as the last campfire is extinguished, they'll have no more business income for the year in question. Therefore, Lisa's year-end income statement will read like this:

LISA'S LEMONADE AND COOKIE STAND
INCOME STATEMENT—YEAR ENDING 12/31/XX

Sales	$ 25.00
Total revenue	$ 25.00
Costs of goods sold	$ 9.66
Selling, general, and administrative costs	5.00
Total costs and expenses	$ 14.66
Profit before taxes	$ 10.34
Less federal, state and city taxes	$ −4.86
(assuming a 47% tax rate, $10.34 × .47)	
Net income	$ 5.48

Now that may not be the most impressive bottom line in history, but keep in mind that Lisa and Christine are only six years old. Whenever kids that age manage to earn money on their own (rather than collecting a weekly allowance) it's an accomplishment they'll remember for the rest of their lives. I'll certainly never forget that very first business I owned and operated roughly 30 years ago!

UNDERSTANDING PROFIT MARGINS

Spending just a few minutes with pocket calculator in hand, I can teach Lisa about the three most important margins of her lemonade and cookie stand—or, for that matter, of *any* business in which she invests.

1. *Gross Profit Margin* (Gross Margin) is equal to *Sales* minus *Costs of Goods Sold,* divided by *Sales*

    = $25.00 minus $ 9.66, divided by $25.00
    = $15.34, divided by $25.00
    = $61.36%.

2. *Operating Profit Margin* (Operating Margin) is equal to *Sales* minus *Costs of Goods Sold,* minus *Sales and General Administrative Expenses,* divided by *Sales*

    = $25.00 minus $9.66, minus $5.00, divided by $25.00
    = $10.34 divided by $25.00
    = $41.36%.

3. *Net Profit Margin* (Net Margin) is equal to *After-Tax Profit* divided by *Sales*

    = $25.00 minus $9.66, minus $5.00, minus $4.86, divided by $25.00
    = $5.48 divided by $25.00
    = 21.92%.

You've probably noticed that our net profit margin has shrunk considerably, from the 32.56% calculation in Lisa's initial plan to a mere 21.92% based on her decision to expand the business. Often, as an entrepreneur tries to expand his or her operations, additional dollars must be spent which won't "come down to the bottom line." The initial expenses connected with expansion (in this case, wages for Christine and the newspaper ad) prove well worth it in the long run, however. I'm reminded of my economics teacher's admonition to "Hang in there, baby!"

The title of this chapter is *"How to Pick Winners—And Avoid the Losers."* You may be wondering why I just devoted a few pages to Lisa's hypothetical lemonade and cookie stand. Why do you suppose my "pretend daughter" and I sat down at the kitchen table and worked out all these figures before we actually put the plan into action? It was essential that Lisa and I carefully review all the basic fundamentals of starting up our business, to make certain that her food and beverage stand would be a winner rather than an ill-advised loser *before* we invested our time and money in it!

It Pays to Do Your Homework

Let me tell you more about a very smart "little old lady" from Brooklyn who knew how to do her homework—and then some! Her name was Anne Scheiber, and she was born into a large family on October 1, 1893. Anne's father died when she was quite young, so she worked by day as a bookkeeper while earning her high school diploma at night. All of her hard work and studies eventually paid off, however, and in time she even managed to obtain a law degree—an uncommon accomplishment for women of Anne's era. Eventually she settled for full-time employment as a tax auditor for the Internal Revenue Service. While one by one her male colleagues at the IRS advanced to the ranks of management, Anne found herself passed over time and time again when promotions or raises were handed out.

Ms. Scheiber retired in 1943 with a rather insignificant monthly pension of $83 and $5,000 in savings. What happened next? This remarkable Brooklynite resolved to put that monthly pension check of hers to the best possible use. Not content to rock away the rest of her life, she took up a retirement hobby that proved far more profitable than doing needlework: she began to do a little homework on the subject of investments.

How can we be certain that Ms. Scheiber did her homework? Suffice it to say that, by the time she'd reached the ripe old age of 101, this "little old lady" had managed to acquire an investment portfolio worth a whopping $22 million! (At the reading of Anne's last will and testament, it was learned that her vast fortune was left to Yeshiva University in support of the education of Jewish women of merit.)

Follow the Money

Should you contemplate starting up or investing in a business where the most you stand to lose in a worst-case scenario is $4.83, that sum is not likely to make or break you. But now that my six-year-old Lisa has an understanding of how to read her own income statement, she should have no real problem translating a similar statement with a bottom line involving *billions* of dollars. Regardless of whether you're six or sixty, you should have no real problem, either.

What if the gentleman who lives next door is so impressed with Lisa's talent at running her lemonade and cookie stand that he proposes to cut himself in on the action by offering her $100 as an investment? With this unexpected windfall, Lisa can hire several additional employees, and also purchase nearly 20 times the amount of raw ingredients we originally put in our shopping cart. Naturally, our neighbor has every right to expect a nice return for such a considerable investment, but Lisa also stands to profit from the arrangement. In the end, she should rake in many times the $5.48 in net income she was capable of earning from operating only two stands.

A really *shrewd* potential investor might take a nice, long walk around the neighborhood to see if other youngsters have even better operating margins. Should our neighbor happen to run across another young entrepreneur whose business demonstrates a consistent growth in sales and even more enticing margins, that $100 bankroll would likely go to Lisa's competitor instead. (As they say, that's the way the cookie crumbles!)

Real-life investing on Wall Street is conducted in much the same competitive way. Wall Streeters carefully examine a company's financials to make sure a firm has a healthy measure of sales growth, as well as increases in the three margins we've been discussing for the past few pages. The firm whose prospects look the best gets the investment dollar. The approach to analyzing the financials remains the same whether the company in question makes and sells lemonade and cookies, fax machines, or silicon chips. But the most savvy researchers on Wall Street know that each industry tends to have somewhat different margins. Accordingly, as each individual business is put under the microscope, its margins are compared with those of other firms within its own industry.

Enough about cookies and lemonade: Let's move on to a gigantic corporation with a 1995 annual report reflecting a net income of nearly $4 billion. Having read and digested all the information in the previous chapter, you can take pride in already owning a piece of this particular firm's "action" yourself (at least on paper), since I'm referring to none other than Intel. As an educated investor, you know how important it is to ask your broker for the facts, rather than let him or her regale you with hype based on nothing more than the need to bank your commission dollar. All the facts you'll need to know about Intel (or any other company being pitched to you) should be readily available to your broker, and therefore just as readily available to you.

You should insist on seeing Intel's most recent income statement before you put any of your hard-earned savings into the company's stock. Assuming that you had no problem understanding Lisa's Lemonade and Cookie Stand's income statement, you should be equally adept at deciphering Intel's. Again, there's virtually no difference between the two, save that the latter firm enjoys a bottom line (net income) that's nearly a billion times higher.

Here's a condensed version of Intel's income statement. Perhaps you'll see why it wasn't a bad idea to add Intel to your portfolio in the previous chapter:

INTEL

INCOME STATEMENT—YEAR ENDING 12/30/95

Net sales (of microprocessors)	$16,202,000,000
Costs of goods sold (manufacturing costs)	7,811,000,000
Gross profit	8,391,000,000
Gross profit margin	
(The ratio of gross profit margin divided by sales)	51.79%

Fairly impressive numbers, don't you agree? From the first two items on this statement, we can easily extrapolate both the *sales* of Intel and how much it costs physically to manufacture all the microprocessors the firm so successfully markets worldwide. With even the cheapest pocket calculator in hand, we can compute the *gross profit margin* in a matter of seconds, and a margin of 51% is pretty darned good!

What follows is a step-by-step breakdown of Intel's income statement for the same year. Don't let the enormous numbers frighten you. You now know the underlying principles behind them from our experience in the cookie and lemonade racket.

INTEL
INCOME STATEMENT—YEAR ENDING 12/30/95

Net sales	$16,202,000,000
Costs of goods sold	− 7,811,000,000
Gross profit	$ 8,391,000,000
Research and development	− 1,296,000,000
	$ 7,095,000,000
Selling, general, and administrative costs	− 1,843,000,000
Operating income	$ 5,252,000,000
Nonoperating income	+ 415,000,000
Earnings before interest and taxes	$ 5,667,000,000
Interest expense	− 29,000,000
Income before taxes	$ 5,638,000,000
Provision for income taxes	− 2,072,000,000
Net income	$ 3,566,000,000

You can analyze the financial health of a company the same way that medical doctors perform a general health checkup on a patient. Wall Streeters refer to this process as *fundamental analysis,* a series of tests used to measure the numbers in a firm's three major financial statements. You're already acquainted with the *income statement,* and we soon take a good, hard look at what's known as a *balance sheet.* The third major statement (which we don't discuss in the book) is referred to as the *statement of cash flow.* That's a bit more difficult to master, but can nonetheless be quite helpful at times.

JUST THE FACTS, MA'AM: WHAT THE NUMBERS TELL YOU

Having already analyzed the three most important margins of Lisa's Lemonade and Cookie Stand, let's do the same for Intel. Don't panic if you don't have a calculator at arm's reach. None of the math involved is that complex, despite the huge numbers involved.

As already mentioned, a company's *gross margin* is useful whenever we want to look at its gross profit solely from the basic manufacturing angle. We already know the formula for calculating gross margins, so all that's left is to plug in the appropriate figures from the foregoing chart: Intel's *gross profit* (8,391,000,000) divided by *sales* (16,202,000,000) equals a gross margin of 51.79%. Should Intel not have to pay its sales staff, or make expenditures relating to advertising or anything else, the firm would make 51.79 cents on each dollar spent manufacturing its product. But Intel is hardly a lemonade stand with a volunteer army of moms slaving away in vast kitchens somewhere—nor can the firm rely on a $3 newspaper ad to bring in a sales figure of more than $16 billion! It follows that very high selling and administrative expenses must be taken into account.

Therefore, the next step in our financial analysis involves scrutinizing the firm's *operating profit margin,* and the first number we need to consider is Intel's *operating income.* This figure takes into account: (1) the manufacturing costs of all the products sold during the year in question, (2) the selling and general administrative expenses of running Intel, and (3) all the firm's research and development costs. (Technology companies invariably spend large amounts of money each year on research and development—as do pharmaceutical firms.) Using the equation already learned from the cookies and lemonade exercise: Intel's *operating profit margin* equals *operating income* (5,252,000,000) divided by *sales* (16,202,000,000), which comes to 32.42%.

There's only one more margin to calculate, that is, how much money Intel has left after Uncle Sam gets what's coming to him. You'll recall that *net profit margin* is equal to *net income* (3,566,000,000) divided by *sales* (16,202,000,000), so it only takes a few punches on the calculator to arrive at a figure of 22.01%. This tells us that Intel made 22 cents on every dollar of sales—an extremely impressive number when you consider that most American companies have net profit margins somewhere between 6 and 10%.

We've discussed gross profit margin, operating profit margin, and net profit margin, but investors want to see more than just decent margins in each of these categories, which is why analysts also scrutinize a firm's *earnings growth*. Of the three margins we've covered thus far, the operating profit margin is the one that analysts pay most attention to. (Nonoperating income refers to income the company realizes through means other than sales of its products. Nonoperating income may include money a firm is awarded in the settlement of a lawsuit or income from the sale of one of its buildings.) Although these funds are always considered income, they are unlikely to be available next year. These kinds of extraordinary events should therefore be discounted, since this portion of a firm's total income won't reflect the earnings investors can expect in the future from the normal course of business operations. A firm's operating profit margin, then, is key because it reflects only what we refer to as the "main line" of day-to-day operations.

To illustrate the point, let's go back to our lemonade and cookie stand example for a moment: Suppose one of Lisa's customers is the generous sort who hands her a $5 bill for a 50 cent purchase, and says "Keep the change!" Lisa is ecstatic, to say the least, but can hardly count on that sort of tip on each and every sale. The $4.50 of additional income would therefore be categorized in Lisa's income statement as *nonoperating income.* Should this unexpected tip be accounted for in any other way, it would distort the information used by potential investors who want to project Lisa's earnings over the long run.

Investors want to see a firm's earnings grow at the same time its three profit margins expand, which means that the company will earn progressively more money on each sale it makes. Earnings are reported on a quarterly basis (four times per year) by the chief financial officer of all firms that offer stock for sale in the marketplace. Wall Street professionals compare the results with the same quarter's earnings for the preceding year.

For example, Intel's fourth quarter earnings for 1996 will be compared to its fourth quarter earnings for 1995. The computer industry and many other retail businesses experience an increase in sales for the final quarter of each year, as the firm's products are bought and gift-wrapped for the holidays. On the other hand, Lisa's Lemonade and Cookie Stand experiences its peak earnings during the summertime.

IS YOUR STOCK A "DARLING OF THE DAY"?:
INVESTING FOR GROWTH

Each firm listed on any of the three exchanges must issue a quarterly report; the many thousands of analysts who work on Wall Street quite literally "tune in." The company's chief financial officer (CFO) generally makes a speech in which he or she details items in the firm's financial statements, then offers explanations and answers questions. He or she offers the firm's projections for the next quarter, in terms as optimistic as possible. Each analyst then tries to separate fact from fiction (that is, wishful thinking on the part of the CFO). The analyst in turn formulates his or her own opinion as to whether the company is headed in the right direction, and whether the stock seems to be a good or poor investment in the weeks and months to come.

Some major firms such as IBM hold an actual in-person press conference in a massive meeting room at one of New York's more opulent hotels. The future movement of IBM's stock can probably be forecast in part by its CFO's choice of wardrobe (right down to the color of the shirt and tie he wears), regardless of the figures reflected on the balance sheet. The vast majority of firms make their quarterly reports via conference call; even the intonation of the CFO's voice during this call can have a dramatic impact on the upward or downward price fluctuation of that company's stock. Should the poor man (or woman) be feeling a bit "under the weather" and happen to sneeze at an inopportune moment, it's *conceivable* that the company's stock might go down five points or so in the aftermath!

Obviously, analysts want to hear more than that a firm's earnings are in good shape for the moment. They're eager for total reassurance that earnings will continue to grow in the future.

At this writing, Intel is clearly one of Wall Street's "darlings." There's no way to be certain that it will continue to enjoy such high favor in the long run, however. Who knows? Perhaps the firm will be run out of business by some extraordinary new competitor, even before this book goes to press! (Always bear in mind the caveat that past performance is no guarantee of future results.) Let's loyally stick with Intel for the remainder of this chapter, however, because we're about to embark on the exercise of comparing this particular stock's performance (that is, "price") with the bottom line of Intel's income statements for the past three years.

Let's first take a look at the price of Intel at the conclusion of each year's final day of trading:

December 31, 1993	31.5
December 31, 1994	31.9375
December 29, 1995	56.75
December 31, 1996	130.9375

You may be amazed that the price of Intel stock remained more or less unchanged from the close of 1993 to the last trade of 1994, then rose dramatically in 1995 and more than doubled in 1996. These are the facts that led the most savvy brokers and researchers to believe that Intel's future looked promising way back in 1993 and 1994, long before the rest of the world had a clue.

As discussed, investors in the stock market are really buying future earnings of the firms they choose to add to their portfolios— so the key is knowing what formula to use to determine whether earnings are likely to increase from quarter to quarter or from year to year. It's this simple: a good growth rate in a firm's earnings is almost invariably rewarded by a corresponding increase in the price of its stock. So let's put Intel under the microscope again, this time examining both its earnings and profit margins for the previous three years.

Intel's full income statement for 1996 is not available at this writing, so I won't include any of the firm's 1996 figures in the comparison chart that follows. Rest assured, however, that the first three quarters of 1996 indicate more than a decent rate in Intel's earnings growth. (Had this not been the case, the price of Intel's stock would hardly have skyrocketed from a 1995 year-end price of 56.75 to a whopping 130.9375 by the time the closing bell marked the end of trading in 1996.) In January of 1997, Intel announced a two-for-one stock split. (This means that an investor who owned 100 shares at the price of 140, for example, would now own 200 shares valued at 70.) Virtually all analysts on Wall Street are projecting a further increase in earnings growth for the firm in 1997, so chances are good that Intel will still be one of Wall Street's "darlings" by the time this book hits the shelves.

We're about to take a look at Intel's *sales growth,* which can be calculated by way of a math formula no more difficult than the sort you mastered in grade school. But first we'll need to know Intel's net sales figures as reported on its annual income statements for 1993, 1994, and 1995, respectively:

	1993	*1994*	*1995*
Net sales	8,782,000,000	11,521,000,000	16,202,000,000
Operating income	3,392,000,000	3,387,000,000	5,252,000,000
Net income	2,295,000,000	2,288,000,000	3,566,000,000

Taking an in-depth look at these numbers in terms of *sales growth* helps provide the first important piece of information we need in order to understand why Intel's price remained virtually unchanged between 1993 and 1994, then began to heat up so dramatically throughout 1995 and 1996. It's now time to rely on the trusty formula I mentioned earlier.

Intel's *1994 sales growth* is equal to its *1994 sales* (11,521,000,000) minus its *1993 sales* (8,782,000,000), divided by *1993 sales* (which is again the figure 8,782,000,000). If you don't have a calculator handy, the math is easy enough to do on paper: start with 11,521,000,000, then subtract 8,782,000,000, arriving at the difference of 2,739,000,000. Divide 2,739,000,000 by 8,782,000,000. The result is 31.19% when rounded to the nearest two decimal points. Therefore, Intel's sales growth for 1994 was an impressive 31.19%.

You might well ask why the price of Intel's stock remained stable even though sales grew at the rate of 31.19%. The answer is that an increase in sales is relatively meaningless unless it is accompanied by a substantial increase in earnings! So, let's proceed by calculating Intel's 1994 earnings growth, applying another simple mathematical formula: Intel's *1994 earnings growth* is equal to its *1994 net income* (2,288,000,000) minus *1993 net income* (2,295,000,000), divided by *1993 net income* (2,295,000,000). A few clicks on the calculator or longhand scribbles on a notepad yields a 1994 earnings growth rate of a negative .31%! This tells us that the rate of earnings actually slipped from 1993 to 1994 (although the difference is less than 1%), and explains why there was no movement in the year-end price of the stock from 1993 to 1994—despite the impressive sales growth.

Moving to Intel's results for 1995, let's calculate its *1995 sales growth*. We first take the firm's *1995 sales* (16,202,000,000) minus *1994 sales* (11,521,000,000) and come up with 4,681,000,000. We divide that figure by *1994 sales* (again, 11,521,000,000), and the result tells us that Intel's 1995 sales growth was 40.63%.

Using the second formula just mastered, we can easily calculate Intel's *1995 earnings growth:* Intel's *1995 net income* (3,566,000,000) minus *1994 net income* (2,288,000,000), divided by *1994 net income* (2,288,000,000) gives us a 1995 earnings growth rate of 55.86%. And we can't help but notice that there was an extraordinary difference in Intel's earnings growth in 1994 (a negative .31%) and its blissfully positive earnings growth of 55.86% in 1995!

We can therefore congratulate ourselves for playing "Nancy Drew" and cracking the riddle of why the price of Intel jumped from 31.9375 at the end of 1994 to 56.75 at the close of the last trading day of 1995. As shown by our examination of Intel, a positive move in earnings growth is normally rewarded by a corresponding appreciation in the stock's price.

Wall Street analysts also make sure to examine a company's operating margin—a formula that should be old hat now that you've applied it to Lisa's Cookie and Lemonade Stand. Let's see if we can figure out the direction of Intel's operating margin (whether it's expanding or contracting), beginning with fiscal year 1993. Intel's *1993 operating margin* is equal to the firm's *1993 operating profit* (3,392,000,000) divided by *1993 sales* (8,782,000,000), which gives us a result of 38.62%.

Likewise, Intel's *1994 operating margin* is equal to its *1994 operating profit* (3,387,000,000) divided by *1994 sales* (11,521,000,000), which works out to 29.40%.

To bring us up to date (as much as possible, since the 1996 annual income statement isn't available at this writing), let's also

calculate *Intel's 1995 operating margin:* The *1995 operating profit* (5,252,000,000) divided by *1995 sales* (16,202,000,000) is equal
to 32.42%.

Intel's operating margin actually shrank (that is, contracted)
in 1994, although it bounced back quite a bit in 1995. Any analysts worth their salt could have told us that Intel poured an
incredible amount of cash into research and development during
the course of 1994, in the expectation that such expenditures
would pay off big-time in 1995. Those investors who kept faith
(by sticking with the stock over the long run) were eventually
able to enjoy substantially higher earnings than would have been
possible without the allocation of Intel's 1994 research and
development costs.

In 1995 alone, we saw a 40.6% sales growth accompanied by an
expansion in Intel's operating margin from 29.40% to 32.42%—and
that's a winning combination by anyone's standards!

To summarize, what all investors want to see is a consistent
growth rate—not just sales and earnings, but an expansion of operating margins as well. Unless you do all the homework on your
own, it's essential to ask brokers the following questions about any
stock they happen to be pitching: (1) What is the firm's sales
growth? (2) What is its earnings growth? and (3) What is its operating margin, and how does this number compare to that of the previous year? There are no hard-and-fast rules, but William J. O'Neil
(publisher of *Investor's Daily*) recommends that investors in the
stock market look for firms that have an annual earnings growth
rate somewhere between 15 and 50%. The bottom line is that,
whenever brokers try to sell you a so-called "growth stock," they
should show you a track record of growth to back up their claims
about the firm.

A Delicate Balance: Value Investing

An alternative to "growth investing" is an investment style known as
value investing. Again, veritable armies of analysts specialize in
sniffing out especially good buys in the marketplace—even among

firms that don't have demonstrable track records of growth. These analysts are on a constant lookout for stocks not yet identified as Wall Street "darlings." When a firm's balance sheet indicates undervalued assets, it's a sign there may be "gold in them hills"!

Understanding the many nuances of a firm's balance sheet is not merely a science, but an art form. Yet in principle, the balance sheet of any given company is not much different than what you and I might draw up in order to get a proper understanding of our own finances. Most of us have a certain number of personal assets, including whatever equity we may have in a home or automobile, as well as whatever cash we have on hand, our investments in stocks and bonds, the furniture in our homes, whatever jewelry we own, and so forth.

So much for our assets, which can be thought of as the "good news" portion of the balance sheet. The "bad news" is that most of us carry certain debts (also known as liabilities) of one sort or another. Such debts often include our rent or home mortgage payments, as well as a car loan and/or various credit card balances. (The average American family is in hock for thousands of dollars charged on the handy plastic utensils we carry around in our pocketbooks.) Simply put, the term *assets* refers to whatever monetary value can be assigned to everything we own, while our *liabilities* are the total of what we owe to others.

It follows that *assets* minus *liabilities* equals *net worth,* an equation that holds true for private individuals just as it does for the firms listed on the Wall Street exchanges. In corporate terminology, however, the total of a firm's assets minus liabilities is known as *shareholders' equity*. Fully understanding the balance sheet of a firm and ascertaining that its earnings are being generated on a fiscally sound basis are prerequisites to giving so much as a second thought to investing in the company's stock.

The investor receives no benefit whatsoever if the firm into which she sinks money has taken on overwhelming debt simply to generate income because the piper must be paid eventually. Should there be an unexpected general downturn in the economy or a dramatic decrease in sales for the particular product(s) the firm manufactures, it would be extremely difficult if not impossible for the company to weather the storm.

On a firm's balance sheet, assets are invariably broken down into two separate and distinct categories: (1) *current assets,* and (2) *long-term assets. Current assets* include any items that can easily be converted into cash within a 12-month period; all other assets fall into the latter grouping. To illustrate this principle, let's once again turn to Intel.

INTEL
BALANCE SHEET
(CURRENT ASSETS)
12/30/95

Cash	1,463,000,000
Marketable securities	995,000,000
Receivables	3,116,000,000
Inventories	2,004,000,000
Other current assets	519,000,000
Total current assets:	8,097,000,000

Cash simply refers to what any bank will accept at face value. *Marketable securities* include commercial paper, bankers' acceptances, and Treasury bills. The *receivables* category includes all amounts presently owed to Intel for the services or products it has already sold. In other words, a great many computer manufacturers (such as Compaq, Dell, and IBM) purchase Intel's Pentium processors for installation in their own PCs. You might think of receivables as amounts that are owed to Intel in the normal course of doing business, as there's normally some lag time between the date on which goods are purchased and the date on which payment is made.

Inventories include whatever finished products are currently on the shelves of Intel's warehouses waiting to be sold, in addition to those products not quite finished (which might be thought of as work in progress) and the raw materials on hand for the manufacture of more Pentium processors. The *other current assets* category includes anything and everything the firm owns that can be readily converted into cash within a year's time—including such relatively insignificant items as postage stamps or mailing labels the firm may have on hand.

It's now time to turn our attention to Intel's *long-term assets:*

INTEL
BALANCE SHEET
(LONG-TERM ASSETS)
DECEMBER 30, 1995

Property, plant, and equipment	$11,792,000,000
Accumulated depreciation	− 4,321,000,000
Net property, plant, and equipment	7,471,000,000
Investments	1,653,000,000
Deposits and other assets	283,000,000
Long-term assets	$ 9,407,000,000
Current assets	8,097,000,000
Total assets	$17,504,000,000

These assets *cannot* easily be converted into cash within a 12-month period. In Intel's case such long-term assets include property, buildings, manufacturing plants, and other items referred to in accounting terms as *intangibles*. The latter category includes difficult-to-quantify items such as patents, copyrights, trademarks, and even something known as goodwill.

Goodwill is the rather subjective value assigned to a company for having had a good track record dealing with its customers over a significant period of time. Whenever I think of goodwill, I remember that I invariably look for Tropicana products at the supermarket because I've always been pleased with them. Sure, I could probably save some money by purchasing a lesser-known brand instead. (For all I know, a lot of companies sell juice that tastes the same or even better.) Being a creature of habit, though, and a satisfied Tropicana customer for many years, I don't mind paying a bit more for Tropicana, if need be.

Chances are that most of you have similar consumer loyalties to certain products. Stop for a moment and consider how many name brands you choose as a result of the corporate goodwill you've experienced in the past. For example, do you head into an unfamiliar diner when you get the urge for a hamburger, or point your car straight for the nearest Wendy's or McDonald's? When it comes to a company's balance sheet, however, the goodwill factor we've just discussed is a mere bookkeeping device. (In fact, it's normally taken into account only when a firm is purchased, sold, or blended into a combination of other companies.)

Accumulated depreciation is another bookkeeping device, one related to the passing of time and its eroding effect on the general usefulness of a firm's manufacturing plant(s) and equipment. Should Intel still own a plant it built in the seventies, it's probably not nearly as sturdy or useful as one the company designed and constructed 20-some years later. Outdated plants and equipment eventually need to be replaced. Accumulated depreciation is a commonly used accounting technique by which we allocate wear and tear over the expected lifetime of a company's long-term assets. The subtotal immediately below accumulated depreciation in Intel's balance sheet on page 87 is labeled *net property, plant, and equipment,* and takes into consideration the net value of these long-term assets once the appropriate depreciation has been calculated.

So much for the good news about Intel's assets (both current and long term). Now it's time to brace ourselves for the section of the balance sheet that outlines Intel's liabilities:

INTEL
BALANCE SHEET
(ANNUAL LIABILITIES)
DECEMBER 30, 1995

Notes payable	$ 346,000,000
Accounts payable	$ 864,000,000
Accrued expenses	$1,304,000,000
Income taxes	$ 801,000,000
Other current liabilities	$ 304,000,000
Total current liabilities	$3,619,000,000
Deferred charges	$ 620,000,000
Long-term debt	$ 400,000,000
Other long-term liabilities	$ 725,000,000
Total long-term liabilities	$1,745,000,000
Total liabilities	$5,364,000,000

Intel's "bad news" is broken down into the same categories—that is, current (moneys owed within 12 months) and long-term (debts that come due at some point thereafter). Intel's *current liabilities* of

$3,619,000,000 include all debts that must be paid off within the 12-month period ahead, such as taxes, wages, and so forth. Intel's *long-term liabilities* of $1,745,000,000 reflect a wide assortment of debts that needn't be paid until another full year has passed.

All that remains is to determine whether the good news outweighs the bad news.

Just as if Intel were an individual person, the company's net worth is equal to its assets minus its liabilities.

INTEL
BALANCE SHEET
(SHAREHOLDERS' EQUITY)
12/30/95

Assets	$17,504,000,000
Liabilities	5,364,000,000
Net worth	$12,140,000,000

The net worth of any business is represented as its *shareholders' equity*. The extremely good news in Intel's case is that its shareholders literally "own" more than $12 billion in real assets! This figure for shareholders' equity is reflected on Intel's balance sheet as follows:

Common stock net	$ 2,583,000,000
Retained earnings	9,557,000,000
Total shareholders' equity	$12,140,000,000

Common stock net refers to the basic ownership equity of the company. *Retained earnings* represents the accumulation of undistributed earnings, that is, the earnings not distributed as dividends, since the company was originally founded. You might think of this category as a savings account from which dividends can eventually be distributed to shareholders. I should point out, however, that Intel is a so-called growth company, which means that the firm doesn't choose to pay out its earnings at this point in its life cycle.

Instead, Intel plows all of those undistributed earnings back into its coffers in order to stimulate continued growth. While this strategy creates a low-dividend yield in the short term, it has some decided advantages in the long run.

What does this mean to you as an individual investor in the firm? For one thing, you're required to take a certain leap of faith, to believe that Intel can increase its earnings more than you could, had you received a sizable quarterly dividend check. You alone can decide whether your money would make more future earnings held in Intel's coffers or your own.

One final warning: Although Intel's shareholders "own" more than $12 billion in assets, they are nonetheless exposed to the maximum risk in terms of the future profitability of the firm. Each shareholder's respective degree of ownership is an entitlement that can be enjoyed only after all *other* obligations of the firm have been satisfied.

Weighing the Good News Against the Bad

So far we've examined the income statement and balance sheet—the two most important financial statements. Now comes the moment of truth, as we weigh the good news against the bad to decide whether the stock in question is a bona fide contender for our investment dollar or merely a pretender to the crown.

Analysts have several extremely handy "tests" they like to administer once a firm's quarterly announcement has been made and its appropriate financial statements duly filed. Experts use a wide variety of tests, but I cover only the four I believe are most effective in ascertaining the health of a firm and the prospect for its continued well-being. The basic math involved in these checkups is no more difficult than the simple addition, subtraction, and division chores you've already mastered—and this section concludes the "toughest" basic math portion of the book! So, take heart, and sharpen your pencil as we take the final plunge.

1. **Current ratio.** The *current ratio* is equal to *current assets* divided by *current liabilities*. In Intel's case, this works out as follows: $8,097,000,000 divided by $3,619,000,000 is equal to

2.2374. A ratio of 2 or higher is considered by most analysts to indicate financial health, so Intel once again passes muster.

2. **Acid test ratio.** The *acid test ratio* is equal to *current assets* minus *inventories,* divided by *current liabilities.* In Intel's case, $8,097,000,000 minus $2,004,000,000, divided by $3,619,000,000 is equal to 1.6836. Most analysts look for a ratio of 1.5 or more as an indication of health. This test is performed to make sure that inventories don't make up a major portion of a firm's current assets. An extremely high inventory may well indicate that the company is having a hard time selling its product.

3. **Capitalization ratio.** The *capitalization ratio* is equal to *long-term debt* divided by *total capitalization. Total capitalization* equals *long-term debt* plus *shareholders' equity.* Bearing that in mind, the *capitalization ratio* is equal to *long-term debt* divided by *total capitalization*—although the percentages relating to *shareholders' equity* and *long-term debt* are always examined separately.

   In Intel's case, a glance at the complete balance sheet will tell us that the firm's *long-term debt* is $400,000,000 and *shareholders' equity* is $12,140,000,000. *Total capitalization* equals $12,540,000,000. This information permits us to calculate Intel's *capitalization ratio:* $400,000,000 divided by $12,540,000,000 equals 3.19%.

   Shareholders' equity as a percentage of *total capitalization* is equal to $12,140,000,000 divided by $12,540,000,000, which results in a figure of 96.81%. This means that nearly 100% of Intel's total capitalization is shareholders' equity, with only about 3% financed through long-term debt. (If you were a homeowner with only 3% of your mortgage payments left, you would have an even greater appreciation of Intel's enviable equity position.)

   A rule of thumb is that a greater ratio of debt to capital involves the stockholder in greater the risk. We don't want to invest our hard-earned cash in a company conducting its business primarily on money it owes to others. (That firm would be extremely vulnerable if business took a significant downturn.) If the company were unable to keep up with its interest payments, which often account for a considerable chunk of its current debts, its assets may well wind up in the hands of its creditors.

4. **Return on equity.** *Return on equity* is determined by dividing a firm's *net earnings* (net income) by its *shareholders' equity*. In Intel's case, we simply divide $3,566,000,000 by $12,140,000,000, and come up with a figure of 29.37%. This means that Intel is presently profiting to the tune of nearly 30 cents on every dollar of total shareholders' equity. (Another common term for shareholders' equity is *book value*.)

You've just managed to digest some "tricks of the trade" with which the average broker isn't fully acquainted after working for 30 years or more on Wall Street. So congratulations! And, once again, you have my assurance that this chapter is as mathematically tough as this book is going to get!

Is Your Broker's Tip Hot—Or Not?

I've lost more money than I care to think about over the years by believing someone else's hot tip rather than conducting my own independent research on a firm and its financial statements. That's why I never—but *never*—listen to the advice of a financial correspondent or broker whom I don't know. The "rumor *du jour*" always sounds like a veritable gold mine until you take a close look at the margins and ratios we've just discussed. You may discover that the only "gold" to be mined from the transaction is your own hard-earned investment dollar, plus a hefty commission fee.

Any truly intelligent investor must take full responsibility for carefully examining each firm in which he or she plans to invest— a process that necessitates a thorough perusal of the financial statements and track record of its management. A potential investor should also make sure that he or she understands the overall industry itself. (Don't forget to check out what any potential competitors of the firm in question may have up their collective sleeves.) You'll be ahead of the game if you have a reliable broker and a full-service brokerage house equipped with honest and diligent analysts. I suggest that you not only read the reports and financial opinions they generate for you, but do some good old-fashioned homework on your own as well.

Did you know that you can simply pick up the phone and ask for the investors' relations division of any firm in which you contemplate making an investment? The company will be glad to mail its financial statements to you directly, and you can take the time to analyze them on your own. Should your own brokerage firm participate as the underwriter of any given stock, its team of analysts may bend the truth about the firm's future earnings potential (as well as underplay any potential threat from competitors). The sad truth is that several analysts over the years have confided to me that their jobs have been put in serious jeopardy whenever they've failed to put out a favorable report on one of the stocks underwritten by their employers. In one particular instance I'll never forget, an analyst friend of mine was actually instructed to commit securities fraud in order to sell a deal—which prompted his immediate resignation.

Although the telling of out-and-out lies about the financial health and well-being of a company constitutes the most serious act of fraud—the sort that's punishable by substantial fines *and* imprisonment—it's a disgustingly time-honored Wall Street tradition that takes place every day. The proliferation of unscrupulous analysts is what makes investing in the stock market such a blindfolded "crap shoot." Without being well-briefed on what makes Wall Street tick *before* writing that very first investment check, a novice investor is almost sure to lose his or her shirt in the market.

FIGURES DON'T LIE

I'm like Hetty Robinson Green in at least one sense: *I simply hate to lose money!* That's why I don't mind doing my own homework rather than get suckered into believing someone else's rumor-mongering. I'd much rather make a major mistake on my own and have only myself to blame for it. On the other hand, if any of the homework I do happens to turn up a big winner, then I've only myself to congratulate.

MARKET CAPITALIZATION

By thoroughly checking out a firm's balance sheet and income statement, we determined its net worth and yearly profit or loss. The term *market capitalization* takes into consideration the overall market's belief in the future of the company, the future of the industry as a whole, and the future of the national economy. As complicated as all that may appear at first glance, the actual formula by which we determine market capitalization is as simple as the other equations we've already tucked under our belts:

Market Capitalization = Numbers of Shares Outstanding × Price of Stock

Remember that at the end of 1995 the *shareholders' equity* in Intel was $12,104,000,000. The market capitalization number (often referred to as *market valuation*) for Intel is simply the amount of money that would be required at any given moment to buy up each and every share of the firm's outstanding stock. Since at the end of 1995 Intel had 821,000,000 shares of stock outstanding, all we need do is multiply that number by $56.75 (the price of a single share at the end of that same year). This provides us with the figure for Intel's market capitalization, which works out to be $46,591,750,000.

Analysts then extrapolate a few more useful ratios, each of which is based on this market cap number; one by one, let's examine the last three tools that prove most useful in determining whether your broker's tip is "hot," or not.

1. **Price/earnings ratio:** To arrive at the earnings per share value (a number normally spelled out for you on the income statement), we divide a firm's *net income* by *the number of shares outstanding.* In Intel's case, 3,566,000,000 divided by 821,000,000 is equal to $4.34 per share. *Price* divided by *earnings* equals 56.75 (the price of one share of Intel stock at the end of 1995), divided by $4.34 (earnings per share), which gives us a *price/earnings ratio* of 13. Price/earnings ratios are rounded to the nearest whole number.

2. **Price-to-sales ratio:** To find the *price-to-sales ratio* (a figure you *won't* find on the income statement), first take $16,202,000,000 (Intel's *1995 sales*) and divide it by 821,000,000 (*the number of shares outstanding*). The resulting figure is $19.73 per share. *Price* divided by *sales* equals 56.75 divided by $19.73. We've just arrived at a *price-to-sales ratio* of 2.89.

3. **Price-to-book ratio:** Keep in mind that *book value* always refers to *total shareholders' equity,* which in this case is $12,140,000,000. Divide that figure by 821,000,000 (*the number of shares outstanding*), and you arrive at a dollar amount of

$14.79 per share. The *price-to-book ratio* equals 56.75 divided by $14.78, which is 3.83.

Each industry is different, however, as you may weary of me reminding you. The proverbial warning flag should pop up whenever any of the three ratios I've just mentioned is abnormally high. For example, one rule of thumb is that *price-to-sales ratio* should not be higher than 3. Here's another tip: according to Peter Lynch (the investment guru who managed Fidelity's highly successful Magellan Fund), a stock's *P/E ratio* should always be at or below its *growth rate*. Should a stock demonstrate a 20% growth rate, a P/E ratio of anything less than 20 is adequate. In the case of Intel, 1995 earnings grew at 55.8% and the P/E ratio was roughly 13. By applying Lynch's theory, any smart broker or individual investor would have known that Intel was a good buy long before its stock price began to skyrocket. And those are the folk who can congratulate themselves on owning Intel as it rose to the astonishing level of 130.9375 per share!

Selecting Smart: What Savvy Investors Look For

What is the best way to sum up this entire chapter on picking winners and avoiding losers? The following are the most important traits sought by smart investors each time they select a stock:

Growth rate (on a year-to-year basis as well as a quarterly comparison) of 15% or more

Price-to-earnings (P/E) ratio lower than the growth rate just mentioned

Price-to-sales ratio of less than 3

Current ratio more than 2

Acid test ratio more than 1.5

Capitalization ratio as small as possible. Remember that this represents long-term debt versus shareholders' equity.

Operating margin as high as possible (the higher the better), although this margin must always be compared with those of other firms within the same industry. We want to see expansion, unless the company has made an active, purposeful decision to pump cash back into the firm at the present time in order to ensure greater earnings in the long run.

No guarantees are possible, of course, but these guidelines serve as excellent health indicators. Companies with poor financials sometimes discover a revolutionary new technology or pharmaceutical drug that causes a level of growth that couldn't have been anticipated. In other instances, one firm purchases another that appears (on paper) to be in financial distress, but a wonderful synergy occurs between the two companies that couldn't be reflected in numbers alone.

Finally, extraordinarily gifted analysts are able to see opportunities for value investing by carefully scrutinizing nuances most people overlook when examining a firm's balance sheet. Picking the best stock in the marketplace at any given time isn't easy—or we'd all be as rich as Hetty Robinson Green! But even the most novice investors can find a winner on their own. In any case, the information provided in the pages of this chapter will arm you with all the right questions to put to your broker—who will no doubt go into deep shock when you bandy about such technical terms as *acid ratio* and *price-to-book*. The bottom line is this: if your broker is unable (or unwilling) to provide all the information to which you have every right, avoid sinking your hard-earned cash into any of the losers he or she may try to sell you.

chapter 5

WHO NEEDS CHARTS? YOU DO! A BEGINNER'S GUIDE TO TECHNICAL ANALYSIS

I'm a bit ashamed to confess that I worked on Wall Street for a full ten years before learning how to read and analyze the charts that plot out the price history of various commodities, indices and individual stocks. In my case, it was "better late than never." My best advice to readers of this book is, the sooner, the better! The benefits can be enormous.

Most of the information I've thrown your way thus far (particularly in the preceding chapter) concerns *fundamental analysis*. It focuses on examining the fundamental health of a company in terms of earnings and other factors that affect the firm's operations and balance sheet. For example, fundamental analysis considers whether Intel's new Pentium II product will be a big winner in the marketplace. Will Eli Lilly's new drug for schizophrenia be better and safer than others presently available? What will happen to tobacco companies in the aftermath of the recent settlement agreement?

In short, fundamental analysis helps us understand why a stock's price rises and falls. On the other hand, *technical analysis* makes not even the slightest pretense of explaining *why* the price of a stock moves the way it does. A technician's focus is on the price movement itself, with the assumption that, more often than not, history will repeat itself.

The Magic of Technical Analysis

Before I learned to understand the charts, I thought of technical analysis as something akin to black magic or voodoo. Once I became an avid practitioner of the art, however, I found that I made better investment calls. Moreover, my global understanding of the way the market works improved dramatically.

Technical analysis is a tool all of us can use to enhance our overall knowledge. However, this tool should serve as an *aid* to the decision-making process, rather than as the sole determinant of which investments we eventually make. As a personal rule of thumb I wager money on the results of technical analysis only if it reinforces my own fundamental view of a particular stock or of the overall market.

We can trace the roots of technical analysis in the United States to Charles H. Dow of Dow Jones and Company. As mentioned earlier, Dow was also the cofounder of *The Wall Street Journal*. This remarkable man devoted a great deal of his life to the study of stock market averages. Dow Theory assumes that the majority of stocks follow the major trend of the market. At the time, Mr. Dow used two indices which he named the Industrial Average and the Rail Average (called the Dow Jones Transportation Average).

The six major assumptions made by Dow theorists follow:

1. Closing prices reflect the aggregate judgment and emotions of all participants in the marketplace.

2. The stock market displays three distinct trends:

   ▸ *Major market trends.* Also known as *primary trends,* these generally last for more than one year—and, indeed, often for many years. Primary bull markets (that is, markets that rise over a long term) historically last for roughly two years. Conversely, bear markets (the inevitable "downers") are characterized by substantial decline in prices. The worst decline in recent history was during 1973–74, when stocks lost 43% of total value.

   ▸ *Secondary trends.* The market also experiences *correction phases,* which normally last from three weeks to many months. Prices may fluctuate from 33 to 66% on a temporary basis, even while the long-term primary trend remains in place. For example, the Dow Jones Industrial Average may go from 4,000 to 6,000—then retrace anywhere from one-third of 2,000 (666) to two-thirds of 2,000 (1,332 points) before reasserting the primary movement upward.

▶ *Minor correction phases.* These periods tend to last somewhere between a few hours and a couple of weeks.

3. Major market trends are generally characterized by three phases:

▶ *Accumulation phase.* Price levels are relatively low and informed investors tend to buy the stock.

▶ *Second phase (bull market model).* More buyers enter the marketplace, and prices begin to move rapidly. At some point (generally after the stock market has been on the rise for a couple of years or more), lower-quality stocks begin to move up right along with the higher-quality stocks.

▶ *Distribution phase.* Prices become extremely high, and sophisticated investors begin to sell off their positions.

4. To support a bull market, the Dow Jones Industrial and Transportation averages must confirm each other. In other words, you want to see both the industrial and transportation stocks experience new highs at the same time. You also want to see higher lows on a *selloff* (known in financial circles as a *pullback*). The Industrial Average represents the manufacturing firms, and the Transportation Average represents those companies that move the goods to market. If the economy is doing well, a healthy Transportation Average indicates that both groups are profiting.

5. The volume of shares being traded in the market at any given time is an extremely important factor when it comes to confirming a trend. You want to see stocks advancing on increasing volume and retreating on low volume.

6. Trends continue until a reversal occurs. Predicting a reversal is extremely difficult—and extraordinarily profitable!

Always remember that the trend is your "friend." In other words, don't fight either a bull market or a bear market. It's far wiser to "go with the flow."

Charting the Course: Using Charts to Depict the Marketplace

Technicians use three major types of charts: bar charts, point and figure charts, and Japanese candlesticks. For our purposes, however, it's necessary to take an in-depth look only at the basic bar chart. Figure 5-1 is a one-month bar chart for Intel. Each vertical line represents the trading range for that day. The horizontal line indicates the closing price on the day in question.

This bar chart indicates that on February 28, 1997, Intel traded between 137 and 147. On March 26, 1997, the same stock traded between 134 and 141. These are one-day swings, so you could expect a price fluctuation for Intel of as much as 10 points or more on any given day in the future.

As you can see, a substantial fluctuation in price occurs during the course of a single day's trading. Should you be unable to stomach the anxiety that accompanies such sharp rises and falls, you probably want to find a stock with considerably less volatility. Otherwise, Murphy's law will come into play, and you'll probably wind up bailing out when the price dips to a low point. Both winners and losers fluctuate in price, so it's important to acquaint yourself with a stock's trading history and the normal range of fluctuation.

Technical analysis enables you to view the history of "pure movement" in stock prices, and determine whether or not any given issue is too volatile for your personal portfolio. Because history tends to repeat itself, technical analysis is helpful when it comes to predicting price fluctuations accurately. Making you an expert technician would take a great deal more than a single chapter. (Indeed, many a sizable book is filled with an overview of only the basics.) I *would* like to acquaint you with a few of the terms and principles used by technicians, in the hope that this introduction will whet your appetite to learn more about it so that when you read articles or hear analysts talking about technicals or see a chart in the papers you'll be able to evaluate the information presented.

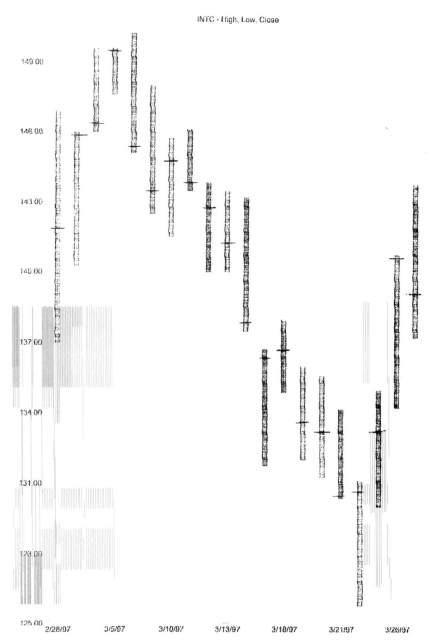

FIGURE 5.1. INTEL BAR CHART: HIGH, LOW, AND CLOSE.

Getting Acquainted with the Tools of a Technician's Trade

Technicians use a variety of charts to follow stock price movements and trends. A discussion of those most commonly used follows.

When analyzing a given stock issue or market, most technicians examine charts representing each of three different timelines:

1. *Daily bar chart*. This normally depicts six months of trading.

2. *Intermediate-term chart*. Such a chart normally covers a two-year period, with trading tracked on a weekly basis. High, low, and closing prices are indicated for each week.

3. *Long-term chart*. This type of chart represents five or more years of trading, and provides high, low, and closing prices on a monthly basis.

Attached to these price movements are daily, weekly, and/or monthly figures indicating the volume of shares traded—depending on the type of chart. In a sense, these charts serve as a snapshot of supply and demand for a given stock during the course of a particular time period. Given today's advanced technology, most charts are created via computer. Happily, most internet services now offer hookups to various chart services, which means that individual investors are able to do technical analysis from the comfort of home. If you are not yet plugged in—don't worry. Your broker can provide you with just about any chart you need before you make an investment in the market.

DRAWING THE TRENDLINE

There are three types of stock movement: uptrend, downtrend, and neutral (also known as oscillating). An *uptrend* is indicated by an upward trendline, which depicts an ascending pattern of highs and lows—with higher lows accompanying higher highs. A *downtrend* depicts descending highs and lows. Finally, a *neutral* or *oscillating trend* indicates that the stock's highs and lows remain more or less constant. See Figures 5-2A, 5-2B, and 5-2C.

INTC - High, Low, Close

FIGURE 5-2A.   AN UPTREND.

FLH - High, Low, Close

FIGURE 5-2B.   A DOWNTREND.

BUD - High, Low, Close

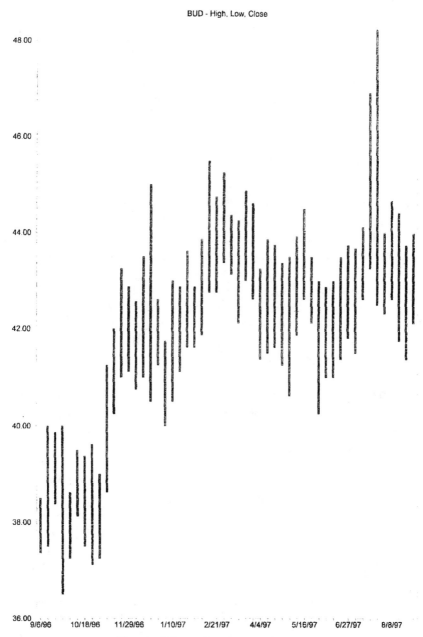

FIGURE 5-2C.   A NEUTRAL TREND.

To study the movement of price, a technician connects the two lowest points in a series of uptrend charts or the two highest points in a series of downtrend charts. An uptrend is confirmed when the focus remains above the trendline that's been drawn. A broken line is a warning signal that the trend is reversing itself. Although intra-day penetration of a trendline is usually insignificant, closing penetration is more indicative that the trend is winding down.

SUPPORT AND RESISTANCE

Additional tools of a technician's trade are measurements known as support and resistance. We use the term *support* to indicate the level at which declining prices meet with demand (buying) and bounce back. This is also referred to as a *reaction low* point, at which the public's interest in buying a stock overcomes the pressures felt by the stock's present owners to sell. On the other hand, *resistance* is the area in which accelerating prices meet with supply (selling), and represents the price at which stock's owners desire to sell over-comes the buying enthusiasm of others. See Figure 5-3.

For me, the most fascinating aspect of the support and resistance phenomenon is the inevitable reversal of roles once the levels have been penetrated. For example, Intel's old resistance was approximately $80 to $81 per share. Once that price is penetrated, $80 to $81 becomes the new support. If, with the passage of time, this support level is penetrated by the increased enthusiasm of sellers, support once again becomes resistance.

We use the term *breakout* to indicate that a stock has broken its resistance level. (Even the best analysts are fooled from time to time. The breakout they think they see turns out to be a "fake-out" instead!) A breakout is particularly significant when it is marked by all-time highs in a stock's price—especially when this is confirmed by a large volume of trades. For example, let's say that XYZ has been trading for the past six months at an average volume of 150,000 shares per day. If the trading volume suddenly soared to 500,000 on XYZ's breakout day, that sign would be extremely bullish.

A *violation of support* is referred to as a *downside breakout*. This sign, too, should be confirmed by an increased volume of trading.

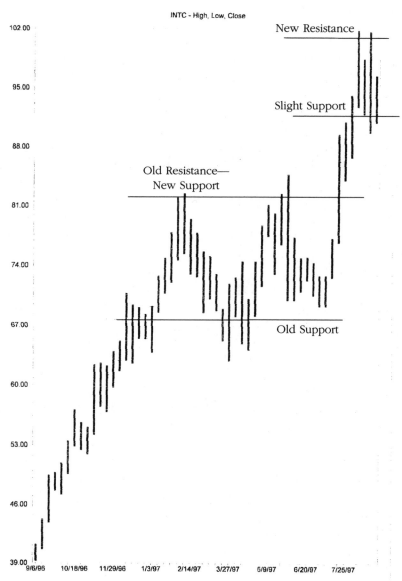

INTC - High, Low, Close

FIGURE 5-3.   RESISTANCE AND SUPPORT AREAS.
(Copyright 1996-1997 America Online, Inc. All rights reserved.)

CHARTING THE PHASES OF STOCK MOVEMENT

Previously, we discussed the overall movement of the market according to Dow Theory. Most technicians, on the other hand, believe that the price of stocks generally moves through four distinct phases that can be identified through graphic patterns:

1. *Accumulation phase.* This period generally lasts for about six months, as supply and demand compete in the marketplace, with the demand side winning in the end. It normally follows a decline in a stock's price that results in the establishment of a price *bottom*. The graphic patterns that result are as follows: rectangular base, saucer, head-and-shoulders bottom, V-bottom, double bottom (W pattern), triple bottom, and island reversal.

2. *Markup phase.* A major upward trend begins, as a breakout occurs that crosses the line of resistance. Trading volume is normally quite high when this happens. Technical analysts look for these patterns instead: falling flag, pennant, coil, ascending triangle, falling wedge, and upside blowoff.

3. *Distribution phase.* Selling begins to dominate throughout this phase, which occurs immediately before the actual price markdown. It's graphically indicated by the following patterns: V-top, double top, triple top, head-and-shoulders top, broadening top, rounding top and island reversal top.

4. *Markdown phase.* Once support has been violated at the close of the distribution phase, it's generally accompanied by an equal (or greater) volume on the sell side. Whenever the stock's price starts to rally on the upswing, however, the volume of trading tends to fall. Technicians can spot the markdown phase by noting the following patterns: rising flag, pennant, coil, descending triangle, and blowoff (selling climax).

PLOTTING MOVING AVERAGES

What are known as *moving averages* are also helpful to the technician in terms of deciphering the pure movement of a stock. These numbers represent the total of closing prices experienced on a specified number of trading days. For example, one would divide the last 50 days' trading prices by 50 in order to ascertain a particular stock's moving average. On an intermediate-term basis, many technicians chart both the 50-day and 200-day averages.

Briefly put, a *moving average* is a mathematical depiction of a trendline. A stock that's rising in price often meets support at the moving average, whereas a declining stock meets resistance at the moving average. In either event, the violation of a moving average indicates that a change in trend may be taking place. A rising moving average represents a strength in price, whereas a declining moving average indicates weakness.

DETERMINING RELATIVE STRENGTH

Another tool used by technical analysts to examine individual stocks is something known as *relative strength.* This measurement device enables a technician to compare a stock or index to the overall market. A falling relative strength line means that the stock (or index) is underperforming the S&P 500 Index, whereas a rising line indicates that it is outperforming the S&P 500. New highs in the stock price should be accompanied by new highs in the relative strength line. If not, the sign shows *negative divergence*—a warning that a stock's upward trend may be slipping.

ANALYZING DIFFERENCES: THE ADVANCE/DECLINE LINE

An *advance/decline line* is what helps technicians analyze the difference between the number of New York Stock Exchange issues that advance and those that decline. The advance/decline line tends to move in sympathy with the Dow Jones Industrial Average. Should this line not correlate with the Dow Jones, however, this sign of divergence may foreshadow the breaking of a trend.

THE TRENDING OR OSCILLATING MARKET

Before leaving the subject of technical terminology, I should point out that analysts invariably refer to the market as either trending or oscillating. A *trending* market is clearly moving in one direction or the other, while an *oscillating* market reflects the fact that prices appear to be fluctuating randomly within a given trading range.

USING THE CHARTS

Becoming a technician can be a full-time occupation and then some. However, you *can* apply some of this information to your actual stock picks. Before I buy any stock, I take a good hard look at the chart. I want to buy stocks that are either in an uptrend or are beginning to break out of a neutral pattern. I don't want to enter into a position in a downtrend. Deciphering trends can be useful to each investor. Repeating an old adage on Wall Street, "The trend is your friend."

Living with the Bulls and the Bears: Predicting the Ups and Downs

"Tulip mania" is only one illustration of the fact that the mass psychology of investors should neither be overlooked nor underestimated. Given the proliferation of media covering the investment world these days, it's not unusual to see the stock market turn from wildly bullish to bearish in a single day.

My father, now happily retired, has a new hobby he enjoys very much: he tunes his television set to CNBC's Wall Street from opening bell at 9:30 through the final trades of each day. Although Dad's not the most expert investor on the planet, he thinks that financial newscasts are extremely dramatic and fun to watch. (They cease being fun only when the stocks in his own portfolio take a substantial beating.) "Why is everybody wildly bullish one day, but the bottom falls out of the stock market the next?" he asked me recently. "How can a small investor like me cope with price swings like that?"

As I've been told, Dad, "Perception is 90% of reality." With the advent of continuous global coverage of Wall Street—all instantaneous—investors are more susceptible than ever to whatever mania or panic prevails at a given moment. If we make a bad investment decision, we can hardly hold the media responsible. The best advice I had to offer my father was: "Listen to the guys and gals who actually manage the money." The various salespeople on the Street are fed a constant stream of information coming from the marketers, but money managers have to live with their decisions from day to day, month to month, and year to year. It follows that they wouldn't have attained any appreciable degree of success and standing in the business had they not managed to rack up some rather impressive performance statistics over time.

Caveat Emptor! Less-than-scrupulous money managers use the media to their advantage by planting news items to hype whatever stocks they happen to be pushing. They then sell into a rally once a demand has been created. Needless to say, the stock's price tumbles the moment the buying frenzy burns out. (I once invested in Novell Systems after hearing a rumor that the company was being bought, only to watch the price fall from a high of roughly 20 to 23 points all the way down to 7-1/2.)

SENTIMENT INDICATORS

An entire branch of technical analysis is based on information received from *sentiment indicators* that constantly monitor the pulse and psychology of investors everywhere. Experts at using such indicators operate on the general premise that the vast majority of investors become optimistic as the market reaches new highs, and pessimistic as the market begins to tumble. Although few have been tested in any methodical fashion, the sentiment indicators used by technicians include the short-interest ratio, public specialist's ratio, advisory service's sentiments, mutual funds flow, put/call ratio, and (perhaps most useful of all) insider transactions.

Insiders are stockholders who own in excess of 5% of the voting stock of a corporation. Also included in this category are corporate officers and employees who have access to information that's unavailable to the rest of us. (That's why they generally tend to be correct in their buying and selling strategies!) Insiders know when a new product is coming out, for example, and are privy to a company's sales figures long before they're announced to the general public. Should you notice that a *group* of insiders is selling their positions in a stock, you should either go with the flow and sell your own position or (at the very least) avoid making additional purchases. Conversely, large purchases by insiders of additional shares of a stock should boost your confidence in that stock.

From time to time just about everyone on the planet needs to raise money, however, for a variety of different reasons. Before you panic, make sure that more than a single insider is selling his or her position before you follow suit! I always try to ascertain how much stock is in the hands of the chairman of the board and/or president, and whether they're trying to buy more stock or unload what they already have. (If a firm's officers don't have much confidence in the future of their company, then why should investors?) *Barron's* financial weekly is particularly expert at reporting insider transactions; such features are well worth reading.

What the Indicators Mean: Tips from Master Technicians

I'd like to credit an expert technician and teacher named Ralph Acampora for having inspired me to become an avid reader of charts. A good friend named Cynthia Medric urged me to enroll in a course Ralph taught at the New York Institute of Finance about six years ago—a learning experience that dramatically changed my life. Cynthia, a former student of Ralph's, is presently the senior technical analyst at Weiss, Peck & Greer's hedge fund.

MEET A WALL STREET "ELF"

You may already be familiar with Ralph from his many appearances on the PBS television network—most notably as one of the "elves" on Louis Rukeyser's *Wall Street Week*. (For those unacquainted with this long-running show, each of the "elves" predicts the direction of the stock market for the next three months.) In 1995, Ralph insisted that the stock market would rise from what was then roughly 4,100 points to at least 7,000 by 1997. At the time, such a prediction seemed hopelessly bullish, but much to my surprise, Ralph was right on the money!

Ralph got his start in the business in 1966 after being involved in a serious car accident. While in the hospital recovering, he was exposed to the field of technical analysis by his father's friend, Bill Downey. Once Ralph was on his feet again, he spied an ad in the help wanted section that read "Junior analyst sought, no experience necessary." Ralph didn't know it at the time, but he was on his way to becoming one of the nation's leading experts in technical analysis. He presently serves as Managing Director/Head of Technical Research at Prudential Securities.

In the early stages of training, Ralph spent most of his afternoons updating point-and-figure charts for his boss, a man by the name of Harold Schreider. (Mr. Schreider had the distinction of having served as economic advisor to President Eisenhower.) The thought that kept running through his mind was, "Why am I putting little *X*s on a chart?"—a question he finally asked his employer.

"Did you ever feed chickens?" asked Mr. Schreider, launching into a detailed discourse on the subject. "If you throw chicken feed over your right shoulder," he said, "the chickens will run to your right. Throw the feed over your left shoulder, and they'll run to the left. Look straight down at the ground, and you'll see a lot of tiny *X*s—and that's how you know which way the chickens went!"

The *X*s on a chart or graph tell us where the money is going— a lesson Ralph never forgot. His whole life since that day has been spent following the *X*s by analyzing trends, operating on the assumption that the market knows where it's headed. (His theory is: "Determine the direction first, and ask questions later.") I knew that readers of this book would enjoy meeting Ralph, so I was delighted when he accepted my invitation to offer some sage counsel and advice on the subject of how best to use technical analysis.

Ralph is careful to point out that a company and its stock are two altogether different entities. The firm itself may be doing well financially, while the stock behaves poorly—or vice versa! The first decision each of us must make as investors is to define our objectives. A professional trader should rely more on near-term charts (three to six months), whereas individual investors should scrutinize charts that cover at least two years.

Ralph likes to identify which stocks are breaking out either on an intermediate basis (as indicated by a two-year chart) or over the longer term. He stresses that a breakout should always be confirmed by an upturn in the volume of sales. Ralph's personal rule of thumb is that the breakout should be accompanied by twice the daily volume average (as calculated over a six-month period). In other words, if the average volume of trading for a given stock is 100,000, its breakout day should warrant a volume of at least 200,000 shares.

Better yet is when the breakout is confirmed by what Ralph calls group action. He insists that a *group breakout* (that is, breakouts experienced by more than one stock in the same industry) is extremely telling, and can only bode well. For example, if Mobil experienced a breakout, Ralph would like to see the other oil companies doing well also.

Ralph monitors trendlines, and points out that a violation of a trendline on a weekly chart can be quite significant. If a particular stock closes below the trendline on high volume, you should think about selling.

On the subject of insider buying, Ralph says he likes to spot that sort of trading long before the breakout, particularly if it occurs in the accumulation phase. Another positive indicator is insider buying of a stock that has been heavily shorted. This means that many investors are trying to profit from their perception that the stock will decrease, rather than increase, in value—a concept we address more thoroughly in Chapter 9.

Ralph also stresses that when a lot of insiders are selling—especially if one of them is the firm's chairperson—you should seriously consider doing the same (particularly if the stock is breaking its support level). Always assume that insiders know more than you. Also pay attention to institutional ownership—those mutual funds, banks, investment advisors, hedge funds, insurance companies, and pension plans that hold the stock. Should a particular stock increase in price and the firm's insiders start to sell, institutions holding major positions in the stock will want to follow suit. If institutional ownership is high, however, few other institutions would be willing to buy. You should consider it a good sign when insiders begin to buy up a stock that's not heavily owned by institutions, because those institutions will eventually wish to buy—especially if the stock is included in the S&P 500 Index.

Ralph's philosophy is that a trader can base decisions on technical analysis alone, but that an individual investor should think of research as a "four-legged stool," factoring in: (1) the present state of the economy; (2) whether a particular industry is likely to do well in this part of the economic cycle; (3) the fundamentals that influence the balance sheet of a particular firm; and, finally, (4) whether the technicals support the investment decision.

I asked Ralph how he manages to keep his cool despite the obvious pressures of the business, especially when he's bombarded by so much information and by widely differing points of view. He confesses to tuning into CNN and CNBC in the morning, reading the daily papers, and listening to the opinion of virtually everyone he meets on his way in to work. The moment he enters the chart room at Prudential, however, he shuts the door and tunes out all other information—which in the final analysis would only serve to cloud his judgment. When all is said and done, his job as a technician is to identity the trend and predict when it will stop trending.

In closing, Ralph's advice to the individual investor is two-fold: Start with quality and stay with quality. In other words, make sure you do your homework and choose quality stocks for inclusion in your portfolio, then stay with them over the long haul.

MORE TECHNICAL WIZARDRY

Another master technician, Cindy Medric, suggests using *Investor's Business Daily* to assist you in finding interesting stocks and avoiding losers. The paper graphically depicts the stocks in the news. It displays weekly charts for stocks traded on the New York Stock Exchange, the American Stock Exchange, and NASDAQ. These include stocks trading over $12 that hit or were near new highs or had the greatest percentages in increased volume. As you screen for stocks, if you see four or five companies in one industry making new highs, you might be able to catch a major move in a trend. *Investor's Business Daily* also has the top 15 stocks with the highest rises in volume for the three markets. Because volume usually precedes price, this list might also help you screen for winners. Stocks with falling relative strength are also tracked, and this could signal a downturn in one of your stocks. If you see a position with falling relative strength, you might want to check this out with your broker. In all cases, these tools are just helpful starting points for your research into stocks.

What to Ask Your Broker

With this brief summary of the factors that make a stock tick, you can find your own winners. You have been exposed to the fundamentals and technicals of stock selection: the fundamentals tell you *why to buy a stock* and the technicals tell you *when*. Now that you are versed in the two schools of thought, you can make sound decisions about your broker's recommendations.

No one expects you to have total recall of the massive amount of information already covered, but you should now be armed with a veritable arsenal of questions to ask your broker. Here are 25 to get you started:

1. Is the particular stock an investment for growth, or an investment for value?

2. What is the firm's capitalization?

3. What are the company's revenues? What is the growth rate of those revenues?

4. What was the previous year's price/earnings ratio? What price/earnings ratio is projected for the future?

5. What growth in earnings has been experienced in the past? What sort of earnings growth is expected in the future? (Remember, the earnings growth rate should be higher than the price/earnings ratio, if the investment in question is a growth stock.)

6. How does the firm in question compare with others in the industry? What sort of goodwill factor is attached to the company? Conversely, do consumers feel any ill will toward the firm?

7. What sort of competition does the company face from others within the same industry? Has the possibility of competition been factored into the firm's earnings forecast? Is there any chance that its products or services will be made obsolete? What barriers to entry face new competitors? Can one merely hang out a shingle, or do would-be contenders need to build a huge manufacturing plant in order to compete?

8. Is the investment banker underwriting the stock associated with the brokerage recommending it? (If so, let the buyer beware!)

9. What are the company's gross margins, operating margins, and net margins? How do these numbers compare with the margins of others in the same industry?

10. With reference to the firm's balance sheet, is the current ratio above 2? Is the acid test ratio above 1.5?

11. Who makes up the firm's management team? Does its president and/or chairman of the board have a solid track record of past successes? (By all means avoid the fly-by-night managers who jump from one company to the next without achieving substantial results.) Are top executives overpaid, or is their level of compensation tied into the overall performance of the company?

12. How does the firm treat its personnel? What is the staff turnover rate? Is the company an equal opportunity employer, or does it practice discrimination of any sort? (Keep in mind that a major lawsuit against the firm could irreparably damage its reputation or even drive the company into bankruptcy.)

13. What is the reputation of the stock's underwriter? (It's a good sign if the underwriter is well-respected in the financial industry, but this factor alone cannot guarantee the performance of a stock—since even the best underwriters introduce losers to the marketplace from time to time.)

14. What is the track record of the financial analyst recommending the stock to the broker who is recommending it to you? (A good broker knows which analysts have a record of telling out-and-out lies about the prospects of a stock simply to please the investment banking division responsible for underwriting the issue.)

15. How does the stock look in terms of technical analysis? Is it presently in an uptrend, downtrend, or neutral/oscillating channel?

16. Is the relative strength line moving up or down?

17. Is the stock close to a breakout and, if so, is trading volume increasing?

18. Are insiders (including corporate officers) presently buying up more shares, or are they trying to unload what they already own?

19. What is the support level?

20. At which price is there resistance?

21. Where is the trendline at present?

22. What is the 50-day moving average? What is the 200-day moving average?

23. How does the stock's earnings cycle fit in with America's overall economic cycle? (For example, when the Federal Reserve Bank is trying to stimulate the economy, it's a good time to invest in firms engaged in manufacturing homes, automobiles, and other "big-ticket" items.)

24. What is the ratio of a firm's "earnings before interest and taxes" to its "total interest expense"? (To ascertain this number, simply divide the former by the latter.) It's a good sign if the result is 8 or more, as it indicates that the company should be able to make timely interest payments.

25. How does Standard & Poor's rate the company's credit? (This concept is discussed at length in Chapter 7.)

Any broker who's worth his or her salt, that is, commission fee, should be willing and able to answer all of these questions. If not, I suggest you find yourself another broker!

chapter 6

SAFETY FIRST: "WORRY-FREE" INVESTMENT TOOLS

Chapter 1 began with the mention of three financial geniuses who rank as veritable wizards of Wall Street, but J. P. Morgan was perhaps the greatest (and certainly the most eccentric) of the lot.

You may know J. P. Morgan as the founder of several powerful firms that thrive quite nicely to this very day. Chances are you've heard of the three major institutions bearing his name: Morgan Stanley, J. P. Morgan & Co. (also known as Morgan Guaranty) and Morgan Grenfell. Although the impressive financial legacy he left behind ensured that Morgan would remain a household name throughout America and much of the world for centuries to come, the immense contribution he made to the security of all of our bank accounts is largely forgotten.

Lessons from One of America's Bravest Financial Wizards

John Pierpont Morgan (1837–1913) had the good fortune to be born into an internationally prominent family of bankers. As a young man, J. P. became known as the driving force behind industrial towers of strength such as U.S. Steel and General Electric, but it wasn't until Morgan reached the ripe old age of 70 that he was asked to serve his country by bailing it out of a crisis unlike any it had faced before. To do this, he gave of his own personal resources and wielded his mighty political influence to an extent that no other man (or woman) of his era would have been able to.

For a variety of reasons, as the twentieth century rolled around, Hamilton's original dream of a central bank strong enough to play a leadership role in regulating America's overall economic policies had yet to be realized. Not surprisingly, in the intervening years, an epidemic of financial "panics" and various banking crises cropped up throughout America. In fact, until the Federal Reserve System was finally established in 1913, the national economy behaved much as a manic depressive yet to discover the right medication. Whenever America's industries enjoyed booming business, a period of feverish speculation ensued—and investor optimism knew no bounds. Before long the pendulum would swing suddenly just as hard in the other direction, resulting in long and agonizing periods of recession such as the one that occurred in 1903. This era would then give way to another extreme of expansion, speculation, and higher stock prices. This was the prevailing pattern in the 1900s. The 1903 recession gave way to a "boom," but, by the autumn of 1907, the pendulum stood ready to swing back the other way. Tragically, few investors expected the sort of catastrophic downturn in the economy that would bring this great nation to the brink of financial ruin.

More than 8,000 companies failed in the first nine months of 1907 alone. The catalyst that set off this disastrous chain of events was the action of a New York financier named F. Augustus Heinz. Using his position as president of The Mercantile National Bank, Heinz misused his depositors' funds in what proved a futile attempt to take over the United Copper Company. After 15 minutes of frenzied trading on the New York Stock Exchange, Heinz had succeeded in becoming a massive shareholder in United Copper, all the while running the stock up in price from an opening quote of 39-7/8 to a whopping $60 per share. In the end his takeover bid failed and the stock plummeted to $10 per share—which meant that United Copper was trading at roughly one-quarter of its value before Heinz's ill-advised interference.

The Mercantile National Bank suddenly found the majority of its holdings invested in shares of United Cooper purchased at prices between $40 and $60, but worth only $10. Heinz's unfortunate gambit (financed with other people's money) had thrown Mercantile National into bankruptcy, and the two brokerage houses that helped Heinz in his takeover attempt were also forced to shut their doors. The stock market was shaken to the core by Heinz's folly; in no time at all the overall value of stocks listed on the exchanges spiraled downward to a four-year low!

A similar panic began shortly after, on October 21, 1907. Knickerbocker Trust Company's president, Charles Barney, was a known associate of Heinz. For this reason, depositors at Knickerbocker feared their funds also would be lost in the United Copper fiasco. They proceeded to remove a total of $8 million in cash before Knickerbocker's doors were slammed shut and bolted the next afternoon. Word quickly spread to depositors of another institution, The Trust Company of America, which held a major block of Knickerbocker shares. Many people reasoned that, since Knickerbocker had gone bankrupt, The Trust Company of America might soon do the same. Its president urgently requested an audience with J. P. Morgan and begged J. P. Morgan for a sufficiently substantial injection of cash to permit The Trust Company of America to remain in business. Although Morgan strongly disapproved of trust companies, he decided to serve the best interest of the public. After quickly reviewing the trust's financial statements, Morgan rounded up $10 million in cash from a group of wealthy and influential friends. Morgan knew full well the sort of domino effect likely to occur should three financial companies go bankrupt one after the other, so he acted swiftly to ensure that The Trust Company of America remained solvent.

Many investors at other trusts panicked nonetheless, and it became clear that the efforts of one man alone couldn't save the entire financial industry. Roughly 48 hours after Morgan stepped in, the federal government followed his lead, coming up with $25 million. Even this further injection of cash into the banks of New York City failed to convince people that it wasn't safer to keep all their cash tucked into their mattress linings. It soon appeared that not even the New York Stock Exchange would have enough funds to remain in business. Morgan realized that, were the NYSE to close, the disastrous impact on the national economy would be completely irreversible. Minutes after being informed of this further crisis, our great and powerful "wizard deluxe" rounded up an additional $25 million in cash—the amount required to keep the doors of the exchange open. He then formed a coalition of New York's most prominent spiritual leaders, urging them to preach sermons of faith and optimism in the future of America and the sanctity of the financial basis on which our democracy had been founded.

As each day of the next two weeks passed, however, the government of New York City itself edged ever closer to a state of bankruptcy, and our public officials found themselves pleading with Morgan for the sort of financial aid he alone could provide. Once again, J. P. answered the call, organizing a banking syndicate able to muster a collective pool of resources large enough to serve as a "tourniquet" to prevent New York's coffers from being bled to death. To cut straight to the bottom line, November 6th marked an end to the devastating crisis, and Morgan deserved the grateful thanks of the entire nation.

J. P. Morgan died at the age of 75, just a few years after saving New York City—and America itself—from what would have surely proved the worst financial disaster in history. The estate he left behind was valued at a full $68.3 million.

Soon after Morgan's death in 1913 the Federal Reserve Act created what became known as the *Federal Reserve System* to monitor the nation's economic health. However, no power on earth was strong enough to prevent the even more catastrophic Wall Street crash of 1929. Eventually, under the Roosevelt administration, the Federal Deposit Insurance Corporation (FDIC) was set up to guarantee the savings of depositors. I suppose that federal guarantee is as good as any of us can expect from life, aside from the oft-mentioned certainty of death and taxes!

Safe and Sure: Checking and Savings Accounts

Each of the "worry-free" investment tools we're about to cover in this chapter is referred to as *cash*. That umbrella term is used in financial circles to describe a wide variety of financial instruments that reach full maturity within a year of original issue.

Our most liquid asset of all is the balance (whether great or small) each of us maintains in checking and/or savings accounts. The interest rate offered on such accounts by our neighborhood banks is generally lower than those associated with other investment options. So much for the bad news: The good news is that, in most banks, our checking and savings accounts are insured by the

FDIC up to a total of $100,000 per customer, per bank. (Make certain that every institution with which you do business has on prominent display a notice attesting to that fact.)

Want Higher Interest on Your Hard-Earned Dollar?

Although checking and savings accounts are useful, a number of equally worry-free investment vehicles offer considerably more bang for the buck.

UNDERSTANDING YIELD CURVES

A *yield curve* is a graphic depiction of how maturity (always indicated by a horizontal line) relates to interest rates (as shown on the vertical line) of any fixed income investment. Thus, a yield curve measures the interest rate the issuer is willing to pay for borrowing your funds, according to the terms of the loan's maturity.

The key to unlocking the mysteries of the yield curve is what's known as the Federal Reserve *discount rate*. This is simply the interest rate charged by the Federal Reserve for the "overnight" loans it makes to member banks. This all-important discount rate in turn influences the federal funds rate, which is what banks charge each other for the loan of their reserves. (The term *reserves* refers to the amount of actual cash being held on deposit at any given time.)

Another important fact to bear in mind is that the U.S. government borrows money, through the sale of its securities issues, for periods of time ranging from a minimum of 3 months to a maximum of 30 years. Therefore, different interest rates apply according to the length of time involved, that is, the *maturity of the issue*. This gives rise to the concept of the yield curve as an essential tool used by investors and analysts everywhere.

Over the course of American history, we've seen five different types of yield curves. For the average person reading this book today, however, it's only important to acquaint oneself with the following three:

1. The *standard yield curve* has dominated throughout most of our history. This curve reflects the fact that the issuer of a bill, note or bond (in this case, the U.S. government) has normally been willing to pay a higher interest rate for loans that bear longer maturities. For example, at this writing, the government is willing to pay a 6.72% interest rate for a 30-year bond; 6.42% for a 10-year bond; and 5.10% for a 6-month Treasury bill.

2. A *flat yield curve* indicates that the U.S. government is willing to pay precisely the same interest rate, whether for a 1-year Treasury bill or a 30-year bond. The most recent flat yield curve came into play in 1989, when the government offered the same interest rate (8.5%) for both a 1-year bill and a 30-year bond.

3. An *inverted yield curve* signifies that the issuer (again, the U.S. government) is willing to pay more for short-term borrowing via Treasury bills than for long-term bonds. The most recent inverted yield curve occurred in 1981, when the government paid 14.8% for 1-year Treasury bills and 13.4% for 30-year bonds. An inverted yield curve is most likely to occur in an economic climate of abnormally high interest rates, something we haven't experienced as a nation for the past 15 years.

Keep the Faith: U.S. Treasury Bills

The very safest investment we can make is to put our money into Treasury bills backed by the full faith and credit of the U.S. government. If our representatives in Congress behave as responsible adults, America will never default on its debts. Should a default occur, the legal tender in your wallet may not be worth much more than the paper on which it's printed—and not even the likes of J. P. Morgan could bail us out of that sort of economic disaster!

Should you decide to purchase a U.S. Treasury bill, you might think of the transaction as lending money to a friend. Your friend faithfully promises to pay your money back in full—perhaps with a bit of interest—on or before a certain date. But what if your friend isn't as creditworthy as you thought? Suppose the agreed-on period of time passes by, but the friend pleads poverty and asks for additional leeway. What choice do you have but to extend more time for repayment? At this point you may realize that your "friend in need" is somewhat less than a "friend indeed" for not having kept the original promise. Even if you eventually recoup the money you were generous enough to lend out, you'll likely think twice before extending such loans in the future. Consequently, the friend's credit rating (in your own view, at least) may suffer a downward spiral.

As Americans, we can count ourselves fortunate that the U.S. government has an extremely good credit rating—despite the fact that our national debt is quickly approaching the $6 trillion mark. (Believe it or not, our credit rating is better than that of any other nation in the world.) We can therefore remain confident that any personal funds we choose to invest in Treasury bills will be fully repaid at the appropriate date of maturity. The bottom line is that interest rates are dictated by the creditworthiness of the borrower—whether a personal friend or national entity. Should there be any element of uncertainty about the repayment of the cash at maturity, however, we have every right to demand a higher interest rate in return for the risk involved.

As mentioned earlier, U.S. Treasury bills are considered by most to be the soundest investment vehicle of all—which is why we who work on Wall Street think of the interest rate associated with T-bills as completely synonymous with the term *risk-free*.

Aside from the safety factor we've just discussed, a few additional points to keep in mind about Treasury bills include:

1. the maturity date is one year or less from the date of issue;

2. the minimum denomination of bills that can be purchased is $10,000; and

3. T-bills can be purchased from your local bank as well as through your broker.

Should you wish to avoid commission fees altogether, you can buy them directly from the U.S. Treasury. A total of 12 Federal Reserve Banks are located in various cities throughout the nation, and it's quite simple to purchase Treasury bills in person. Once an initial account has been set up, you can make future transactions by mail—always on a commission-free basis. Whether purchases are made in person or via mail, this method is known as using *Treasury Direct*.

Treasury bills are issued at what we call a *discount;* they eventually mature at full value. The amount of interest that a T-bill investor receives is the difference between the bill's maturity value and its face value. Suppose, for example, you purchase a 1-year Treasury bill with an interest rate (also known as *yield*) of 6%. You're actually buying a face-value bill of $10,000, but at a discount of $9,400. To work this equation (with the help of your trusty pocket calculator):

$$\text{The Price of the Treasury Bill} = \text{Face Value} - \text{Discount Amount}$$
$$= \$10,000 - (\$10,000 \times .06)$$
$$= 10,0000 - \$600$$
$$= \$9,400$$

Interest rates vary, but the formula always stays the same. Should the Treasury bill carry a yield of 6%, you'll earn a total of $600 in interest. On a bill with a 10% yield, you receive $1,000 in interest at the maturity date.

The equation gets slightly more complicated when you buy Treasury bills with maturities less than one full year. In this case you need to factor in the appropriate "days till maturity" to determine the total price you should expect to pay. For all fixed income investments, a 360-day year is assumed. (Please don't ask me where the other five or six calendar days disappear to; frankly I haven't a clue!) Should you hold a 6% Treasury bill with a face value of $10,000 for 6 months, you need to factor in a "days till maturity" figure of 180. Therefore,

$$\text{Total Price} = \text{Face Value} - [(\text{Face Value} \times \text{Yield} \times \text{DTM}) \div 360]$$

By plugging in the appropriate numbers, you can solve the equation easily on your own:

$$\text{Price of the Treasury Bill} = \$10,000 - [(\$10,000 \times .06 \times 180) \div 360]$$
$$= \$10,000 - \$300$$
$$= \$9,700$$

The U.S. Treasury issues bills that carry maturities of three months, six months, and one year. Virtually no credit risk is involved, which makes T-bills the most liquid of all cash-equivalent investment tools. The news gets even better: Treasury bills aren't subject to taxation on either the state or local level.

The only real disadvantage is that Treasury bills normally carry the lowest interest rate of all the money market instruments available. The average Treasury bill rate (1926–1995) has been about 3.7%. The maximum yield during this 69-year period was offered in 1981 (14.71%), and the minimum return was slightly less than zero (in other words, "zilch"!) in 1938.

It's All in the Timing: Certificates of Deposit

Most readers of this book have at least heard of CDs—and I don't mean compact discs! You may have noticed the going interest rates for certificates of deposit on display in the windows of your local bank. A negotiable certificate of deposit is nothing more than a receipt from a bank guaranteeing that a certain amount of interest will be paid on an agreed-on amount of principal over a specified amount of time.

At present, more than 200 banks all across America issue certificates of deposit. The first $100,000 of CDs issued to an individual bank customer are fully insured by the FDIC. (But always check for those four all-important initials on display at your bank teller's window.)

One does not buy a certificate of deposit at a discount as is the case with Treasury bills. Instead, the transaction is made at face value. CDs can be issued with a maturity of more than one year, and that's generally the case in the present marketplace. Such CDs are subject to interest rate risk because after making your purchase, interest rates may take an upward turn. In that case, had you held onto your money to invest it elsewhere, you could have shopped around for an investment with a higher interest rate.

All CDs with maturities of *less than one year* pay interest only at maturity. On the other hand, for any CD with a maturity date of *one year or more* interest payments are made on a semiannual basis. For example, suppose you purchase a $100,000 CD with an interest rate of 6% and a maturity date of one year. Here's how to calculate what you'll receive at maturity:

$$\text{Proceeds at Maturity} = \text{Face Value} + \text{Interest}$$
$$= \$100,000 + [\$100,000 \times .06]$$
$$= \$106,000$$

Should you buy a $100,000 CD with an interest rate of 6% for 6 months, you'll need to factor in a figure of 180 as its DTM—or days till maturity—as follows:

$$\text{Proceeds at Maturity} = \$100,000 + [(\$100,000 \times .06 \times 180) \div 360]$$
$$= \$100,000 + \$3,000$$
$$= \$103,000$$

CDs with maturities of more than one year pay interest on a semiannual basis. You receive the original face value on eventual redemption. With this in mind, let's look at a third and final example before we close out this section on certificates of deposit.

Assume you bought a $100,000 CD with an interest rate of 6% and a maturity of five years. The interest payments you can expect to receive are as follows:

$$\text{Semiannual Interest} = (\$100,000 \times .06) \div 2$$
$$= \$3,000$$

The bad news is that all the interest you earn by investing in CDs is fully taxable at both the state and local level. The good news, however, is that the interest rate you earn is normally somewhat higher than that for U.S. Treasury bills.

Cash in with General Money Market Funds

The now booming money market fund industry first came into being in 1972, enabling private investors to benefit from the sort of high interest rates previously available only to the "big boys." Before money market funds were created, "small fry" like you and me had little choice but to invest our savings in a personal bank account where the interest our money would earn was rather tightly restricted by something known as *Regulation Q*. That legislation gave the already rich a decided advantage over the rest of us. Thanks to all the money market funds now available, however, low- and middle-income investors can deal themselves into a higher-stakes game.

Fidelity established itself as an aggressive leader in this new product soon after it was introduced to the marketplace. In 1974, Fidelity came out with The Fidelity Daily Income Trust. This was the first money market fund to offer user-friendly accounts (complete with check-writing privileges) as a "perk" to potential investors. Not surprisingly, Fidelity immediately earned a reputation within the industry as the most promising "new kid" on the block.

Again, the money market game is one at which all investors, large or small, can play. Money market funds can be purchased through various mutual fund "complexes" such as Fidelity, Dreyfus, Vanguard, Strong, and T. Rowe Price. They can also be purchased through a number of banks, as well as from registered reps at most brokerage houses.

Money market funds have been widely heralded for their expertise at pursuing three separate goals simultaneously:

1. To safely preserve the total capital invested in the fund;

2. To retain a high degree of *liquidity*, that is, the ability to move in and out of a wide assortment of securities; and

3. To reap the highest possible income for investors, while at the same time keeping risk to an absolute minimum.

In sports terminology, that's what you'd call a triple play.

Time for another easy formula: The *net asset value* of a money market fund is invariably $1 per share. And that $1 per share always equals the fund's total assets minus liabilities, divided by the number of shares outstanding.

The primary objective of a money market fund is to ensure that its price per share never falls below $1. This means that the price of your shares forever remains at $1, while the amount of interest you earn on the fund permits you to buy additional shares. Life holds few guarantees, however. It's certainly *possible* for a fund to let its price per share fall below the $1 mark—although virtually all retail money funds over the past 15 years have managed to hold steadfastly to the $1-per-share pledge that is the norm in such funds.

The most common variety of money market fund is the taxable sort, of which there are two types. We refer to these as *first-tier* and *second-tier funds*. The former are more common by far, and are legally restricted to holding commercial paper that's been issued by companies with high credit ratings. On the other hand, second-tier funds are allowed to invest up to 5% of their assets in commercial paper issued by firms that offer higher interest rates but are ranked lower in terms of creditworthiness. Greater risk is associated with second-tier money market funds than with funds of the first-tier variety.

Both tiers of money market funds are carefully regulated by the Securities and Exchange Commission. All funds are restricted to holding a mixture of commercial paper with an overall maximum average maturity of 90 days or less. Additionally, by law no single issue is permitted to comprise more than 5% of the money market fund's portfolio.

Should less-than-top-grade commercial paper play a part in the fund's portfolio, however, such lower-ranked paper cannot comprise more than 1% of the fund's total assets. Money market funds are also permitted to hold various securities issued by the U.S. government. Because no credit risk is attached to such holdings, no restrictions are imposed on the amount of U.S government securities a fund can hold as a percent of its total assets.

Remember the theory of diversification touched on in Chapter 2? You might say that money market funds take particular care not to put all their eggs in one basket. In fact, the average fund owns more than 30 individual issues at any given time in order to ensure that, should one "egg" crack, the entire fund won't "crack up" with it!

Last but not least of the worry-free investment tools addressed in this chapter is one that may seem heaven-sent for the "risk-averse" investor. If that description fits you, you're bound to love what's coming next.

Government Money Market Funds: A Sure Thing

Government money market funds invest only in securities issued by, or at least fully guaranteed by, the U.S. government. Should a dyed-in-the-wool conservative wish to enter the marketplace despite her severe aversion to risk, no more attractive investment vehicle is available.

What's known as *Treasury-only money market funds* pay somewhat less in terms of yield than general first-tier or second-tier funds, but you can congratulate yourself that your conservative investment in Treasury-only funds won't be subject to taxation at the state or local levels. If you live in a state that imposes a hefty state income tax, the purchase of these funds is probably your best bet. Your after-tax yield should, in fact, be greater than if you had invested in a general money market fund. At the same time your investment is as safe and worry free as it gets!

Although some government money market funds hold investments in U.S. Treasury bills and other government-guaranteed securities, they also sink money into securities issued by various federal agencies, for example, the Federal Home Loan Mortgage Corporation and the Student Loan Marketing Association. Such agency securities are similar to those officially backed by the FDIC in the sense that they are at least "morally" backed by the U.S. government. However, these securities *are* subject to state and local income taxes.

Again, we can thank our lucky "stars" (such as Hamilton, Morgan, and Roosevelt) that any investment we make in government money market funds is quite safe and worry free.

Shopping for the Right Cash Investments

Modern women are fortunate to have role models such as Marcia Beck, who until recently served as president of the Goldman Sachs mutual fund complex. One of her responsibilities at that prestigious firm involved overseeing in excess of $20 billion in cash, and that's more than even the most devoted shopper among us could spend in the course of a lifetime! Marcia earned her MBA degree from Columbia University and has been a major player at the Wall Street game for the past 16 years. She's certainly "paid her dues" (and then some) in the business world, but has managed to retain both her sense of humor and her charm. She's proof that you should pay no heed to those who say, "You can't have it all." Not only has Marcia attained an enormous degree of success in the often down-and-dirty world of high finance, but she's married with two children.

Today's woman really can have it all, even in a male-dominated society. However, when planning for the golden years of retirement, the question that faces us is, "How can we *keep* it once we've got it?"

The investments overseen by Marcia during her long tenure at Goldman Sachs were a mixture of cash, equity (that is, stocks), and bonds—so, who better to turn to for some sound "shopping tips" on how to make prudent investments? I think you'll find the advice Marcia was kind enough to share with us to be most enlightening. After all, we're going shopping with one of the very best.

Q: Marcia, into which cash investment vehicles do you put your personal savings?

A: For liquidity, I keep a portion in a 100% U.S. Treasury money market fund that's directly linked to my brokerage account. I try to keep all cash amounts that I'm saving and don't need right away invested in U.S. Treasury bills or notes that I buy through Treasury Direct.

Q: Why keep so much cash in Treasuries?

A: Because there's absolutely no chance of default, unless America itself goes into default. I have a real philosophical problem when it comes to taking any risk whatsoever with my cash investments. The additional reward one stands to make by investing cash in anything other than Treasuries is minimal, relative to the additional risk that's involved. Keep in mind that any dividends you receive on a 100% U.S. Treasury money market fund are not subject to taxation on either the state or local level. It's easy to access the cash you keep in a money fund, so you'll be able to enjoy all the benefits of owning Treasuries without sacrificing the liquidity of your cash.

Q: Perhaps the readers of my book will understand this point a bit better if you take a moment to explain liquidity. *What does that term mean to you personally?*

A: Liquidity means that I'm able to access my funds from 8 o'clock in the morning to 3 o'clock in the afternoon, each and every business day. An investor's cash is not put at any market risk whatsoever—assuming of course that the management of the fund in question is doing what they're supposed to. In other words, my shares in the fund always have a constant value. I should add that Treasury Direct is most convenient for investors who want to hold onto their bills until they mature. Any decision that might be made to sell the bills before the appropriate maturity date would necessitate their transfer from Treasury Direct to a brokerage or bank, since there's no way to sell them directly.

Q: How can a potential investor be absolutely certain that a money market fund maintains 100% of its assets in U.S. Treasuries?

A: Make sure to ask the broker or advisor who is trying to sell you the fund whether the totality of its holdings is in Treasuries—and whether or not there are any "repos" in the mix. The "repo" portion of your investment in a fund is invariably subject to state and local taxes. Also subject to such taxes are obligations issued by federal agencies such as the Federal Home Loan Mortgage Corp. or, depending on your state of residence, The Student Loan Marketing Association. By carefully examining the fine print of a fund's prospectus, you should be able to find this information spelled out for you, but if you still have any question in your mind, by all means place a phone call to the fund itself. Should you live in a state that imposes something called an "intangible tax," you should ask your tax advisor how such income will be treated.

Q: What advice do you have for potential investors in municipal money market funds?

A: Most holdings in municipal money market funds are tax exempt at the federal level, but an element of credit risk is involved. Various municipalities have defaulted over the years, but so far no municipal money market fund has allowed its $1 net asset value to break—simply because the investment advisors of the funds in question felt compelled to make sure that investors incurred no losses. Historically speaking, whenever a municipal fund (or other widely available money market fund) has experienced a credit problem that could result in a loss to investors, the mutual fund complex sponsoring the fund has come up with enough cash to make up the difference. They did so out of their own pockets, so to speak, in order to protect their business franchises and reputation in the industry—not from any legal responsibility or guarantee to keep the net asset value of such funds at $1.

Q: That's an extremely good point for readers to bear in mind. Since funds have no legal responsibility to maintain the $1 net asset value, how can we be sure that our investments in such funds are safe?

A: The truth is that you rely on the overall good business judgment of the sponsoring organization itself. By all means make sure that your investment is placed with one of the larger complexes, and that it's been in business for some time. Also, be certain that the fund isn't buying any derivatives with your money. This is highly unlikely, but you never know unless you ask the right questions. If the fund performs more than 0.5% better than the average fund out there, ask the mutual fund why they are outperforming their competition.

Q: Moving on to other cash investments readers might consider, what advice would you offer concerning certificates of deposit?

A: The chief advantage of buying CDs is that they're typically issued by FDIC-insured banks, and therefore insured up to $100,000. Investors can choose whatever date of maturity best suits their personal investment needs. The FDIC insures up to $100,000 per depositor, per bank. In other words, if you had savings, checking, and CD accounts totaling more than $100,000 at XYZ bank, and that institution failed, you would recoup only $100,000 from the FDIC.

Q: Even so, is there any real cause for concern when such investments are purchased from a major bank with the very best of credentials?

A: Although major banks are businesses with globally dynamic credits, their fortunes nonetheless ebb and flow from time to time. At certain periods throughout our nation's history, some of our largest money centers have been rated at less than investment grade and have faced serious financial difficulties. The truly risk averse should never make total investments at any one bank of more than the maximum amount that's completely covered by FDIC insurance.

Q: I'm becoming convinced that you're fairly risk averse when it comes to making cash investments. Am I right?

A: Absolutely! No investment that falls into the category of cash should be subject to an element of risk. Cash you're certain you won't need to touch in the immediate future should either be invested via Treasury Direct or in U.S. Treasury purchases made through your bank or broker. Immediate cash should be kept in a money market fund comprised of Treasury bills. Such money market funds are regulated by the Securities and Exchange Commission, and therefore must stand up to some very specific criteria. Should a fund be unable to meet such criteria completely, it can't legally be called a *money market fund.* Whenever you see a prospectus without those three words on its cover, be sure to ask *why* they don't appear.

Q: Don't you think that's being overly cautious?

A: Again, Marlene, I don't want to take risks with my cash, and you can have defaults or problems with even the best short-term securities. Orange County took most people by surprise.

Q: You've just made your point. But for anyone who missed the headlines at the time, would you provide us with a brief recap?

A: I suppose that many of your readers who live outside Orange County, California, may not be completely aware of what happened there in 1994, but it's quite a fascinating story. Orange County's Treasurer ran the general county pool, which included the funds of the various municipalities within the county. He was in charge of vast sums of money allocated to the region's many public school boards. He made huge investments in risky derivatives, and even borrowed money to wager on the direction of interest rates. In other words, he "bet heavily" on some of the riskiest investments in the marketplace. Guess what? He guessed wrong!

Q: What happened next?

A: Not only was Orange County unable to meet its short-term obligations as they matured, but the salaries of teachers in the public school system were in jeopardy. Don't forget that, prior to this disastrous incident, Orange County had one of the highest short-term credit ratings in the nation. Consequently, quite a number of money market funds—both the taxable and nontaxable varieties—were left holding Orange County debt instruments that had lost a great deal of value overnight. The investment advisory sponsors of such funds quickly stepped in to insulate their investors against the resultant loss by absorbing the losses on those securities. Still, the next time a similar incident occurs, who's to say that the sponsors of such funds will have the financial resources and business willingness to do the same? Remember, they are not legally or morally obligated to do so. That's why my advice to potential investors boils down to this: why bother taking any risks with your cash when you don't have to?

Marcia's final point really "hit home" for me personally about a week after our interview: on phoning the management of my own basic U.S. government money market fund, I was shocked to learn that only 4% of its holdings was invested in U.S. Treasury bills; a full 96% of it was invested in short-term obligations issued by federal agencies. This meant that only 4% of the yield I earned was actually tax exempt on the state and local levels. Worse yet was the fact that the fund yielded less interest than what was currently available in the U.S. Treasury market. Needless to say, I plan to liquidate the account immediately and start shopping for a 100% U.S. Treasury money market fund to take its place—all thanks to Marcia and her excellent advice.

Didn't I tell you we were going shopping with one of the very best?

LENDING YOUR MONEY TO THE BIG BOYS: BUYING BONDS

The decorative highlight of the New York Stock Exchange's majestic Board Room might surprise and astonish you, as it did me. Should you have the chance to set foot in this room, your eyes will be drawn immediately to the priceless eighteenth-century urn gifted to the exchange by a man who was among the most powerful in the world at the time: Czar Nicholas II of Russia. This extravagant display of gratitude was a token of the Czar's thanks to Wall Street's largest exchange for agreeing to list the Imperial Russian Loan as a bond issue shortly after the turn of the twentieth century. The great gift of the Czar undoubtedly will be worth its weight in gold for many centuries to come, yet those who purchased bonds in support of His Imperial Highness's stern-fisted dictatorship would have been wise to invest their hard-earned "rubles" elsewhere.

Lessons from Imperial Russia: Things Change

I'm reminded by this wondrous *objet d'art* (designed by the legendary Carl Fabergé) that even the mightiest empires run the risk of one day being reduced to ashes.

According to a report issued by the archives of the New York Stock Exchange, an application to list the Imperial Russian Loan was filed on August 6, 1902. Its distinguished group of underwriters included J. P. Morgan and Co., August Belmont and Co., Baring

Magoun and Co., and The National City Bank. The massive debt to be financed by the bond's issue (2,310,000,000 rubles) was the equivalent of more than $1 billion in U.S. currency. Eight days after the application was made, the bonds were officially listed on the exchange. The bad news came in over the wires a bit more than 15 years later: the bloody Bolshevik Revolution of October 1917 succeeded in ousting the all-mighty Czar from the tremendous position of power he'd held for decades.

The devastating blow for investors in Russia's Imperial Bonds was that the Bolsheviks immediately disavowed all financial obligations made under the rule of Czar Nicholas II. The new Communist regime announced that it would honor none of the agreements entered into by "His Imperial Highness, the Emperor of All Russia"—it's hard to explain why the suddenly worthless bonds continued to trade on the exchange for even an hour after this proclamation had been made. (Perhaps a few desperate investors held onto their bonds in the slim hope that the Czar would eventually return to power.) The next three years passed under ever-strengthening Bolshevik rule until even the most optimistic of the bonds' investors decided to throw in the towel. The Czar's bonds were officially removed from the New York Stock Exchange's listings on January 27, 1921. The beautiful Fabergé urn is all that's left to show for the Imperial Russian Loan.

This illustrates the fact that the only absolute certainty is that there are no real certainties in life. A degree of risk always exists, no matter how secure the world's governments and municipalities may seem. Business enterprises incur even greater degrees of risk. It's absolutely essential to weigh the wisdom of investing in any bond issue against such factors as the applicable maturity date and the likelihood that the issuer (whether government or corporate) will be solvent enough to pay off the loan in full when the appropriate time comes.

The Higher the Risk, the More You Earn

Would you believe that a number of major corporations have begun to issue bonds with maturities of a full 100 years? An individual investor must take a gigantic leap of faith to sink his or her money into the future earnings of a firm that may go bankrupt long before a full century passes by. As mentioned in the previous chapter, bonds issued by the U.S. government promise to be the most risk-free source of future income for our retirement years and for bequeathing to our children and grandchildren.

In order to accumulate wealth, a portion of every investment strategy includes purchasing bonds of the government, corporate, or municipal varieties. If you're completely unable to live with the vicissitudes of the stock market, you can still build a portfolio of high-quality bonds to achieve a higher degree of income than keeping your money in worry-free cash. But to do this well, you need to become thoroughly acquainted with five distinct forms of investment risk.

Interest-Rate Risk

The Federal Reserve sets interest rates through what's known as the Federal Reserve discount rate. Although this is a short-term rate, every aspect of the American economy revolves around this "magic number" set by the Fed. Okay, so it's not really a "magic" number, but the Fed's discount rate *does* function as a mighty baton by which the Federal Reserve orchestrates the entire American economy.

As do stock prices, interest rates fluctuate upward and downward. Because bonds are tied to interest rates, their prices are not static by nature. In other words, the value (or price) of all bond issues available in the marketplace inevitably rises and falls according to the interest rate prevailing in the American economy at a given moment.

Because bonds are issued with maturity dates of more than one year, payments are made on a semiannual basis in the form of *coupons*. (By definition, the term *bond* refers to most investment vehicles that mature at points between slightly more than one year and 30 years from the date of issue.) Hence, a $10,000 bond with a coupon of 6% and a maturity date of 30 years would make twice-yearly payments according to the following formula:

$$\text{Annual Yield} = \$10,000 \times .06$$
$$\text{Semiannual Payment} = \$600 \div 2$$
$$= \$300$$

The investor in such a 6% coupon bond would therefore receive payments of $300 twice a year. As time passes by, however, things change. For the sake of illustration suppose that interest rates rise dramatically over the next two years, with the result that newly issued 30-year bonds carry a yield of 8-1/2%. A $10,000 bond would warrant coupon payments of $425 twice a year. We arrive at that figure using the same formula we used a moment ago; we merely substitute an interest rate of 8-1/2%. Let's give it a try:

$$\text{Annual Yield} = \$10,000 \times .085$$
$$\text{Semiannual Payment} = \$850 \div 2$$
$$= \$425$$

The foregoing scenario serves as a perfect example of the frustrating dilemma faced from time to time by all investors in the bond market: a bond that once was purchased at a 6% yield is no longer as attractive as the 8-1/2% bond currently issued in the marketplace. The investor would be wise to sell the 6% issue to another investor and use the money to buy a new bond at the currently prevailing yield of 8-1/2%. But, you might well ask, "Who would want to buy a 6% bond under such conditions?" The answer, of course, is "no one!"

Consequently, if the investor wants to sell the less attractive 6% bond, he or she will have to bite the bullet and sell the bond at less than its original price, in order to make up the difference between the lower interest rate of, say, two years ago and that of the presently available yield. The investor will be forced to part with the original $10,000 bond at a discount, by selling the instrument at less than its face value of $10,000.

The investor has no obligation to sell the original 6% bond, however, and can bank on receiving a total of $10,000 when it comes time to redeem the bond at the applicable maturity date. Assuming, of course, that the bond's issuer is still solvent by the time such maturity date rolls around, the investor will always receive what's known as *par* (the bond's original face value). Having already received semiannual coupon payments of 6% over the course of the bond's lifetime, the investor has already pocketed in full the agreed-on amount of interest.

To play devil's advocate, however, let's assume that the opposite scenario occurs: an investor owns a note worth $10,000 at 6%

bearing a 30-year maturity, and interest rates take a downward turn to 4-1/2%! If the bond owner decides to "hang in there," he or she could count on receiving the twice-annual coupon payments of $300. However, if that investor resolves to sell the instrument, current market conditions would dictate that the bond holder receive a premium on the interest he or she would be missing at the prevailing interest rate. You're already familiar with the formula, so join me in "cracking" the equation for a bond issued with a coupon rate of 4-1/2%. Just what will our semiannual coupon payment be?

$$\text{Annual Payment} = \$10,000 \times .045$$
$$\text{Semiannual Payment} = \$450 \div 2$$
$$= \$225$$

Obviously, the 6% bond the investor purchased some time ago is worth more in terms of yield than the bonds currently available at 4-1/2%. If the investor sells the 6% bond, he or she would have every right to expect a premium, that is, a price more than the $10,000 face value originally paid.

The following points summarize the three scenarios we've just examined:

‣ Should the 6% interest rate (or yield) neither rise nor fall, the bond is considered *trading at par* since it is worth the original face value of $10,000.

‣ Should the 6% interest rate that prevailed at time of purchase move upwards to 8-1/2%, the bond is considered to be *trading at a discount,* since it is worth less than the original face value of $10,000.

‣ Should the 6% interest rate that prevailed at the time of purchase move downward to 4-1/2%, the bond is considered to be *trading at a premium* since it is worth more than the original face value of $10,000.

As long as the bond's issuer remains solvent (which was *not* the case with His Imperial Highness, the Czar of Russia), an investor receives full face value of the bond at the maturity date, regardless of what the going interest rate is at that time.

According to Ibbottson Data, long-term government bonds bearing maturity dates of roughly 20 years have experienced what's known as a *compound annual growth rate* of approximately 5.2%. But such bonds have fluctuated over the years from a high of 13-1/2% in 1982 to lows of 2.5% during the forties.

Interest rate risk affects each and every bond for sale in the marketplace—whether federal, municipal, or corporate—and is therefore the single most important factor in evaluating bonds. The term we use for measuring the effect of a change in interest rates on a bond's price is *duration*. (And, believe me, the jaw of any slick bond salesman is bound to drop big-time the instant he hears a question like, "So what's the bond's duration?" from someone assumed to be a first-time female investor.) Never forget to ask this question when considering the purchase of any bond, or bond fund (that is, a mutual fund composed exclusively of bonds). The average duration of the bond or bond fund is an all-important factor in weighing your decision either to buy into the investment or "pass" on the deal!

Duration refers to the degree to which a bond changes in value with an accompanying upward or downward movement in overall interest rates. Should a bond (or bond portfolio) have a duration of 6.2, its value changes by 6.2% for each 1% fluctuation in the prevailing interest rate.

To illustrate the point, let's turn to the example of a 6% bond with a face value of $10,000. If the bond had a 6.2 duration, your $10,000 investment would be worth only $9,380 if the interest rate increased by 1%. You won't need a calculator to deduce that 6.2% of $10,000 = $620. Simply subtract the $620 from the original face value as follows: $10,000 − $620 = $9,380.

On the other hand, if interest rates dropped by 1%, the bond (or bond portfolio) could be expected to increase in value by 6.2%. So, instead of subtracting $620 from the $10,000 face value, we would add the same amount instead, arriving at a value of $10,620.

It doesn't take a rocket scientist to recognize that the higher the duration of a bond, the more a change in interest rates will affect its actual value. Duration depends on such factors as the maturity of the bond, the pattern of cash flow (coupons), and the original price paid for the bond.

Credit Risk

Credit risk is the second most important risk factor in evaluating bonds. This type of risk is issue-specific, that is, it's a value judgment made by analysts as to the likelihood that any specific issuer will default on payments for the bond or its eventual redemption in full. The U.S. government has yet to default on its debts, so America's credit rating simply can't be beat. (Yet, even that is not irreversibly etched in stone when one remembers that things change with the passage of time.) Nevertheless, we assume that the spirit of America residing in the hearts of its countrymen—and women—will ensure that our great nation remains solvent and creditworthy for the immediate future. For now, then, let's hold firm in our assumption that bonds issued by the U.S. government carry virtually no credit risk.

However, credit risk is a very important factor to consider when making investments in corporate and/or municipal bonds, which is why both varieties are "rated" by one or more of the nation's credit agencies. The major corporate bond rating agencies are Moody's Investor Services, Standard & Poor's, Fitch Investors Service, and Duff & Phelps. The information provided by Standard & Poor's and Moody's generally carries the most weight in the marketplace, but I myself pay more attention to the ratings provided by S&P. (Sorry, Moody's!) If you look up the S&P ratings, you see something that looks like a report card similar to those you received in grade school. The following table shows the "marks" assigned to bonds and what those marks mean to investors and Wall Street analysts:

AAA	Indicates highest quality
AA+ AA AA−	Indicates high quality
A+ A A−	Indicates medium grade
BBB+ BBB BBB−	Indicates lower-medium credit quality

Any rating below the level of BBB– is referred to as less than Investment Grade.

BB+ BB BB–	} Indicates low quality
B+ B B–	} Indicates that the bond is speculative
CCC CC C	} High risk of default
D	Already in default

Credit rating agencies are generally careful about doing their homework, but they are by no means infallible. It's a given that mistakes due to human error occur from time to time, but the major agencies listed in the foregoing are fairly reliable at providing quality information to potential investors.

Individual investors should stay with corporate bonds with at least a AA– rating. In municipals, I don't buy anything below A. For safety's sake, it's important to stay with higher quality bonds. If you want a higher yield, I recommend putting your money in a high yield bond fund with a number of full-time analysts watching the company's credit and diversification. Their advice may help you avoid disaster.

Liquidity Risk

Remember the scenario in which an investor might want to unload a 6% bond at a discount because the prevailing interest rate had risen to 8-1/2%? Should you find yourself in a similar situation, there's no guarantee that you'll be able to find a buyer for the bond in question, even at an enticing discount rate. Particularly if the bond you're holding is one that's been "thinly issued" (which means that not too many other investors are holding it), you're likely to have a bit of trouble selling it. Wall Street refers to this as *liquidity risk*—since the bond in question has become a difficult asset for the investor to *liquidate*.

Don't worry about not being able to sell that 6% bond at all, however, although you may be forced to sell at a price significantly lower than face value. Assuming that the issuer remains both solvent and creditworthy, you'll find some broker on Wall Street who's willing to get rid of it for you, but the discount at which the broker may need to sell the bond may not be to your liking.

To conclude this section on liquidity risk, I should point out that such risk does not normally apply to bonds issued by the U.S. government. But you could from time to time find yourself with a liquidity problem with various corporate or municipal bonds.

Call Risk

Corporations often issue bonds with an interest rate higher than that currently prevailing in the marketplace (that's the good news), but with something known as a *call provision* (that's the bad part). If interest rates were to decrease from that of the issuer's original coupon rate, with the result that the bond's value increased significantly, the issuer would reserve the option to "call" the bonds back in. This is a legal way for a corporation to ensure that "take-backs are allowed!"

Naturally, the bond's issuer must pay the original purchaser either a *par* (face value) or *premium* (above face value) price any time such a security is called back before the appropriate maturity date. It follows that the only reason the issuing corporation would recall the bonds was if management became fairly certain that it would be able to issue new bonds at a significantly lower interest rate—one more in line with the current prevailing bond market.

Each bond offered in the marketplace comes with a formal agreement between the issuer and purchaser, something known as an *indenture*. If call risk is an element included in such an agreement, you'll find somewhere in the fine print a reference to a specific call date as well as to whether the bond would be redeemed by the issuer at par value or at a premium under such circumstances. The element of call risk comes into play because, once the bond is recalled, the investor may be unable to replace the bond's originally promised yield with another bond of similar quality.

Event Risk

There's not much to say about this final sort of risk, except that there's always the chance that an unforeseeable event may downgrade a company's market value. Again, the one real certainty in life is that things change—often in the most dramatic ways imaginable.

In December of 1996, one of America's premier toy companies (Mattel Inc.) found itself slapped with lawsuits resulting from one of its newest products on the market. Mattel no doubt expected its new Cabbage Patch Snacktime Kid doll to be one of the year's biggest moneymakers, but just as the executive team was congratulating itself on the sale of more than 500,000 units, reports began to come that the dolls craved locks of hair! The toy manufacturer swiftly offered a $40 refund to purchasers, but that gesture might not prevent angry parents from suing Mattel for having traumatized their toddlers.

All sorts of totally unforeseen disasters, ranging from acts of God to such "acts of man" as corruption in the ranks of its management team, can wreak havoc with a corporation's bottom line. Who's to say that a firm's manufacturing plant might not suddenly explode, due to human error or a meteorite from outer space?

Choosing Bonds that Fit Your Needs

Now that we've become acquainted with all five types of risk that may come into play in the bond market, let's discuss the various types of bonds vying for our hard-earned cash. To paraphrase the title of one of Woody Allen's earliest films, you're about to learn "everything you've always wanted to know about bonds—but were afraid to ask." One by one we tackle seven major categories of bonds, beginning with the most risk free.

U.S. GOVERNMENT BONDS

The U.S. government issues both long- and intermediate-term debt obligations, and both varieties are similar to the Treasury bills we've already discussed at length in the previous chapter.

1. Long-term debt obligations are known as *Treasury bonds* and refer to securities that bear maturities of ten years or more. They have a minimum face value of $1,000.

2. Intermediate-term debt obligations are known as *Treasury notes,* but fall into the bond category nonetheless. Treasury notes are issued with maturity dates ranging from one to ten years into the future. They bear a minimum face value of $5,000 for two-, three-, and five-year maturities, and a minimum of $1,000 for those that mature at seven or ten years.

Both Treasury bonds and notes are traded all over the world, which means that action occurs in the marketplace literally 24 hours a day. Most of these trades take place over the counter at brokerage firms that bear a considerable resemblance to NASDAQ, but a degree of trading takes place on virtually all the major exchanges worldwide.

The U.S. Treasury offers all this debt by means of auctions of Treasury bills, notes, and bonds. Prior to the auction, the Treasury announces the size of the particular Treasury issue to be sold. Banks and brokerage firms bidding on these securities can place their bids in either a competitive or noncompetitive fashion. Should you choose to bid competitively through your broker, he or she specifies the face value and yield at which you're willing to invest money. Conversely, a noncompetitive bid is one that states the desired face value, then expresses a willingness to purchase the security at whatever the weighted average of the competitive bids turns out to be. Once the auction has actually taken place, the coupon rate of the security is established by the U.S. Treasury based on the average of all bids.

Treasury notes and bonds work a bit differently than T-bills, in that the interest rate you receive is always the stated coupon rate. For example, suppose a Treasury note or bond has an 8% coupon rate and bears a face value of $10,000. It takes only a moment with a pocket calculator to determine how much money you'll receive in interest:

$$\text{Interest Received} = \$10,000 \times .08$$
$$\text{Semiannual Payment} = \$800 \div 2$$
$$= \$400$$

As noted earlier, the value of the bond or note fluctuates with each rise or fall in the market's prevailing interest rate. Should the interest rate increase, the value of the bond would decrease. Therefore, a $1,000 bond or note issued at the prevailing interest rate invariably sells at par, that represents the face value of the security at 100%. Should the interest rate go up, the bond or note would be less than par, and would therefore be represented as a percent of par value, that is, at something less than 100%.

To continue this exercise a bit further, let's say that the $1,000 bond or note you bought at a lower interest rate soon becomes worth a mere $957.50. Oddly enough, this sum would be represented as 95.24—although the reason won't be readily apparent to those uninitiated in bond vernacular. You see, one unusual feature of the way such percentages are tracked is that the bond's listing is always stated in 32nd increments of a single percentage point! (Using a calculator once again, 24/32 is the mathematical equivalent of .75, should we want to express this number via decimals.) In this case, the security would be valued at 95-24/32 of its $1,000 face value, a sum calculated using the following equation:

$$.9575 \times 1,000 = 957.50$$

You already know what would happen should the prevailing interest rate move downward over the course of time: your bond or note would be valued at more than its original face value. Should your original security priced at $1,000 now be valued at 101-20/32, the worth would be expressed as 101.20. The figure appearing next to the bond's name in the market listings of your investment daily would be derived by applying the same arithmetic formula that we used in the previous example.

$$1.01625 \times 1,000 = 1016.25$$

The bond or note in question would therefore trade at 1016.25. For most readers of this book, I'll bet that's the first time you've ever had to think in 32nd increments! To sum up this section on government notes and bonds, I'll remind you that the three chief advantages offered by this sort of investment are: (1) there's no credit risk, so they're the safest investments one can make; (2) U.S. Treasury notes and bonds are the most liquid of all securities available in the marketplace; and (3) they're not subject to state or local income taxes. That's a winning combination by anyone's standards—although investors normally receive a lower yield in exchange for all this safety and liquidity.

One final note: Should a Treasury bond or note be sold any time between coupon dates (that is, when the semiannual payments fall due), the interest accrued since the most recent coupon date would be paid to the security's seller at the time of settlement rather than to the new owner. In other words, whoever purchases your government-issued note or bond gets a "fresh start," and the clock starts ticking anew on the yield from the very moment he or she becomes the new owner of the security. (Didn't I promise to teach you everything you always wanted to know about bonds, but were afraid to ask?)

FEDERALLY SPONSORED CREDIT AGENCY BONDS

Federally sponsored credit agency bonds are another form of fixed income securities connected to the U.S. government—at least in the sense that Congress originally legislated a total of eight such institutions. (I should point out, however, that these agencies are now privately owned.) Just what do these agencies do, you ask? They're in the business of making loans to private lenders, who in turn make loans to individuals and corporations. Of these eight agencies, the following are the best known:

1. The Federal National Mortgage Association, which goes by the nickname "Fannie Mae"

2. The Student Loan Marketing Association, known as "Sallie Mae"

3. The Federal Home Loan Mortgage Corp., also known as "Freddie Mac"

Whoever thought these somewhat silly-sounding "pseudonyms" up in the first place, I wonder? Still, to borrow from Shakespeare, they certainly fall "trippingly on the tongue"!

CORPORATE BONDS

Most corporations issue debt as well as equity (that is, stock) in the form of corporate bonds that trade over the counter at most brokerage houses in America, as well as elsewhere around the globe. Some are also listed on the New York Stock Exchange.

Such bonds are typically listed in terms of a percent of par, with par at $1,000. Most corporate bond issuers make payments on a semiannual basis. As with U.S. bonds and notes, when trades occur between coupon dates, the interest accrued to that point is paid directly to the seller rather than to the security's new owner.

These bonds, referred to as *corporates,* are otherwise quite dissimilar from those issued by the U.S. government, with credit risk being the main difference between the two. As each of us is aware, the financial health of virtually any corporation can be blown by the wind—rising or falling when a competitor discovers a new product, or the firm suffers a temporary reversal of fortune.

The ratings assigned to bonds, as well as their maturity dates, are extremely important factors for any potential investor to bear in mind. The expression, "The bigger they are, the harder they fall," serves to remind us that even the giants of industry can topple over time. A company worthy of Standard & Poor's highest ranking (AAA) today may rate a D on its report card ten years from now, or perhaps even tomorrow! To cite just one example, do you recall how one of America's greatest automobile manufacturers, Chrysler, almost went bankrupt in the early eighties? Were it not for the intervention of Lee Iacocca and the U.S. government, the great Chrysler corporation might well have turned into an automotive "dinosaur." (For that matter, do you remember what happened with the Edsel?)

I personally don't buy corporate bonds with maturities of more than 5 to 7 years, and I don't even think about putting my money into anything with an S&P rating less than AAA or AA. Although I enjoy owning bonds considered to be strong and sound investments, I find it difficult to take that leap of faith believing that any firm will be around and blissfully solvent for a period more than seven years into the future. Only when interest rates are unusually high (above 9%), do I buy longer-term U.S. government bonds of ten- to fifteen-year maturities.

Wall Street measures the spread between AAA corporates and government bonds. In the last twenty years the spread between the ten-year government and corporate has been roughly between .5 and 1.5%. I don't think this slight increase in yields is worth the added risk for long-term paper. Also, after taxes, governments are not taxed at the state and local level.

The sort of unforeseen event that made the Imperial Bonds of Russia worthless in the early twentieth century is a fact that each of us should bear in mind whenever we purchase a bond of the corporate variety. Again, life offers no guarantees—who knows whether the planet itself will still be habitable by the turn of the twenty-first century? That's why I warn investors to stay away from corporate bonds with maturities of seven years or more. Since I usually buy bonds with the intention of holding them until their maturity date rolls around, I'd like to have at least some degree of confidence that the issuer will still be in business to redeem them. That's why my personal "rule of thumb" vis-à-vis corporate bond maturity dates is seven years.

I've already acquainted you with the term *indenture,* which refers to the various terms and conditions that are part and parcel of the bond purchase agreement itself. In order to verify that the indenture of any given bond is strictly legal—and that these terms are upheld for the entire lifetime of the bond—someone known as a bond trustee is appointed to monitor the security's issuer carefully on a day-to-day basis.

Many corporations have some sort of collateral backing their bond issues, such as property holdings, manufacturing equipment, corporate stock, or perhaps other bonds that are pledged as security. The most common type of corporate bond is something called a *subordinated debenture,* which is backed only by the overall creditworthiness of the security's issuer. Therefore it's essential to examine the firm's credit rating and resist the urge to sink your capital into a bond issued by any corporation that scores less than a high quality rating! Again, don't take a leap of faith too far into the future.

What do credit agencies look for when rating bonds? They examine every minute detail of the firm's financial statements and past track record and thoroughly evaluate the quality of the management team behind it. They look at the overall industry in which the firm is engaged, and keep an eye out for any competitors in the marketplace who might pose a threat to the bond issuer in the future. As mentioned earlier, however, credit agencies are staffed by human beings and subject to human error. Again, the buck stops with you, the investor, in terms of evaluating the bond issuer in

question, as well as the track record of the credit agency that's issuing the firm's report card.

For inquiring minds who want to know, one insightful study
released by Moody's indicated a default rate of less than one percent (.7%, to be exact) on bonds ranked high quality as expressed
by an AAA report card from Standard & Poor's and Aaa by Moody's.
Compare that percentage to a whopping 14.3% default rate on
bonds with ratings less than BB from the experts at S&P or Ba from
the team at Moody's. Unless your desktop comes equipped with a
crystal ball guaranteed to offer more reliable investment advice, it's
a good idea to pay attention to what the top credit agencies have to
say about the issuer of any corporate bond in which you plan to
invest. By no means let yourself get suckered into buying bonds
with more than a short-term or intermediate-term maturity date,
because not even the best credit agencies have crystal balls good
enough to peer that far into the future!

MUNICIPAL BONDS

We now turn to the subject of municipals. This variety of bonds represents the issuance of debt instruments by either a state or local
government. These bonds are often used to raise money for special
projects such as the construction of hospitals or highways. The most
common type of municipal is known as a *general obligation bond*
and is backed by the full faith and credit of the state or local government that issues it. Unfortunately, such full faith and credit has
from time to time proven considerably less than that of the U.S. government. That's why, before proceeding any further in discussing
municipal bonds, I caution you that an element of risk is definitely
involved in this type of investment.

As you know, a few state and local governments have declared
bankruptcy over the course of America's history, and more are
bound to do so in our nation's future. The value of holding any general obligation bond is directly dependent on what the municipality involved is able to collect in taxes.

My biggest philosophical problem with investing in municipal
bonds is that I question the personal integrity of far too many of
the men and women whom we as voters elect to positions of public office.

That said, I have on a number of occasions forced myself to put a little of my own personal cash into this type of security—if for no other reason than to diversify my investments as much as possible. To date, the default rate on the municipal bonds I've added to my portfolio has been reassuringly low (knock on wood). The default rate is very low for the overall country. Still, I find myself with nervous stomach pains each time I'm confronted by front-page headlines questioning the integrity of the state and local officials running the show! So, remember that a definite risk is involved with municipals, and decide for yourself whether this sort of investment carries more risk than you can comfortably "stomach."

Again, some good news goes along with the bad: as compensation for the element of risk involved in municipal bonds (as compared with that of U.S.-backed securities), the federal government has historically decreed most municipals to be tax exempt. Therefore, any interest you earn on municipals issued for public purposes is not taxed by the IRS. On the other hand, municipal bonds issued for private purposes (such as housing developments) are taxed by the IRS unless the tax-exempt nature is expressly spelled out in the terms of the bond's indenture. Happily, most municipals are exempt at all three levels of taxation—assuming that the investor is a resident of the state or local municipality introducing the bond to the marketplace.

If your sixth sense is warning you that another yield formula is in store before we go further, then you have a good built-in "crystal ball" indeed! Pull out that trusty pocket calculator of yours one more time, because we're about to use both a coupon rate and marginal tax rate in order to examine what's known as the *equivalent taxable yield* on municipal bonds.

As our first example, suppose that the municipal bond you've purchased pays a yield of 5-1/2% and bears a maturity date of five years. For the purpose of this exercise, assume that you're subject to a marginal tax rate of 36%. The *equivalent taxable yield* on your municipal bond would therefore be equal to your tax-exempt yield divided by a factor of 1 minus your marginal tax rate, as follows:

$$\text{Equivalent Taxable Yield} = 5.5 \div [1 - .36] = 8.59\%$$

Further suppose that the current prevailing rate on a U.S. bond or note is only 6-1/2%. For a potential investor who hasn't familiarized herself with this formula, that 6-1/2% is clearly more tempting than the 5-1/2% offered by the municipal. But, the moment that a potential investor realizes that the U.S.-backed bond or note will be taxed on the federal level, while the municipal bond will not, the latter type of security seems more attractive because it actually means more cash in the investor's pocket at year end.

For investors in high tax brackets, the purchase of municipals becomes the more attractive option. As noted earlier, most municipals are of the general obligation variety (also known as *GO bonds*). For what it's worth, my personal advice to investors in such securities is to make sure that they buy only *standard GO bonds,* backed by the ability of the state or local issuer to ensure the eventual redemption of the bond by means of taxation.

Let's review the steps each investor should take before investing in any municipal bond:

1. Acquaint yourself with your personal marginal tax rate. (Don't worry about this for the moment, because I explain in detail how to calculate this in Chapter 13, but be sure to double-check your calculations with your accountant.)

2. Use the formula I've just provided to calculate the taxable equivalent yield.

3. Don't be tempted by any variety of municipal bond other than the standard general obligation, unless you're confronted with overwhelming evidence that another sort of municipal bond is a totally safe bet.

For added protection, you may even want to concentrate on municipal bonds that come with an actual insurance policy attached! The following six firms issue such insurance:

1. AMBAC Indemnity Corp. (AMBAC)

2. Capital Guaranty Insurance Co. (CGIC)

3. Municipal Bond Assurance Corp.

4. Connie Lee Insurance Co.

5. Financial Guaranty Insurance Co. (FGIC)

6. Financial Security Assurance Corp. (FSA)

Another way to invest in municipal bonds is to participate in special *municipal money markets,* the sort offered by most mutual fund complexes. When choosing among funds of this type, the key is to draw comparisons among their respective equivalent taxable yields.

Before rounding off this section of the chapter, I should point out that any future changes in the way our tax system works will obviously have a dramatic impact on the municipal bond market. For example, should America adopt the sort of flat tax that's been the subject of much discussion lately, the tax advantages of owning municipal bonds would be eliminated. Municipal bonds already issued at that point in time would retain their tax-exemption, of course, but the overall effect on the future viability of municipals might well be devastating. The bottom line is that it's anyone's guess how our federal tax system will evolve in the years ahead, especially given the mysterious nature of the "collective mind" of our Congress.

HIGH-YIELD ("JUNK") BONDS

Remember the eighties and the notorious "junk bond king" named Michael Milken? Despite the drama and press headlines conjured up by the mere mention of his name, this perhaps misguided "maestro" of Wall Street single-handedly created a brand new industry. Before Milken came onto the scene, high-yield bonds were known in the industry as "fallen angels." Very few brokers or investors gave them a second thought.

"Fallen angels" were bonds that had enjoyed an investment-grade credit rating at the time of issuance, but subsequently fell from grace (so to speak) to an S&P rating of BB+ or below. Milken examined a number of such securities and concluded that they had considerable investment potential in the marketplace, nonetheless. He then crafted a well-thought-out plan by which he could issue new bonds based on such firms, despite their lower-than-investment-grade credit ratings. How did he pull it off, you ask? He simply compensated the investors in such securities by promising higher yields. These high-yield or "junk" bonds soon became the means by which countless takeovers were financed throughout the eighties. In fact, a great many such bonds helped finance companies that did astonishingly well in the long run. (Where, for example, would

Ted Turner and Turner Broadcasting be today were it not for Milken and the junk bond industry?)

The court verdict went against Milken in the end, and he served a number of years in a low-security prison to repay a debt to society for his alleged crimes. Yet, many still protest that Milken did nothing wrong. With the passage of enough time, Milken may eventually be vindicated. He may even be remembered by historians as a true genius who did a great deal more good than bad for the American economy as a whole. One thing's for sure: whether you think of them as high-yield bonds or junk, these investment tools still enjoy a prominent place in the American economy and are held in high esteem by many investors the world over.

Assuming you don't have the time required for you to become an expert in "junk" analysis, I strongly advise you to avoid purchasing such bonds on an individual basis. Instead, consider participating only in the sort of diversified portfolio available through one of the trustworthy mutual funds that make it their business to specialize in high-yield instruments. The following list includes four such funds, each of which enjoys a five-star rating, along with their five-year annualized returns as of September 30, 1997, and a toll-free number, should you care to phone for a prospectus and account application.

Mutual Fund	Annualized Five-Year Return	Telephone Number
Fidelity Spartan Income	14.38%	800-544-8888
Northeast Investors	14.93%	800-225-6704
Fidelity Capital & Income	12.57%	800-544-8888
Value Line Aggressive Income	12.75%	800-223-0818

We discuss Morningstar's ratings in some detail in Chapter 8, where we take an in-depth look at the mutual fund industry.

CONVERTIBLE BONDS

Convertible bonds are the sort of corporate bond that can be exchanged for equity (that is, stock) at a specific price, and which normally carry a coupon rate that's lower than that of the average corporate bond. The bad news is offset by an unusual "perk": should the issuer's stock perform above the conversion price, the value of the convertible bond moves up in direct correlation with the stock.

This provision makes for a much greater upside potential than is offered by run-of-the-mill corporate bonds. However, issuers of convertible bonds are often firms with less than the highest credit ratings. Again, since most of us don't have the time to become experts at credit analysis, it's wiser to purchase this type of security through a mutual fund that specializes in convertibles.

Although the junk bonds we listed in the previous table ranked five-star ratings from Morningstar—the highest score the firm gives out—the best-performing no load mutual funds specializing in convertibles merit no more than four stars. (I save the definition of *no load* for Chapter 8.) This list, as of September 30, 1997, is as follows:

FIVE-YEAR AVERAGE

Mutual Fund	Rating	Annualized Return	Telephone Number
Fidelity Convertible Securities	****	15.78	800-544-8888
Vanguard Convertible	**	12.73	800-662-7447
Value Line Convertible	***	15.34	800-223-0818
Key SBSF Convertible Securities	***	14.63	800-539-3863

ZERO COUPON BONDS

Last but not least of the major bond types with which you need to be acquainted is the zero coupon variety. Much like U.S. Treasury bills, these bonds are sold at a discount, then appreciate over the course of time until they can be redeemed at full face value. Another similarity to Treasury bills is that the interest is not paid out to the bondholder.

The major difference between the two is that zero coupon bonds are not taxed in the same manner as Treasury bills. Instead, the bondholder actually "owes" the IRS whatever interest is accrued each year, with the proviso that the investor can't collect such interest until the actual maturity date rolls around.

Why would anyone want to buy zero coupon bonds, rather than those offering a steady income on a semiannual basis? Suppose a parent wants to put away money for the college tuition of a child. What better way to make sure that the necessary money becomes available at just the right time than by setting up a zero coupon bond that matures just as the child is ready to enter his or her freshman year?

However, I should point out that zero coupon bonds are an extremely volatile investment tool—and that timing is everything. Since their duration is normally much longer than that of other bonds with the same maturity, zero coupon bonds are more sensitive to changes in interest rates. Should the long-term movement of interest rates work out in your favor, nothing could be finer either for building a future nest egg for retirement or for putting your offspring through college.

On the other hand, should interest rates go up significantly, you'll not only lose out in terms of interest, but you stand to take a substantial loss on your original principal as well—but only if you sell before the maturity date. Again, timing is everything, and it's wise to have a specific goal in mind before investing your money in zero coupon bonds.

Congratulations! You've just survived a rather thorough briefing on a total of *five* types of risk and *seven* categories of bonds—all squeezed into the pages of a single chapter. In short, you've become an expert on the subject of lending money to the "big boys." I've thrown an incredible amount of information your way; you may well know just as much now (if not more) about these subjects than do most of the registered reps you're likely to meet at your local brokerage firm. Before any of them have the chance to "arm-wrestle" you into purchasing less than the best-quality bonds for sale in the marketplace, I've made sure that you're well armed with all the right questions!

SHOPPING AROUND FOR MUTUAL FUNDS

"The apple doesn't fall far from the tree," as the saying goes. I seem to have inherited my fascination with money from none other than dear, old Dad. When I was little more than a toddler, my father and I would rev up the family auto and head for the local bank every Saturday morning. Once there, we would each deposit funds into our respective savings accounts. I needed a bit of a boost up to the level of the teller's cage when my turn rolled around, but it proved well worth my father's effort. Today, he's proud of having taken the time to teach me important lessons about money at such an early age—lessons for which I'll always be extremely grateful.

As you might imagine, dad's average account balance was considerably greater than that of his darling daughter. Still, I always experienced a thrill when depositing whatever small change I had managed to accumulate the previous week. (No small-time piggy bank was good enough for me as a child.) Yet, the best, most exciting, aspect of this weekly routine was seeing a little "free money" stamped onto my passbook, as if by magic! If nothing else, I learned that savings accounts earned something called interest, whereas the piggy banks resting on the bedside night stands of most of my friends did not.

I was equally fascinated by how diligently my dad shopped around for better interest rates, and occasionally made a higher-than-normal deposit in order to earn a free gift of some sort. We would take home a small appliance for the family kitchen, proudly congratulating ourselves that it hadn't really "cost" us anything. On the other hand, my father's expertise in matters financial had certain limitations, and (as do *all* investors) he made an occasional costly blunder! Dad was invariably successful in the "toaster" department at our local bank, but I'm sad to report that he didn't have nearly as much luck when it came to investing in stocks.

Were the "Good Old Days" Really All That Great?

Back in the fifties, one of my dad's neighbors (a roofer by trade) encouraged him to invest some of his savings in IBM, Xerox, and Loew's Theaters, all of which turned out to be stellar picks over the long run. Would you believe it? More than 40 years later, my father is *still* kicking himself for buying stock in Pan Am at the suggestion of a know-it-all co-worker instead of heeding the sage counsel of the guy next-door. (Pan Am took a rather spectacular nose dive in the seventies before it eventually "crashed and burned" altogether in the eighties.)

Like my dad, even the most astute and savvy investor picks the occasional big-time loser. We could all drive ourselves crazy with regret about the countless "would haves," "could haves," and "should haves" we missed over the years. Important lessons can be learned from past errors, but the time comes to move on once those lessons have been learned! The fact is that *no one* is able to go through life without regrets.

For investors of my dad's generation, buying stocks was mostly a hit-or-miss endeavor. You wagered your money and prayed that you'd made a good guess about the future earnings of the company in question. Today, ordinary folk like you and me can tap into a global database of financial information heretofore available only to an exclusive and elite group of analysts on Wall Street. We can call up an entire library of resource material without ever leaving the comfortable privacy of our own homes! All it takes is a PC and modem that's hooked into one of many Internet services—and that technology is becoming increasingly affordable with each passing year. For example, I just bought a state-of-the-art PC and printer for roughly $2,500, and I'm able to enjoy unlimited access to the Internet via America Online for only $20 per month.

For those who have yet to take the full plunge into today's Information Society, the same sort of investment information is telecast via CNBC and other cable networks. Consequently, none of us need rely solely on the advice of some commission-hungry broker or even a friendly, well-intentioned neighbor or co-worker. Anyone willing to take the time to monitor the right television broadcasts and keep abreast of the news printed in one or more investment dailies and magazines can profit from the same sort of research materials previously available only to the most powerful Wall Street pros.

But more important even than access to information, the main reason private individuals of my dad's generation couldn't cash in on the stock market was that they lacked any real ability to diversify their investments. My father would choose to invest in a single stock—sometimes unwisely, as proved the case with Pan Am— and his own financial security became inseparably tied to that of the company itself rather than to the overall growth in the marketplace. It was therefore extremely difficult for any low- or middle-income investor to diversify his or her holdings. But the great news for investors in the nineties is that the proliferation of mutual funds nowadays enables virtually anyone with savings to profit via stock diversification.

At present, there are as many mutual funds to choose from as there are individual stocks in the marketplace. I hasten to add that you should never use the "dart-throwing" method for selecting one, because all mutual funds are *not* created equal! It is essential to do some diligent shopping and check out the merchandise before you hand over your savings to any particular fund manager (or to more than one fund should you decide to diversify your portfolio further).

What Makes a Mutual Fund "Tick"

Mutual funds have actually been around since before the Great Depression—not that very many folk knew about their existence until the seventies. The major reason for the tremendous surge in popularity of such funds over the past two decades is that so many private individuals have become better-educated investors.

In the fifties, the entire mutual fund industry held assets worth approximately $4 billion. Compare that figure to the $53 billion presently managed by a *single* fund today! (I'm referring, of course, to The Fidelity Magellan Fund, which for some time was expertly managed by a legendary investment guru, Peter Lynch.) Other mutual funds have enjoyed spectacular track records of late. For example, The Fidelity Contra Fund and Vanguard Windsor now control approximately $23 billion and $15 billion in assets, respectively. Frankly, were the three funds mentioned here the *only* funds from which to choose, there would be no real need for a full chapter on mutual funds. But (would you believe it?) there are at least another 7,500 presently available in the marketplace.

That's why I want to share with you some important industry secrets. You should always consider a great many factors before investing in mutual funds—and very few brokers and investment advisors are willing to take the time to explain these things thoroughly to a novice investor. So prepare to take a crash course in mutual funds that includes in-depth briefings on such topics as performance, styles of investment management, what to look for in a portfolio manager, how to review properly the costs and mechanics of a mutual fund, and how to measure the risk involved. I ask only that you promise *not* to keep this information strictly between the two of us, but rather share what you learn with your investor friends.

Evaluation of the Fund's Price Tag

Without further ado, we begin by asking a loaded question—pun intended!

IS THE MUTUAL FUND OF THE "LOAD" OR "NO LOAD" VARIETY?

The first important fact you should know about mutual funds is that each of the 7,500-plus funds in the marketplace is bound to fall into either the "load" or "no load" category. By definition, the term *load* refers to nothing more or less than a sales commission. *No load* funds are those on which no commission fees apply. Generally speaking, load funds impose sales fees up front—

meaning that such charges are automatically added on to the tab at the time the initial investment is made. Normally, this load amounts to somewhere between 4 and 8% of the total capital involved in the transaction.

On average, however, you should expect to pay only 4 to 5% as a sales load. Should the load amount to 4%, for example, and you had a total of $10,000 to invest in a particular mutual fund, here's the simple formula you'll need by which to calculate the appropriate sales charge:

$$\text{Amount of Sales Load} = \text{Amount of Capital Invested} \times \text{Percent of Load}$$
$$= \$10,000 \times .04$$
$$= \$400$$

What this means is that only $9,600 of the total capital you originally planned to invest is actually working for you in the mutual fund, with the $400 difference disappearing straight into the linings of your broker's pocket. (What is good news for the broker is bad news for you.) A number of funds may actually be worth a load of 4%—but that this is generally *not* the case.

Only when a mutual fund has a truly stunning performance record should you pay such a hefty "cover charge" for "inviting yourself to the party," so to speak. Most readers of this book probably have at least one memory of paying a substantial cover charge to gain entrance into a nightclub or disco from which—for one reason or another—they wanted to "run like hell" within the first few minutes. That's why I caution that, when faced with the prospect of a 4% sales load, a potential investor should do enough research to make sure that attending such a costly affair will prove a pleasant experience in the long run.

When all is said and done, many low load or no load mutual funds are likely to make just as much money for you, and will no doubt prove better investments by virtue of a minimal (or nonexistent) sales charge attached to them. Quite a few no load funds perform appreciably better than many of the load funds. Moreover, you profit by having every cent of your original capital hard at work for you from the outset. If, in the example just cited, the fund had no sales load, all $10,000 of your investment would be in play from the moment you bought the fund, rather than just $9,600 of it with the 4% load fund.

One recent *Consumer Reports* study indicated that the average annual return on no load mutual funds was 13.5%, while the average return on load funds was a slightly *poorer* return of 13.3%. The results of this study, which tracked the earnings performance of 1,000 different equity funds over a five-year period (1988–1992), should make any potential investor give considerable thought before shelling out a hefty sales load for mutual funds.

Before moving on, I should point out that some funds carry something known as a *back-end sales load*. Instead of reaching for your pocketbook when you "arrive at the party," you don't have to ante up until your broker demands the "cover charge" at the exit door. As always in the financial industry, commissions are the name of the game—so there'll be the "devil" to pay either way.

WHAT SORT OF MANAGEMENT FEES ARE ATTACHED TO THE FUND?

Every mutual fund in the marketplace levies some sort of annual charge for the management of your money, which usually ranges from .5 to 1.5% of your holdings in the fund. On average, this *management fee* is closer to the 1% mark, but—no matter what fee is charged—your money is well-spent if the fund's manager performs his or her job in an admirable fashion. As you can imagine, the best portfolio managers in the business (the ones who control millions or even billions of dollars) make a quite comfortable living. (It's "nice work, if you can get it.")

DOES THE MUTUAL FUND CARRY A 12B-1 FEE?

To avoid compensating a salesperson (broker) for his or her ability to "pitch" funds to private investors through the sales load method, a number of mutual funds impose a sales and marketing fee instead. In the industry this is known as a *12b-1 fee,* and generally amounts to an annual charge between .25 and 1% of the total amount you invest in the fund. Therefore, even if the fund is of the no load variety, don't forget to ask if a 12b-1 fee is involved, and avoid the unpleasant shock.

Now that we've covered several different types of loads and fees associated with mutual funds, you know why it's essential to look before you leap. For my own investment portfolio, I almost invariably select funds of either the no load or low load variety, and avoid the higher-load funds. Only in the rarest of instances, when I'm convinced that the fund's portfolio manager is among the best "party hosts" on the planet, do I allow myself to pay a substantial "cover charge." If a manager has consistently managed to beat his or her benchmark for five years or more, paying a load might prove well worthwhile.

Analyzing the Fund's Style

Let's now move on to analyze the various investment styles employed by mutual funds, as well as the degree to which market capitalization is a factor. In Chapter 3, we touched on the fact that virtually all analysts use the S&P 500 Index as a benchmark when evaluating a portfolio's performance. Most portfolio managers measure the degree of their mutual fund's success (or lack of it) against this globally respected index on a day-to-day basis, but only the true virtuosos manage to beat the S&P. As you'll see in a moment, that fact alone helps us make the next important decision addressed in this chapter: should we as investors select a fund of the passive variety, or is it better to go with an active fund?

WHAT DOES PASSIVE INVESTING MEAN TO MY PORTFOLIO?

Passive investing simply means participating in the stock market via an index fund. By far the most popular are those of the "S&P" variety; Vanguard is clearly the front runner at present. How does a passive mutual fund work? Anyone who takes a close look at the Vanguard S&P 500, for example, discovers that the entirety of the fund's assets are tied up in stocks that make up the S&P 500 Index. The stocks that comprise the fund's portfolio do not change unless the experts at S&P decide to change the makeup of the Index itself. Because the stocks comprising such a fund change so seldom, most of the management fees associated with passively-managed mutual funds are quite low indeed, compared to the fees charged by the actives. Investing in a passive mutual fund is like investing in the stocks comprising the index on which the fund is based. If ordinary folk like you and me had enough money to go out and buy a block of each stock listed in the S&P 500 Index on our own, we wouldn't need to participate in a passive mutual fund tied into the self-same index.

Considering that the folks who run the show at Standard & Poor's are no strangers to the business of picking stocks, this sort of passive investing is a lot like playing follow the leader. (You might even think of it as a no-brainer method by which a great many mutual funds manage their portfolios with a minimum of effort.) The portfolio managers for such funds reckon that they can reap considerably more profit relying on the overall growth of the market, as indicated by the S&P 500, than by relying on their own research abilities.

Why is indexing is so popular? Well, it's based on what's known as the *Efficient Market Theory*. This theory assumes that the market is efficient because it incorporates into the price of a stock any event affecting the value of that security. According to the theory, an individual can't "beat the market" because prices of individual stocks tend to fluctuate dramatically as soon as important new information becomes known to investors. The market at large responds to new information more quickly than individual investors can; thus, no one can consistently buy or sell quickly enought to benefit. By holding a general market portfolio, you benefit from the market's appreciation, but you eliminate much of the risk associated with investing in a single stock.

In addition, people who firmly believe that the stock market will keep rising over the long run view a passive mutual fund as a means to "purify" their investments, since they are not at the mercy of the day-to-day decisions made by a fund's portfolio manager. For those who'd like to eliminate from the equation as much human error as possible, a passive mutual fund is the answer. You can rest assured that it will forever be tied to the long-term performance of a well-known index. The tradeoff, of course, is that investors in passive funds *are* completely at the mercy of the overall stock market itself.

Before going any further, I should emphasize that the S&P 500 is not the only index that's tracked by the various mutual funds in the marketplace. Vanguard has a highly successful fund that's tied to the S&P, but here's a quick look at a few of the other passive funds offered by the same complex:

1. *Extended Market Portfolio.* Vanguard uses this fund to track the Wilshire 4500 Index, which is comprised of small- and medium-sized companies.

2. *Total Stock Market Portfolio.* Vanguard uses this fund to track the movement of the U.S. stock market as a whole, using an index known as the Wilshire 5000, covering nearly all regularly traded U. S. stocks.

3. *Small Capitalization Stock Portfolio.* Want a fund that tracks the small-capitalization companies comprising the Russell 2000 Index? If so, this mutual fund is designed specifically for investors like you. Small-cap stocks have higher volatility, but have outperformed the market on a long-term basis. However, if you are risk averse, this fund may be too much of a roller coaster ride for your tastes.

4. *Value Portfolio.* This fund was set up by Vanguard to track Standard & Poor's Barra Value Index. In the past, value stocks have fared a bit better than growth stocks with a little less volatility.

5. *Growth Portfolio.* This fund is similar to the Value Portfolio, with one slight twist: Vanguard's Growth Portfolio Fund tracks S&P's Barra Growth Index rather than the Barra Value Index.

Should any of these passive mutual funds be of interest, you can phone Vanguard directly at (800) 662-7447 to request additional information. It's definitely to your advantage to arm yourself with enough "shopping catalogues" to fully inform any decision you make *before* you write that very first check.

I don't want to give you the impression that Vanguard has an absolute corner on the market when it comes to passive investing. For example, a firm called Dimensional Fund Advisors (based in Santa Monica) offers a variety of passive or "structured" portfolios, each centered around a specific type of asset class. With Dimensional, you can take your pick from the following: *small-cap, large-cap, international, value,* and *growth.* (And that's not the half of it!) You can contact Dimensional for the full list of their wares at (310) 395-8005. They will steer you to an investment advisor who sells their funds.

Many other large mutual fund complexes offer passive investment vehicles as well. This type of investment not only lets you "purify" your bet on the overall market itself, but enables you to place wagers on both a specific investment style (value versus growth, for example) and degree of market capitalization (small, medium, or large).

The one caveat I should mention has to do with the tax implications of these investments. Most of you are probably familiar with the terms *short-term capital gains* and *long-term capital gains*. The profits an investor makes via index-related mutual funds are usually taxed as the latter, chiefly because trading occurs only when the index itself adds or drops stocks from its roster. (However, since the S&P pays out dividends, a small percentage is taxable as ordinary income.) When it comes time to write out a check to the IRS on April 15th, this actually means some good news for the bottom line of your 1040 form.

Long-term capital gains are presently taxed at a lower rate than short-term gains—at least in most income brackets. For households with high incomes, short-term capital gains are taxed at 39.6% on the federal level, as compared with an 18% to 28% rate for long-term capital gains. Capital gains are taxed at 28% if held between one year and eighteen months. They are taxed at 20% if held between eighteen months and five years, and 18% if held after five years. This makes index-related mutual funds even more attractive to investors. An active mutual fund tends to reap short-term gains. On the other hand, index-related gains are mostly long term and therefore taxed at 20% rather than 39.6%.

WHAT DOES ACTIVE INVESTING MEAN TO MY PORTFOLIO?

Active investing includes not merely selecting the stocks to buy, but also trying accurately to "time" the overall stock market itself. To some extent, active investing is more an art form than a science. All equity portfolio managers want to make themselves look good in the eyes of their investors by selecting just the blend of stocks that will enable their funds *to beat* the combined average of the S&P 500 Index. At the very least, managers hope to hold their own by doing just as well as the S&P—though only the top "gurus" in the industry are able to do so successfully.

Should you choose an actively managed mutual fund, the fund itself—as well as the value of your investment in it at any given moment—depends completely on the portfolio manager's ability to make the best possible decisions about how to invest your money! Whether "win, place, or show," your financial fate is subject to whatever "bets" the portfolio manager chooses to place on your behalf in the daily "horse race" that is the global financial marketplace.

Should you decide to go the route of active investing via mutual funds, it's imperative that you get to know your portfolio manager. (You should also measure the returns of any funds you're considering and examine the risk associated with those returns.) My advice is to look for a portfolio manager who's been in the business for quite some time, and—just as important—has a degree of humility. Nothing worries me more than managers who display a boastful and cocksure attitude toward their jobs! Who needs a rootin', tootin' cowboy (or cowgirl) "busting broncos" in the Wall Street arena at the risk of life and limb, particularly when one's personal financial welfare is at stake? I prefer to cast my lot with "humble" portfolio managers who know how hard the fund's investors worked to earn all the capital that's riding on each decision they make!

Most mutual funds are comprised of a variety of stocks, so it becomes all but impossible for you to research thoroughly each of the companies represented by your investment in the fund. That's why it's essential that portfolio managers (or at the very least competent and trustworthy members of their team) regularly attend the appropriate firm meetings and buckle down to the chores of tackling all the analytical homework that's involved in doing the job properly.

MAKING CHOICES: ACTIVE VS. PASSIVE FUNDS

Which investment style (active or passive) am I more prone to trust when it comes to my own investment portfolio? I'd cast roughly 75% of my vote for the latter when it comes to large-cap growth stocks. After all, the S&P 500 is a constant that's proven fairly reliable over the years; it has about it a certain "machine-like" quality that helps minimize the element of human error. On the other hand, when it comes to small-cap or value investing, or international and sector funds, I feel better served by an active manager.

Portfolio managers are made of flesh and bone, however, which makes them subject to human frailties. Even the best of them make mistakes from time to time. Choosing stocks on a day-to-day basis requires a great deal of hard work, to say the very least—the sort of stamina it takes to bring back a gold medal from the Olympics!

Each individual investor must decide for herself whether it's worth paying a higher management fee for an actively managed fund, or to opt instead for a passively managed fund. Either way, the quality of a fund in large part depends on the ability of the portfolio manager to perform well in the marketplace on behalf of the fund's investors.

Analyzing the Manager's Style

Now that we've examined *what* makes a mutual fund tick, it's time to focus on *who* makes it tick.

A wide assortment of mutual funds are actively managed, so it's always important to examine each from the standpoint of investment style, capitalization, and risk level. As you already know, the two major styles of investing are growth and value. Managers of growth funds are actively seeking growth in both earnings and sales. On the other hand, managers of value funds are constantly looking for a "diamond in the rough" in the form of a presently undervalued stock that, in their opinion, may have significant future value. Let's take a look at each management style before proceeding any further, beginning with what it takes to be a good growth manager.

SHOPPING FOR GROWTH

Today's growth fund managers tend to follow trends in much the same manner as Hetty Green wagered on the Industrial Revolution throughout the late nineteenth century. Such managers focus on industries (and promising firms within those industries) that, on average, enjoy more impressive year-to-year earnings than those in the overall economy. Our friendly nineteenth-century Wall Street "witch" invested heavily in railroads, but that was, of course, before the Wright Brothers demonstrated that people could fly. A full century later, my dad invested in the airline industry (albeit in the wrong airline), and missed his friend's advice to buy Xerox and IBM—the wave of the future. Nowadays, portfolio managers on the lookout for growth investments are focusing their attention largely on "information" picks such as Microsoft, Cisco, and Intel—hoping to ride this remarkable wave of technological advances into the twenty-first century.

Yet, so-called growth firms often crop up in many older and more established industries as well. Remember "daughter" Lisa's first business enterprise? Suppose that Lisa had had the good fortune to come up with a delicious new formula for lemonade—perhaps one with a new and exotic flavor. She may single-handedly have been able to revolutionize the entire thirst-quenching industry, even at the tender age of six! The concept is not really that far-fetched when you consider the remarkable story behind Snapple, which was eventually acquired by Quaker Oats. These days, financial analysts agree that the oatmeal giant paid an excessive price to acquire Snapple a number of years ago. Had you been fortunate enough to have a stake in the young beverage manufacturer before Quaker's scouts snapped it up, you might presently be "feeling your oats" while comfortably ensconced in a luxurious Palm Beach mansion.

New products are often introduced into an already established industry, totally revolutionizing it. On the other hand, an innovative marketing scheme may prove extraordinarily successful, with the result that a whole new sector of the populace becomes eager customers for an old product—one that may have been on the market for decades. Who's to say, for example, that "Internet brokerage houses" won't be giving the major full-service houses a real run for their money before too many years pass? Discount brokers such as Charles Schwab have already managed to win over a significant number of accounts previously handled by the major firms, and that trend may continue until full-service houses are forced to cut their commission fees to stay in business. (Ironically enough, as I key these words into my computer, an advertisement for "e.Schwab" just flashed across my television screen, reminding me that Schwab customers can now make stock transactions over the Internet.)

The job of growth portfolio managers is to seek out new-industry firms, as well as to identify companies with plans to introduce exciting new products into already established industries. They must also keep abreast of whatever innovations in pricing and marketing are on the horizon. It follows that growth managers aren't normally interested in "slow-growing" sectors of the economy—the most "booming" industries of America's yesteryear, such as the railroads of Hetty Green's era, often carry no *real* potential for growth, given the significant passage of time and inevitable advancements in technology.

How do portfolio managers go about evaluating the factor of growth in such an ever-changing world? For starters, they take a good, hard look at a company's year-to-year track record of earnings. For example, suppose that a firm named "Global Gadgets" managed to yield $1 per share in 1995. Earnings of $1.25 during 1996 would indicate an earnings growth rate of 25%, and would also clue us in on the fact that the "gadget" industry was on an upswing.

Moving to a real-world example, Microsoft reported earnings of $741 million (or 57 cents per share) in the most recent quarter of 1996. A portfolio manager would review Microsoft's earnings for the comparable quarter of 1995, which the firm reported at $575 million (equivalent to 45 cents per share), to determine Microsoft's earnings growth rate. It's time to pull out your calculators again and tackle one of the user-friendly formulas I introduced you to in Chapter 4.

Growth Rate = 1996 Net Income − 1995 Net Income ÷ 1995 Net Income
            = $741,000,000 − $575,000,000 ÷ $575,000,000
            = $166,000,000 ÷ $575,000,000
            = 28.87%

Companies that demonstrate a long-term earnings growth rate of 15% or more are considered growth companies by most portfolio managers. Because these managers are normally willing to pay more for growth, firms that fall into this category tend to have higher price/earnings ratios (another concept we tackled in Chapter 4). Be forewarned, however, that growth stocks can be riskier than the majority of other stocks in the marketplace because of their higher P/E ratio.

SHOPPING FOR VALUE

It's been said that women are born shoppers—one generalization to which I personally plead "no contest." I just love finding a fantastic bargain on clothes, even though this inevitably leads to more bargain shopping to properly "accessorize" my wardrobe. I have a weakness for designer shoes that almost borders on a fetish, but I'm too much a spendthrift to pay the retail price of $200 or more for a single pair. Whenever I hear of a great sale going on at Bally, I head straight for the Fifth Avenue shop to see everything they've got in my size. The salesperson brings out one shoe box after another—and, frankly, I couldn't care less if the models I bring home are last year's, since I bought them at half the normal price. When lesser-quality shoes cost $80, and Bally's are sale-priced at $100, I find it hard to resist splurging. That's what I call shopping for value. I'm no slave to fashion, but I know that shoe styles and colors tend to rotate every two years or so. My bargain-priced shoes are bound to come back in fashion again—and I'll get a real sense of satisfaction when next year I see a similar pair on display at the same store for $220.

The investment style known as *value investing* is not very different from shopping for bargains at your local retailer. Value portfolio managers carefully examine a firm's balance sheet, and concern themselves a great deal with the book value of the company in question.

Portfolio managers of value funds take particular note of companies with low price-to-book ratios. (For a quick refresher on these concepts, see Chapter 4.) If a value manager learns that a firm with a book value of $25 per share is presently trading at $20, he or she might well consider it a fantastic bargain. But why would such a company's stock be trading at $20 to begin with, you ask? Perhaps it's experiencing financial difficulties of one sort or another, and has fallen out of favor in the marketplace. Often, investors in the stock market prefer to hold positions in firms that display a degree of vibrancy and upward price momentum, and lose patience and sell out on those that have hit a plateau.

Patience is the middle name of any good value fund portfolio manager, who takes a chance that a company with a low price-to-book ratio is really a bargain. The smart fund manager recognizes that the firm's future prospects are significantly better than what other investors in the marketplace anticipated. To return to my shoe shopping analogy for a moment: suppose Bally has leftover inventories because the color tan fell out of favor. The value manager would buy those tan shoes at bargain prices, believing there's a good chance that tan will be *the* hottest color in the fashion world in the not-too-distant future.

While ordinary folk like you and me (who actually have to work for a living) enjoy the thrill of finding a good deal on relatively small purchases at our local department stores, others with a great deal more money at their disposal pursue bargains in the global marketplace—and they're playing for much higher stakes. I'd like to share one example of this big-time bargain hunting. To appreciate it, you'll need some historical background.

A "Valuable" Lesson: The Citicorp Story. Many readers will recall that Citicorp—one of the most globally respected banks—found itself in dire financial straits as the eighties drew to a close. By 1991, Citicorp stock was trading at the drastically low price of $9 per share. Many of Wall Street's most vocal analysts were predicting that the company would go out of business altogether, although it had been around since 1812 and, by 1981, had become the single largest bank in America. (Not until the 1996 merger of Chemical Bank and Chase Manhattan did Citicorp finally lose its "heavyweight title.")

How, then, did Citicorp almost go bankrupt in the early nineties? Several factors contributed. For one thing, Citicorp made many international loans to nations in South America, and, during the eighties, began to take substantial losses due to defaults on its loan portfolio. As the United States slid into recession in 1990, Citicorp also suffered from the overall collapse of the commercial real estate market. Consequently, the price of Citicorp stock took a tumble throughout 1991 and 1992. The bank's future prospects looked grim but, as most of you know, there was a happy ending. A value investor stepped up to the plate in 1992 and helped Citicorp recapitalize. A total of $2.6 billion was raised, a full 25% of that sum coming from Saudi Prince Al-Waleed bin Talal.

As I type these words into my computer, Citicorp stock is presently trading at 122. The Saudi Prince, who still owns approximately 9% of Citicorp, can heartily congratulate himself on having made a real "killing" in the market. Thanks to his intervention, Citicorp has become one of Wall Street's "darlings"—and is, in fact, the only full-service consumer bank presently operating on a global basis.

All that's required of a good value shopper—particularly the portfolio manager of a value mutual fund—is the ability consistently to recognize good bargains in the marketplace. (Naturally, that ability is important for each of you to acquire, as well.)

Capitalization, Risks, Ratings, and Returns

Let's examine a few key factors that will enable us, as individual investors, to determine whether or not a particular fund is, in fact, a bargain.

A QUESTION OF SIZE: CAPITALIZATION

A mutual fund can be categorized by the capitalization level of the stocks in its portfolio. You're already familiar with the following formula:

Market Capitalization = Stock Price × Number of Shares Outstanding

Portfolio managers (and, indeed, most of us who work in the financial industry) categorize mutual funds into four groups, according to the average market capitalization of the stocks held in their portfolios:

1. Microcaps—less than $50 million

2. Small Capitalization—between $50 million and $200 million

3. Middle Capitalization—between $200 million and $1.5 billion

4. Large Capitalization—more than $1.5 billion

Thus, any given mutual fund can be categorized in terms of both its investment style (either value or growth) and the level of market capitalization of the companies in which it invests.

One study by Roger Ibbotson and Rex Sinquefield reported that the average $1 investment in small-cap stocks in 1926 would be worth $2,440 in 1994, whereas the same $1 invested in stocks that comprise the S&P 500 would be worth a mere $811. As always, past performance is no guarantee of future results, yet it's clear that small-caps have outperformed the large-caps over the long run. Bear in mind, however, that a greater degree of risk is involved when investing in small-cap stocks, because a minor-league firm is more likely to go bankrupt than is a larger, well-established corporation.

A QUESTION OF RISK

It shouldn't surprise you that a somewhat different risk level is attached to each mutual fund in the marketplace. We've already discussed the subject of volatility in Chapter 2, but here we use the term *standard deviation* to describe the volatility of any investment advisor's portfolio.

Do you recall how I assigned a volatility rating to both my accountant friend (Maureen) and my acting pal (Chuck)? Using asset management terminology, we can describe Maureen as someone with a *low standard deviation*—since there's very little volatility or fluctuation of her income from month to month. Chuck, on the other hand, falls into the *high-standard-deviation* grouping: He may star in a Broadway show one day, but be sleeping on my living room couch after having been evicted from his apartment the next. (As they say, "that's show biz!")

Finally, a paticular four-letter-word is often bandied about in financial circles when describing the degree to which a portfolio's volatility measures up against the volatility of the stocks that comprise the S&P 500 Index. A *Beta* factor is assigned to each fund available in the marketplace—with a Beta of 1.0 being equal to the volatility of the S&P at any given point in time. A Beta factor greater than 1.0 indicates that the portfolio is more volatile than the S&P 500. On the other hand, a Beta less than 1.0 indicates less volatility. Should someone trying to peddle a mutual fund take it for granted that you're a novice at the game, you may get his or her jaw to drop simply by asking, "What's its Beta?"

A QUESTION OF RATINGS

As mentioned earlier, Morningstar Inc. specializes in rating the vast array of mutual funds in the marketplace—ranking each in terms of risk and return on a scale of one to five stars. This system may remind you of the method used to rate hotels, in that you can be fairly certain of enjoying a more comfortable stay at a five-star hotel than at one-star lodgings. However, Morningstar's ratings should be used only as a guide—*not* as a substitute for carefully examining the fund on your own.

Bear in mind that Morningstar by no means tries to predict the future, but rather offers its opinion as to each fund's track record of balancing risk versus reward to date. Morningstar's experts assign a different performance score to each fund in terms of both risk and return, then subtract the former from the latter. They employ a handy statistical device known as a *bell curve* to plot both sets of information, in order to arrive at a final score for the fund's performance over a specific period of time.

For many readers, Morningstar's rating system brings back memories of how exams were graded in the college classroom. Using a typical bell curve a professor might give an A to the top 10% in the class (the equivalent of a five-star rating from Morningstar). A full 22.5% of the class had to settle for a B (or four stars); 35% of more-or-less average students received a C (three stars); and those who just didn't do their homework at all (another 22%) deserved nothing better than a D (two stars). The 10% who either failed to show up at class or managed to sleep through most of the lectures flunked the course altogether (the sort of mutual fund to which Morningstar would assign a one-star rating).

Thanks to the wonders of modern technology, Morningstar's ratings are available to individual investors through Internet services or you can request information straight from the source, by writing Morningstar, Inc. at 225 West Wacker Drive, Chicago, Illinois 60606, or by phoning the firm's representatives at (312) 696-6000.

A QUESTION OF RETURNS

Each time I consider investing in a mutual fund, I first arm myself with *The Morningstar Mutual Fund Report,* then take a moment to ring the fund itself and request a prospectus. Using the S&P 500 Index as my benchmark, I do the homework of comparing the overall returns of the stocks represented by that index against the performance of the mutual fund I have in mind. Don't forget that the S&P 500 is made up of large-cap stocks, so it would be unfair to compare its results with the results of a fund that specializes in a different level of market capitalization. Should I be in the mood to place a wager on a small-cap fund, I would compare its year-to-year results with the performance of the Russell 2000 Index instead.

I advise potential investors to examine a mutual fund's returns over a period of at least five years (a 10-year comparison is even better), and to compare its performance to that of the index most appropriate in terms of capitalization.

In a very real sense, the track record of a mutual fund is synonymous with that of the individual portfolio manager who runs it. For that reason, it's important to determine whether the same manager has been on board throughout the five-year (or ten-year) period in question—and to make sure that his or her performance has steadily improved since taking the helm. Where possible, I try to learn a bit of personal information as well. Again, I'd rather trust my money to someone with a little humility, than take a chance on the arrogant sort.

Suppose, for the sake of argument, that I've narrowed down my choice of potential mutual funds in which to invest. At the moment, it looks like the toss of a coin between a fund run by Manager A and another headed by Manager B. Both funds have yielded average returns of 15% over the same five-year period. I'll resist the urge to let the fate of a mutual fund investment depend on a mere coin toss—a little more homework is required.

For the sake of illustration, suppose that each manager starts with $10,000 on January 1, 1993. I begin by plotting out their respective track records on paper, in the following manner:

| | Manager A | | Manager B | |
Year	%	Portfolio Value	%	Portfolio Value
1993	15%	$11,500.00	30%	$13,000.00
1994	15%	$13,225.00	30%	$16,900.00
1995	15%	$15,208.75	30%	$21,970.00
1996	15%	$17,490.06	−50%	$10,985.00
1997	15%	$20,113.56	35%	$14,829.75

Manager B had three extremely good years in a row before letting returns slip substantially in 1996. (In fact, the entire portfolio lost roughly half its value in a single year!) On the other hand, Manager A proves the adage "slow and steady wins the race." Personally, I always look for a good, consistent track record when I choose a mutual fund. It's a lot easier on the nerves and I like to invest for the long term—not the quick "killing."

The Language of Mutual Funds

You've now had an overview of mutual funds and the men and women who have the demanding—albeit lucrative—job of managing them. All that remains is to acquaint you with a few more general terms used by brokers and analysts on Wall Street, so you'll be fluent in the language of mutual funds before you find yourself on the receiving end of that very first in-person or over-the-phone sales pitch.

1. *Aggressive growth funds.* The main objective of an aggressive growth mutual fund is to achieve substantial capital gains. Such funds take greater risks, because they're in the business of investing in more volatile issues. Their portfolio managers are out to choose stocks with the highest possible level of earnings, with the goal of realizing at least 15% growth each year. The downside of such investments, however, is that dividend yields tend to be low.

2. *Small-cap growth funds.* These funds concentrate their investments in firms with small market capitalization—companies that offer a new product or service, for example. Such small-cap businesses enjoy dramatic increases in earnings should the new products or services they introduce prove successful. Although such firms tend to be highly creative and entrepreneurial by nature, they obviously involve an increased element of risk. You should make certain that the portfolio manager is a well-seasoned professional, able to discern between hype and reality when it comes to the wide assortment of initial public offerings introduced in the marketplace each year. (Let's just say that many Wall Streeters stretch the truth from time to time—to put it mildly.) You're wagering on the day-to-day decision-making ability of a fund's portfolio manager, so it's essential to count on the fact that he or she is a person with plenty of good, old-fashioned common sense.

3. *Growth funds.* This sort of mutual fund is keen on achieving capital gains, but proves considerably less volatile than aggressive growth funds. The portfolio managers of growth funds are

in the market for long-term appreciation in a stock's price and normally concentrate on well-known firms. The investor in a growth fund should be interested in long-term appreciation of capital, rather than banking profits in the short term. Some growth fund portfolio managers utilize a mixture of value and growth investment styles. It's therefore important to ask the sales rep "pitching" the fund whether management is looking for value, growth, or has both goals in mind simultaneously.

4. *Growth and income funds.* Portfolio managers of growth and income funds literally want the best of both worlds. They're not satisfied with the mere appreciation of capital, and therefore seek plenty of current income (through dividends) as well. Note that stocks yielding higher dividends are usually more stable than growth stocks. Consequently, the managers of growth and income funds are inclined to be a bit conservative—which is why they're likely to include a number of blue-chip stocks in the fund's portfolio. (Chances are you've heard the expression *blue chip* before, a term used to describe high-quality companies that have been around for a long time.)

5. *Equity income funds.* The primary goal of equity income funds is to seek current income by investing in stocks known to pay high dividends. Therefore, appreciation of capital becomes a secondary consideration. Portfolios of this sort of mutual fund are normally less volatile than the S&P 500 Index. Some equity income funds invest in cash and bonds as well. Income-producing stocks have dividend yields above the average for those comprising the S&P 500 Index.

6. *Balanced funds.* The portfolio of a balanced fund is usually quite diversified—including a mixture of bonds, common stocks, and preferred stocks. The term *preferred stock* is used to describe a class of stock that pays dividends at a specified rate and will have preference over common stock in the event of liquidation. For that reason, preferred stocks bear more resemblance to bonds than to stocks of the common variety.

7. *Sector funds.* Last but not least in this list of mutual fund categories is the sector fund, which specializes in one particular sector of the overall stock market. Some of the most popular funds

concentrate on firms engaged in industries such as technology, banking, telecommunications, leisure, gold, biotechnology, and health care—to list just a few. Chances are good that one of the major mutual fund complexes (Fidelity, for example) offers a fund designed to cover any sector of the economy that interests you.

You are now completely fluent in the somewhat tricky language of the mutual fund industry and, I hope, won't be thrown off guard by any fast-talking broker or investment advisor who uses technical terminology to impress or confuse you. You've learned virtually everything you need to know about shopping for mutual funds, so the only additional information I need share with you is how to "ring up your purchases at the cash register."

How to Buy a Mutual Fund—and Where

The process is similar to the one we went through together (in Chapter 3) when we bought Intel, Disney, and Cablevision Systems. The first step involves becoming acquainted with the appropriate financial listings printed in the various investment dailies, as well as in most major newspapers.

As you know, more than 7,500 different mutual funds are presently available in the marketplace. Let's turn to the listings of any major newspaper and focus on just five of the "family members" offered by a major mutual fund complex known as Janus—all of which are no load funds. Should you wish to receive a prospectus and account application form, by the way, the Janus management team can be reached at (800) 525-8983. In the meantime, let's take a look at the way these five Janus funds were listed in the financial pages as of January 19, 1997:

Fund	Type	NAV	YTD Return	1-Year Return	3-Year Return
Balanced	DH	14.37	+1.6%	+18.9%	+14.1%
Enterprise	SG	29.62	+1.0%	+18.2%	+16.7%
Mercury	MG	17.25	+4.4%	+27.6%	+22.4%
Twenty	LG	28.93	+5.3%	+37.3%	+18.7%
Worldwide	WS	34.83	+3.4%	+30.9%	+17.6%

I'll walk you through what each column signifies, beginning with *type*. The various two-letter combinations that appear under this heading serve to categorize the fund in terms of investment style and level of capitalization. Here's how to translate the two-letter notations of *type* that appear in the table:

DH = Domestic hybrid fund (that is, one composed of stocks and bonds)
SG = Small-cap growth fund
MG = Mid-cap growth fund
LG = Large-cap growth fund
WS = World stock fund

In addition to those in the Janus listings just cited, other abbreviations are commonly used for fund type, for example:

SV = Small-cap value fund
MV = Mid-cap value fund
LV = Large-cap value fund

Immediately to the right of the *type* column, you'll see the initials *NAV*. As you may already have guessed, these letters stand for *net asset value*. I'm sure you'll remember that net asset value is always equal to assets minus liabilities. The *NAV* figure is calculated by first adding up all the fund's assets (including the value of whatever cash is on hand, as well as that of securities held in its portfolio), then subtracting liabilities. All that remains is to divide the resulting figure by the number of shares outstanding, and we arrive at the appropriate total that represents net asset value—the actual price of the mutual fund in question.

The next three columns represent the fund's returns. *YTD return* provides you with the year-to-date percentage of returns. *One-year return* indicates the same percentage for the previous twelve months. Finally, the column for *three-year return* indicates the annualized average return over the past 36 months. The information given in each column normally assumes the reinvestment of all distributions in the form of capital gains and dividends. You can usually find an explanation of how such percentages are calculated somewhere in the fine print of each newspaper or investment daily that provides mutual fund listings. A number of major newspapers provide Morningstar ratings for such funds, as well.

Now that you know how to make an intelligent decision in the vast "supermarket" of mutual funds, and have even mastered how to price them by consulting the financial pages, all that's left is to point you to the "check-out counter." Assume, for the moment, that you won't require the services of a broker or investment advisor. By simply following the few easy steps I lay out for you in the following list, you'll be well-equipped to handle the transaction on your own.

1. Phone the mutual fund to request a prospectus and an account application.

2. Make out a check payable to the fund, or arrange to wire money through your local bank.

3. Redeeming shares in the fund can be done by telephone, as well. The fund can then wire money directly back into your bank account, if you made such an arrangement when filling out the initial account application. Mutual funds invariably ask whether you want to receive dividend income and/or capital gains directly at the appropriate time, or if you prefer to have the money reinvested in the fund—a decision that's up to each individual investor. If you don't need the cash right away, reinvestment is a good way to put more money to work for you, but the choice is yours.

4. A relatively new means through which individuals can purchase mutual funds involves buying shares on a *programmed basis*. You simply instruct your local bank to withdraw from your account(s) on a regular basis money with which to purchase shares in a mutual fund—a method referred to as *dollar-cost averaging*. The bank will automatically purchase, at regular intervals, additional shares on your behalf, regardless of whether the stock market is fluctuating upward or downward. The size of the weekly or monthly amount you choose to invest via dollar-cost averaging is completely up to you. Some investors

elect to be their own "bosses," so to speak, and budget their money without the automatic intervention of a bank—but, again, that's a choice to be made on an individual basis.

MAKING CHOICES: STUDY THE RECORD

Only the top investment gurus of Wall Street are able to "time" the market accurately—that is, to predict which direction it will take from day to day, month to month, and year to year.

The following tables cover some of the best-performing mutual funds in the marketplace, examined over a five-year period. I hasten to remind you once again that past performance does not guarantee future results. Bear firmly in mind that the years covered by these tables have been very good years indeed for the market, and it's impossible to predict with any certainty what the future holds. Finally, don't forget to check out the portfolio manager of each fund on a basis that is close-up and personal. You may be looking at the stellar track record of a portfolio manager who has just changed jobs (a total idiot may now be in charge of this fund with a wonderful track record of past returns). Other portfolio managers may have started up new funds on their own or retired from the business altogether.

Personally, I don't mind volatility when I'm in the mood to make an aggressive bet. On the other hand, I do mind watching what's supposed to be a balanced fund behave in the marketplace like an aggressive fund. To my mind, anyway, a mutual fund should always deliver on the pledges it makes to its investors. Therefore, if a fund promises to operate as a value fund, the last thing I want to see is that fund behaving in the marketplace as an aggressive growth fund.

Of late, much debate in financial circles has been centered on the question of whether a fund can be so huge that it works to its own disadvantage. Some claim that the largest funds are too large, exerting such a powerful force in the marketplace that they trip over themselves as they move in and out of various holdings. The jury is still out, but a number of investors avoid large mutual funds for precisely that reason—I personally prefer investing in mid-size funds.

One final word of caution: At year end, mutual funds make distributions of capital gains. Therefore, if you buy into a fund toward the end of the year, you have to deal with the accompanying tax bite. (You'll be placed in the unfortunate position of paying taxes on other folks' profits.) For this reason it's best to phone the management of any mutual fund you're considering to determine the dates on which such distributions are scheduled to occur, particularly at year end.

To help give you a healthy head-start on your homework, what follows is what I hope proves useful information about a number of mutual funds with excellent track records over the past five years. Each of the funds listed had a Morningstar Rating of at least 3 stars as of September 30, 1997. To request further information and an account application, all it takes is a phone call. Here goes:

AGGRESSIVE GROWTH FUNDS

Fund Name	Rating	Load	5-Year Annualized Returns	Phone
Aim Aggressive Growth	4 Stars	5.50%	31.60%	(800) 347-4246
Putnam New Opportunities	3 Stars	5.75%	27.90%	(800) 225-1581
Kaufmann	4 Stars	(12b-1 Fee)	25.33%	(800) 237-0132
Permanent Port Aggr. Growth	4 Stars	None	24.00%	(800) 531-5142
Aim Constellation A	3 Stars	5.50%	22.56%	(800) 347-4246
Princor Emerging Growth A	4 Stars	4.75%	21.80%	(800) 451-5447
Putnam Voyager A	4 Stars	5.75%	21.67%	(800) 225-1581
American Century/ 20th Century Ultra Investors	4 Stars	(None)	22.70%	(800) 345-2021

SMALL COMPANY (AGGRESSIVE GROWTH) FUNDS

Fund Name	Rating	Load	5-Year Annualized Returns	Phone
American Century/ 20th Century Gift Trust	3 Stars	(None)	26.71%	(800) 345-2021
FPA Capital	5 Stars	6.50%	29.27%	(800) 982-4372
Fidelity Low-Priced Stock	5 Stars	3.00%	23.18%	(800) 544-8888
RSI Retirement Emerging Growth	3 Stars	(None)	28.34%	(800) 772-3615
Skyline Special Equities	5 Stars	(None)	25.50%	(800) 488-5222
Glenmede Small Cap Equity	4 Stars	(None)	24.69%	(800) 442-8299
MFS Emerging Growth B	4 Stars	4.00%	26.08%	(800) 637-2929
Baron Asset	5 Stars	(12b-1)	25.91%	(800) 992-2766

GROWTH FUNDS

Fund Name	Rating	Load	5-Year Annualized Returns	Phone
PBHG Growth Fund	3 Stars	(None)	30.70%	(800) 433-0051
Oakmark	5 Stars	(None)	25.30%	(800) 625-6275
First Eagle Fund of America	4 Stars	(None)	24.99%	(800) 451-3623
Merrill Lynch Growth A	4 Stars	5.25%	27.31%	(800) 637-3863
Spectra	5 Stars	(None)	29.88%	(800) 711-6141
Fidelity Destiny 1	5 Stars	8.67%	23.50%	(800) 544-8888
Mairs & Power Growth	5 Stars	(None)	24.72%	(800) 304-7404
Guardian Park Avenue A	4 Stars	4.50%	24.60%	(800) 221-3253
Brandywine*	5 Stars	(None)	26.70%	(800) 656-3017
Strong Common Stock	5 Stars	(None)	24.03%	(800) 368-1030
T. Rowe Price Mid-Cap Growth	5 Stars	(None)	25.21%	(800) 638-5660
Vanguard/Primecap	5 Stars	(None)	27.90%	(800) 662-7447

*Minimum purchase: $25,000.

GROWTH AND INCOME FUNDS

Fund Name	Rating	Load	5-Year Annualized Returns	Phone
Safeco Equity No-Load	4 Stars	(None)	25.79%	(800) 426-6730
Mutual Qualified Z*	5 Stars	(None)	21.67%	(800) 342-5236
Mutual Beacon Z*	5 Stars	(None)	21.15%	(800) 342-5236
Mutual Shares Z*	5 Stars	(None)	21.46%	(800) 342-5236
Dodge & Cox Stock	5 Stars	(None)	22.93%	(800) 621-3979
Fidelity Growth & Income	5 Stars	(None)	21.48%	(800) 544-8888
First American Stock A	5 Stars	4.50%	22.02%	(800) 637-2548
Evergreen Growth & Income	5 Stars	(None)	22.00%	(800) 807-2940
Oppenheimer Main-Inc & Gr.	4 Stars	5.75%	25.97%	(800) 525-7048
American Cent Inc & Growth	5 Stars	(None)	21.74%	(800) 331-8331

*Michael Price sold his Mutual Fund complex to Franklin, and there may now be a load attached to new investors.

EQUITY INCOME FUNDS

Fund Name	Rating	Load	5-Year Annualized Returns	Phone
Fidelity Equity Income	4 Stars	(None)	21.41%	(800) 544-8888
T. Rowe Price Equity Income	5 Stars	(None)	19.78%	(800) 638-5660
Fidelity Equity Income II	4 Stars	(None)	19.44%	(800) 544-8888
Federated Equity Income A	5 Stars	5.50%	19.56%	(800) 341-7400
Putnam Equity Income A	3 Stars	5.75%	19.82%	(800) 225-1581
Managers Income Equity	4 Stars	(None)	18.39%	(800) 835-3879
Enterprise Equity Income A	4 Stars	4.75%	18.71%	(800) 432-4320
Safeco Income No Load	4 Stars	(None)	17.83%	(800) 426-6730
Vanguard Equity Income	4 Stars	(None)	18.20%	(800) 662-7447
Pimco Renaissance A C	4 Stars	5.50%	21.30%	(800) 426-0107
Prudential Equity Income B	4 Stars	5.00%	20.50%	(800) 225-1852
Gabelli Equity Income	4 Stars	(12b-1)	18.33%	(800) 422-3554

BALANCED FUND

Fund Name	Rating	Load	5-Year Annualized Returns	Phone
Greenspring	4 Stars	(None)	17.17%	(800) 366-3863
Fidelity Puritan	4 Stars	(None)	16.59%	(800) 544-8888
Founders Balanced	4 Stars	(12b-1)	16.66%	(800) 525-2440
Dodge & Cox Balanced	4 Stars	(None)	16.89%	(800) 621-3979
Vanguard Wellington	4 Stars	(None)	16.49%	(800) 662-7447
FBP Contrarian Balanced	4 Stars	(None)	16.14%	(800) 543-0407
Vanguard Star	4 Stars	(None)	15.39%	(800) 662-7447
Merrill Lynch Capital A	4 Stars	5.25%	16.38%	(800) 637-3863

These are some of the top funds, ranked by 10-year annualized returns as of June 30, 1997. As you will see, some of them specialize in certain sectors of the economy—technology and health care being the most common. That's not surprising, since we baby boomers are now starting to turn gray, and technology is revolutionizing the world as we know it.

Some of the Best-Performing Funds Over the Last 10 Years

Fund Name	Rating	Load	10-Year Annualized Returns	Phone
Fidelity Select Home Finance	5 Stars	3.0%	23.12%	(800) 544-8888
20th Century Gift Trust	3 Stars	(No-Load)	18.17%	(800) 345-2021
FPA Capital	5 Stars	6.5%	19.28%	(800) 982-4372
Davis New York Venture A	5 Stars	4.75%	17.72%	(800) 279-0279
Invesco Strategic Health Science	4 Stars	(No-Load)	19.41%	(800) 525-8085
Fidelity Select Regional Banks	5 Stars	3.0%	21.80%	(800) 544-8888
Invesco Strategic Technology	5 Stars	(No-Load)	18.04%	(800) 525-8085
Spectra	5 Stars	(No-Load)	19.53%	(800) 711-6141
Fidelity Contra Fund	4 Stars	3.0%	18.45%	(800) 544-8888
Fidelity Select Food & Ag.	5 Stars	3.0%	17.80%	(800) 544-8888
Skyline Special Equities	4 Stars	(No-Load)	18.37%	(800) 223-6300
20th Century Ultra Investors	4 Stars	(No-Load)	18.39%	(800) 345-2021
Fidelity Select Electronics	5 Stars	3.0%	19.44%	(800) 544-8888
Vanguard Special Health Care	5 Stars	(No-Load)	19.39%	(800) 662-7447
Fidelity Select Health Care	4 Stars	3.0%	18.91%	(800) 544-8888
Aim Value A	4 Stars	5.50%	18.01%	(800) 347-4246
Invesco Strategic Fin'l Services	5 Stars	(No-Load)	21.21%	(800) 525-8085
Kaufmann	5 Stars	(12b-1 Fee)	19.30%	(800) 237-0132

The above information pertains to the fund categories we've already discussed in the pages of this chapter, but I also want to acquaint you with Worldwide Funds. As that connotation implies, these funds invest in firms all over the world, as well as the United States. Worldwide Funds are a relatively new investment tool in the marketplace.

Worldwide Funds

Fund Name	Rating	Load	5-Year Annualized Returns	Phone
Janus Worldwide	5 Stars	(None)	23.50%	(800) 525-8983
GAM Global A	5 Stars	5.00%	21.99%	(800) 426-4685
Templeton World 1	5 Stars	5.75%	20.87%	(800) 292-9293
Templeton Growth 1	5 Stars	5.75%	19.26%	(800) 292-9293
Fidelity Worldwide	5 Stars	(None)	17.22%	(800) 544-8888
Scudder Global	4 Stars	(None)	15.98%	(800) 225-2470
Prudential World Global B	4 Stars	5.00%	17.26%	(800) 225-1852
MFS World Equity B	4 Stars	4.00%	16.58%	(800) 637-2929

While the preceding funds invest both at home and abroad, what follows are a few funds that restrict themselves to international investments:

FOREIGN FUNDS

Fund Name	Rating	Load	3-Year Annualized Returns	5-Year Annualized Returns	Phone
GAM International	5 Stars	5.00%	21.66%	21.76%	(800) 426-4685
Hotchkiss & Wiley International	4 Stars	(None)	15.75%	17.26%	(800) 346-7301
Managers Int'l Equity	4 Stars	(None)	13.93%	16.40%	(800) 835-3879
USAA International	4 Stars	(None)	14.06%	17.03%	(800) 382-8722
Oakmark International	5 Stars	(None)	15.08%	18.41%	(800) 625-6275

BUYING BOND FUNDS

Readers who love to shop around will be delighted to learn that we've yet to experience one other section of the mutual fund supermarket. All the funds we've covered thus far fall into the category of equity funds (meaning that they invest their assets in the stock market); other funds exist that put all of their "eggs" in the bond "basket."

Why put your hard-earned savings into bond funds rather than actual bonds? For one thing, if you have only a small amount of money to invest, the bond fund may be your only choice, since bonds are usually purchased in denominations of $10,000-plus.

Personally, I'm not a great proponent of bond funds because, as an investor in highly rated bonds, you're absolutely guaranteed to receive back all of your principal in full at the bond's maturity date. Unfortunately, this is not always the case when you put your money into a bond fund. No real maturity date is attached to the collective "bond pool" in which your capital is invested; as a result there's a definite element of risk involved. Interest rates fluctuate, and the value of your bond investments will fluctuate as well. (Because we've already discussed duration as a measurement device, you're now familiar with how to gauge the effect of a 1% change in the prevailing interest rate on the value of a bond instrument.)

The key factors to bear in mind when contemplating a bond fund investment are: (1) the fund's average length of maturity; (2) its investment grade; and (3) the expenses charged by the bond fund's management. Regarding the latter, I should warn you that the median expense ratio (that is, management fee) is roughly .7%.

TIMING IS EVERYTHING, OR IS IT?

In July of 1996, a good friend asked for advice about retirement planning. What she had already managed to save was invested in a 401(k) plan, and allocated exclusively to fixed income (that is, bond) instruments.

I suggested that she place 25% of her retirement savings in the mutual fund marketplace, but that she diversify by dividing her investment between at least two or three funds. Consequently, she decided to invest in three separate offerings sponsored by Fidelity. After doing her homework, she chose one of Fidelity's growth funds, another of the growth and income variety, and a third from the small-cap menu.

Just as soon as she'd taken my advice, however, Murphy's law entered the picture. The stock market went into a sudden tailspin, and my friend jumped to the conclusion that she alone was responsible for having adversely affected the entire global economy. (I quickly assured her that such was hardly the case.) Yet, there was no denying that the Dow Jones Industrial Average had plummeted by 300 points (from 5,700 to 5,400) over the course of a single month.

I managed to calm my friend, reminding her that it took only about eight years for the average investor who held on to stock investments after the Wall Street crash of 1929 to recoup those losses (a most reassuring fact to bear in mind when you start to panic over any less drastic downswing in the market). I cautioned her to resist the urge to bail out of the mutual funds she'd selected since, in my opinion, she had made three wise investments that should pan out well over the long run. By October of 1997, the Dow Jones Industrial Average had bounced back and then some, to 8,000. Needless to say, my friend was all smiles again.

As someone who's worked on Wall Street for nearly two decades, I know better than to worry about day-to-day or month-to-month downswings in the stock market—having learned long ago that it's far better to adopt a long-range investment philosophy.

Another aspect of working on Wall Street, however, is getting used to the fact that even your best friend is bound to get a bit angry at you when the market experiences a downturn. (On more than one occasion either a good client relationship or personal friendship came into serious jeopardy as a result of the unpredictable short-term maneuverings of the stock market.)

My advice? Do as much homework as possible, then diversify your investments. Although many experts insist that timing is everything, the only way consistently to sleep well at night is to console yourself with the fact that time heals everything. Be careful not to keep all your eggs in one basket, and don't panic over the short term. It's far better to heed my old economics teacher's advice and "Hang in there, baby!"

HOW I HANDLE MY MUTUAL FUNDS

Here's how I manage my own portfolio of mutual funds:

1. I use S&P 500 Index funds for the large-cap growth portion of my portfolio. However, if a manager consistently outperforms the S&P for five years or more by at least 2 to 3%, I certainly want to invest in his or her fund.

2. I use active managers for my small-cap, value, and international mutual funds.

3. I avoid paying loads, except for the services of a small-cap or value manager who has consistently beat the market for at least seven years.

4. I diversify my investment styles between growth and value.

5. I make sure the fund's present portfolio manager is the one responsible for the good track record of performance that makes investing in the fund an enticing prospect.

6. I buy mutual funds for the long term, rather than trade them in the short term.

Peter Lynch, one of the investment gurus already cited, offered some excellent advice to panic-prone investors in an article co-written with John Rothschild for the September, 1995 issue of *Worth* magazine. At the time, the Dow Jones Industrial Average rested at roughly 4,700, and a number of self-proclaimed "experts" were predicting a 20% downturn. Messrs. Lynch and Rothschild begged to differ, however. What follows is their advice to investors prone to panic over the short term:

> If you invested $2,000 in the S&P 500 on January 1st of every year since 1965, your annual return has been 11%. If you were unlucky and managed to invest $2,000 at the peak of the market in each year, your annual return has been 10.6%. Or, if you were lucky and invested $2,000 at the low point in the market, you ended up with 11.7%. In other words, in the long run it doesn't matter much whether your timing is good or bad. What matters is that you stay invested in stocks.

PLAYING FOR BIGGER STAKES: THE HIGH-ROLLERS CLUB

"Life is like a box of chocolates," according to the wisdom of Forrest Gump, because "you never know what you're going to get." As for me? I entered my freshman year of college determined to become a doctor—a noble ambition that was soon shot to hell when I realized how prone I was to faint at the sight of blood!

Life held other major surprises as well. For example, I've always been a good deal more risk averse than most folk, yet my career on Wall Street has cast me in the role of salesperson for derivatives, one of the riskiest investment tools of all. (And, let me tell you, it's not easy for someone who's hopelessly honest and up front about the downside of putting money into derivatives to be successful at selling them.) So, how did a "nice girl like me" get into this high-flying world?

DEALING YOURSELF INTO THE DERIVATIVES GAME

Everything started with a date. The fellow in question was named Adam, a really nice guy enrolled in Cornell's Graduate School of Business. Yours truly, on the other hand, was a Human Development and Family Studies major turned Nutritional Sciences major with plans to become a doctor.

The small talk on that first date turned to investing, and Adam told me about an investment tool known as listed options, which was relatively new at the time. He assured me that anyone with even a little bit of money set aside could turn small savings into a considerable sum.

Flash forward one year: I had dropped out of my internship in Chicago and returned to New York City, careerless and "clueless."

Still, I was ambitious and willing to do just about anything required to succeed at some sort of career. On one of my visits to various employment agencies, a job counselor mentioned a secretarial opening in Paine Webber's Options Department. I suddenly remembered my date with Adam, and knew in a flash that my true destiny was calling. Determined to get that job no matter what, I began to type away at 60 or 70 words a minute. One thing led to another and the next 18 years of my life were spent toiling away in the derivatives arena.

A *derivative* is a contract whose value is based on the performance of an underlying financial asset, index, or other investment such as commodities or interest rates, including any given cross-correlation of these. The world of derivatives includes listed options, futures contracts, swaps, structured notes, and exotic options.

I'm certainly not going to encourage any reader of this book to sink her hard-earned cash into derivatives. In its simplest form, a *derivative* is the right or obligation to buy or sell a specific stock or index within a specified time period. However, let me quickly add what's by far the most essential part of the definition: *Derivatives are generally* not *for the individual investor!*

ALL BETS ARE ON!

I'm reminded of a scene in the Broadway musical, *Guys and Dolls,* in which Runyanesque gambler Nathan Detroit tries to coax Sky Masterson into wagering on whether the local deli sold more cheesecake or strudel that day. Detroit already knows the day's results, so it's a sucker's bet. Instead of taking the gamble, Masterson places his hand in front of Nathan's necktie and wagers that his friend can't recall its color—which, indeed, he cannot. The point? If you want to make an "offbeat" wager on anything to do with the stock market, then derivatives are definitely the name of the game.

Would you like to wager that General Motors does better than Ford and/or Chrysler on any given day, week, month, year, or any other time frame you care to name? Why stop there? You can just as easily bet on the direction of the U.S. stock market versus that of Hong Kong's market, or even roll the dice on the chance that

Japanese banks will go bankrupt at the same time that U.S. banks outperform the S&P 500 Index. Through the rather peculiar investment tool known as derivatives, you might even care to wager on the health of the London real estate market relative to *the price of rice in China*!

(I can't resist adding that my first real "job" was working behind the counter at Burger King. Their advertising slogan hasn't changed in years. When it comes to derivatives, just as at Burger King, you can definitely "have it your way" by making any wager that your wildest imagination can conjure up. The only catch is that you'll have to pay a sizable premium to whichever investment bank or broker sets up the bet for you.)

After a full 16 years selling derivatives, here's my recommendation to any potential investor: if you don't happen to be the representative of a major institutional account, *stay as far away from such wagers as you can!* The single aspect of derivatives I've even the slightest inclination to recommend to private investors (that is, to retail accounts) is something called the listed options market. Such investments can be advantageous, but only if used in a safe and methodical manner. In other words, do plenty of homework!

Examine Your Options

The only aspect of the derivatives game structured for individuals is the listed options market, where it's possible to use options as a vehicle to hedge a portfolio, obtain a degree of leverage, and/or cap off a particular loss. For my personal portfolio, I use covered call option writing and buy *LEAPS,* which are long-term options. Options give the holder the right to buy or sell a stock or an index at a specific price in the future. Since this is a bit complex, I suggest that, if you want to try options investing, you acquaint yourself with them thoroughly through a course or a book.

The only reason I discuss concepts such as margin accounts, short selling, and derivatives in this chapter is because many folks in the hedge fund universe employ them daily—so it's best to at least familiarize yourself with the terms.

Staying Within the Margins

Another concept you need to know about is *leveraging.* Freely translated, this means getting more bang for your buck. The act of leveraging is accomplished either by borrowing money through a margin account or by employing various investment tools such as derivatives.

Using a margin account is really quite simple. Let's say, for example, that I want to own 100 shares of Microsoft at $100. I could purchase the shares outright, meaning that my total cash outlay would be $10,000 plus commissions, or I could purchase the same number of shares *on margin,* paying for only 50% of the transaction (that is, $5,000) in cash. The additional $5,000 would be automatically "borrowed" from my broker, who would, naturally, charge me something in the way of interest, which is referred to as the *broker loan rate,* in addition to the normal commission.

My *margin requirement* (the amount I borrowed from my broker) would be 50% of the full market value of the security. The broker loan rate is normally a full percentage point above the short-term rates that apply to Treasury bills.

Another term you need to know is *minimum maintenance equity level.* A certain amount of equity must be maintained as a sort of "collateral" in your margin account at all times. The New York Stock Exchange (and all brokerage firms) require that margin accounts maintain equity equal to 25% or more of the full market value of the stocks involved in margin sales, as well as margin requirements of 50%. (These regulations are intended to reduce the odds that there will be another crash such as occurred in 1929.)

THE UPS AND DOWNS OF MARGINS

Should the price of stock(s) held in a margin account rise, everyone involved is delighted. If the stock prices take a dip, however, you receive (normally by phone) what's known as a *margin call* asking you to put up a specific amount of additional money to secure your position.

Personally, I never use margin. However, if you choose to do so remember to factor the broker call rate into your investment decision. If the broker loan rate is 8%, you should be hoping for a much higher rate of return on your stock purchase. If you believe a stock is going to move at least 25%, the 8% cost is reasonable. Remember, never overextend yourself. If you believe a stock is a sure winner, I advise using LEAPS, that is, long-term options.

Investing in Hedge Funds?

As I've said, my particular specialty on Wall Street has been selling derivatives to various *hedge funds*—highly sophisticated, private investment partnerships that are not regulated by the Investment Act of 1940 (in other words, anything goes!). Hedge funds can employ all sorts of investment strategies, and most of them do. Therefore be warned: *as an investor, you have no watchdog agency to protect your interests, and precious little legal recourse should you ever get burned.* The law considers you to be a "sophisticated investor" by virtue of the fact that you sat down with the gamblers at the hedge fund "gaming table" to begin with, and reasons that you should have known the rules (and the risks involved) from the outset.

The law merely requires that you be *accredited*—that is, have a net worth of $1 million or more and an annual income of at least $200,000. Certain funds will require you to be *superaccredited,* which means that you must have more than $5 million invested in the marketplace. So long as you meet those qualifications, you're definitely on your own, free to win (or lose) as much as you'd like!

Most hedge fund managers normally require a minimum investment of $250,000 to $5 million, impose a 1 to 2% management fee, and take 20% of any profits that result. Some managers don't get their "cut" until they reach a certain "high water mark," for example, 6 to 8% as a return on their partners' investments. Other hedge fund managers take that 20% no matter *what* the annual return happens to be! In other words, if they make 5% for you, they take 20% of your 5% (1% of the investment) as their "piece of the action."

Advice: think long and hard before handing over money to a hedge fund manager. After all, you're banking your savings on a manager's ability to take a leveraged bet on anything and everything, from the future price of Intel stock (in either direction) to the performance of the yen relative to that of the deutsche mark!

A good hedge fund manager must be more than merely smart. To succeed, he or she should possess impeccable timing. Always remember that there are absolutely no tests a person must pass in order to open up a hedge fund and accept money from individual investors, so don't be unduly impressed by the fact that someone's job title is *hedge fund manager*. I've known quite a few complete idiots in the business who have all the bravado in the world, but none of the brains. On the other hand, some hedge fund managers are absolutely loaded with both brains *and* bravado. (The bravado means nothing without the brains—except a sure recipe for financial disaster!)

SHORTING A STOCK

Before continuing our discussion of hedge funds, you should understand the concept of shorting a stock. Most hedge funds try to profit from the fact that stocks both appreciate and decline. A bet on the latter occurrence is known as *shorting the stock*. (Going *long on a stock*, on the other hand, is something that millions of folk do every day—actually buying shares of a particular stock at whatever the going rate happens to be.) So, that's the "long and short" of it (couldn't resist!), except to emphasize that shorting a stock is a risky business indeed, because the losses you might suffer are virtually unlimited.

When you short a stock, you try to profit by wagering on a stock whose price, you believe, will go down in value rather than up. How do you make money? Here's an example: Suppose you and I sit down to analyze XYZ Corp., and conclude that it's a terrible company with very little to recommend it. By all indications, the firm will probably go out of business in the near future. Nevertheless, we can actually *profit* from its impending bankruptcy by using the shorting technique.

How would we proceed? Let's assume XYZ is trading at $20 per share. We call our broker and ask to "short" XYZ. In turn, the broker checks on our behalf to ascertain whether or not the stock is borrowable. (*Borrowability* is a requirement for shorting a stock.) If the answer is yes, we can place an order to sell short a hundred or more shares of XYZ.

The transaction would go like this: We sell 100 shares of XYZ at $20, or $2,000. This means that $2,000 is credited to our brokerage account, but we have an obligation to "buy back" those 100 shares of XYZ at some point in the future. Let's take the exercise one step further, and assume that we prove 100% correct in our dire forecast for XYZ, and the company starts to report terrible earnings and practically no sales. The price of the shares drops. Eventually, the stock is trading as low as $5 per share, and we decide to close out the trade. We then buy the 100 shares at $5, which means we pay $500 to buy back the round lot of XYZ we had presold at $2,000. Congratulations are in order all the way around, as we've just made a rather handsome profit of $1,500!

As you might surmise, there is a serious downside to shorting. Let's assume that we were completely *wrong* in our prediction for XYZ's future. Suppose the company brings out a new blockbuster product that causes its sales to skyrocket. Suddenly the price of a share of stock in XYZ rises from $20 to $50. At some point, we'd have to throw in the proverbial towel, and admit we were wrong. We end up buying the now much more expensive 100 shares of stock to replace what we'd "borrowed," losing a great deal of money in the process. Suppose we don't purchase our replacement shares of XYZ until it's selling at $50. In that case we must pay $5,000 for the 100 shares, a net loss of $3,000.

Suppose for a moment that you (or your hedge fund manager for much larger numbers) had "shorted" Intel a few years back. Such a decision would have been financial suicide! And that's just *one* of the risks. Another is the possibility of being called out of the position prematurely at a loss. (There are several technical reasons why this can happen, but for now just know that it can.) Another "land mine" is the risk that the company will be taken over by another firm. Your initial financial analysis may have been right on the money, but your "crystal ball" wasn't equipped to see such an unanticipated event.

Keep Your Eye on the Hedge Fund Manager

A hedge fund manager is usually someone who's been in the market for a long time—either as a broker or money manager—and has decided to go out on his (or her) own. Some of you may be acquainted with the name and reputation of investment guru

George Soros. Ponder this for a moment: had you been fortunate enough to invest $1,000 in the Quantum Hedge Fund that Soros opened back in 1969, your $1,000 would now be worth roughly $2 million. (Talk about taking a "quantum leap"!) Be forewarned, however, that not all hedge funds are as successful, and take great care to look before you leap.

In terms of greatness, you might think of Soros as the "Mozart of the investment world." Such talent in any field is the exception rather than the rule. I've known quite a number of hedge fund managers who have an amazing ability to make an investor's money disappear like magic! One such manager reached the altogether unsound decision back in the eighties that Compaq, Intel, and Microsoft were stocks just ripe for shorting. He soon proved himself a much better magician than David Copperfield, but in the worst possible way: now you see your hard-earned savings ... now you don't!

I've watched from the sidelines as various investment partnerships have "blown up" in a matter of weeks, leaving someone who'd invested $1 million with nothing at all. First impressions can often be deceiving: one hedge fund rose in value by 80% in a single year, only to crash and burn the next. In that case, an individual who had originally invested $1 million took quite a roller coaster ride, with the investment growing to $1,800,000 before being reduced to ashes! The truth is that some hedge funds use leveraging techniques while concentrating (rather than diversifying) their investments—with the result that investors are put at incredible risk without recourse.

The bottom line: many hedge fund managers turn a dollar into a dime with the greatest of ease, while others just as deftly make investors rich beyond their wildest dreams.

A Baker's Dozen of Hedge Funds to Choose From

If you are considering making an investment in hedge funds, you should understand precisely what you're betting on! A "baker's dozen" exists in the marketplace at present, which I'll break down in terms of "investment style" as follows:

1. *Macro*. This type of hedge fund invests in the global market-place via bets on the direction of individual stocks and international market indices, as well as currencies. The most famous macro fund manager is none other than George Soros of The Quantum Fund. The goal of this type of fund is to profit from changes in the global economy with the assistance of leveraging techniques. These funds have been known to place bets on whether various national economies would rise or fall, the direction of their interest rates, the fluctuation of exchange rates, and so forth. (Would you believe that George Soros became world famous by betting *against* the British pound—and profiting to the tune of $1 billion?)

   Macro hedge fund managers take long and short positions in stocks, as do many portfolio managers. Needless to say, the real gurus of the game are quite adept at choosing stocks. Volatility is quite high indeed, and many such funds take short-term bets, which means that much of the profits are in the form of short-term capital gains and, therefore, taxed as ordinary income.

2. *Opportunistic*. The dominant investment theme of an opportunistic hedge fund is trading-oriented. The managers of such funds are looking for special situations or opportunities on which to capitalize from pure fluctuations and/or imbalances.

3. *Growth*. These hedge funds are not much different from growth mutual funds, except that growth hedge fund managers will short stocks when it appears that the growth factor has tapered off and/or started to decline dramatically. They can be a little less volatile, since the shorts may serve to balance the fluctuations of the stock market itself.

4. *Value*. These bear a good deal of similarity to value mutual funds, except that hedge funds have the ability to short companies that they feel are deteriorating in value. Volatility is also a bit more moderate, since the shorts can cushion overall stock market fluctuations.

5. *Short only*. These hedge funds go short on what they believe to be overvalued securities. Remember that the overall trend of the stock market is upward, which means that short-only

hedge funds are taking an unpopular long-term philosophical position. The volatility that can be expected vis-à-vis this sort of hedge fund is quite high, and all shorts are taxed as short-term capital gains. In brief (or, rather, in short), I'd like to offer three simple words of advice: Be extremely careful!

6. *Market neutral.* In theory at least, these funds are trying to neutralize the market's impact. They tend to be 50% long and 50% short on a large and highly diversified portfolio of holdings. No matter what, profitability of the fund still boils down to the fund manager's ability to select stocks—but with this type of hedge fund volatility is usually low and the positions are held for the medium term.

7. *Distressed.* This sort of hedge fund invests in securities of companies that are in reorganization, bankruptcy, or some other type of corporate restructuring.

8. *Convertible arbitrage.* This category is a bit more conservative than most other hedge funds. The managers of such funds tend to go long on convertible bonds and/or preferred stocks, even as they short the underlying common stocks. This sort of hedge fund is a bit less volatile than other types of hedge funds. If the manager has a good understanding of credit, he or she can be quite successful at capturing profits from the discrepancies between various derivative instruments.

9. *Risk arbitrage.* Simply phrased, this style of hedge fund concentrates on buying the stock of companies that are being acquired, then shorting the stocks of their acquirers. (Did I promise that this would be *simply* phrased?) Since some sort of spread exists in the price of the stock between the time the purchase of the company is announced and the culmination date of the purchase, those who manage risk arbitrage hedge funds make their money on the price the market will pay for that risk. Should the merger agreement fall through, however, the trader could be saddled with enormous losses. When reviewing a risk arbitrage fund, it's essential to look for plenty of diversification in the concentration of the fund's positions. Also, be careful to ascertain whether or not the fund uses leveraging techniques. Only after you have such information in

hand can the inherent risks of participating in such a fund be calculated, even approximately!

10. *Fixed income.* The investments of this sort of hedge fund are based on public and private debt instruments with fixed rates, as well as on their derivatives. There have been quite a few major fixed income fund successes (to offset the many debacles in such hedge funds). The expected volatility is quite high.

11. *Emerging markets.* These hedge funds invest in the less-developed financial markets of the world. For the moment, let's table a discussion of these and save it for the final section of this chapter. The one thing to keep in mind at this point, however, is that these funds are extremely volatile!

12. *Sector funds.* Very much like sector mutual funds, this sort of hedge fund specializes in an industry group (for example, health care, technology, and so on).

13. *Funds of funds.* Don't let the name throw you; there is a reasonable explanation. The manager of this sort of hedge fund chooses a wide variety of hedge funds—much like the registered investment advisor who picks a number of different money managers. One of the major attributes of this sort of hedge fund is that the fund-of-funds manager follows the hedge fund managers quite closely and carefully questions any aberrations in their performance. Fund-of-funds managers are always searching for new managers and are not emotionally committed to any manager. One final note: when it comes to hedge funds, the *alpha factor* (which rates the hedge fund manager's skills) is often exaggerated, since the charters of hedge funds give managers the ability to go short as well as to be leveraged.

Keep in mind that the leveraging component vis-à-vis hedge funds make an investor's risks a bit more pronounced than when investing in a more traditional fund. There are exceptions, of course: should the stock market suffer a downswing, hedge fund managers of the short stock pick or market neutral variety should perform better than more traditional money managers, who aren't hedged. Still, it's impossible to know with absolute certainty whether or not one is hedged properly, and if the shorts in play will perform sufficiently well to offset the long side of a portfolio.

The following is a table of the returns and the risk associated with the hedge fund universe. It was prepared by Hennessee Hedge Fund Advisory Group, a division of Hennessee Group LLC, a New York-based hedge fund advisory and investment management firm.

HENNESSEE HEDGE FUND UNIVERSE HISTORICAL RETURNS (1990–1996)

Manager Style	Annualized Returns	Standard Deviation
Macro	18.79%	18.68%
Growth	21.28%	13.46%
Value	16.90%	9.35%
Opportunistic	19.98%	10.78%
Market Neutral	11.05%	4.49%
Emerging Markets	24.57%	26.47%
Distressed	18.71%	8.87%
Short Only	−3.50%	24.82%
Convertible Arbitrage	9.88%	9.59%
Risk Arbitrage	14.80%	8.47%

When it comes to hedge funds, my advice is that you use a professional consultant in choosing managers. Try not to have more than 10% of your net worth with any one manager, and not more than 20% with a variety of hedge fund managers.

Managed Futures: There's No Future in Them!

There's no better way to open this section of the chapter than by stating the following, straight up: not even if I had $1 billion in the bank, would I ever put as much as $100 in a managed futures account. Even if I had substantial amounts of money invested in every *other* market tool mentioned thus far, I still wouldn't sit down to play at the managed futures gaming table. For me, at any rate, there's just no "future" in it!

By definition, *futures* are extremely volatile investment instruments that entail betting on the direction of various markets. For example, there are futures in foreign currencies (such as the yen, deutsche mark, Swiss franc, etc.), commodities (soybeans, orange juice, pork bellies, gold, silver, cattle, and so forth), interest rates, stock markets, and so forth.

All it takes for someone to hang out a shingle and start trading in futures is to pass a Series 3 license exam, but this by no means guarantees that the successful passer of such a test has the *ability* to trade profitably on behalf of investors. To be sure, some very successful folk trade in futures nowadays, but I'm by no means convinced that I could tell a winner from a loser, even if my life depended on it. No track record of excellent past performance precludes futures traders from being totally wiped out in the blink of an eye. (As Murphy's law would have it, that's probably just what would happen the moment you decided to invest in your first futures fund.) As for me? I'm *far* too risk averse to ever take that sort of chance with my own money, or with anybody else's.

INSIDE THE COMMODITIES TRADER

Managed futures accounts make it their business to speculate on various commodities. For example, futures traders may try to purchase gold contracts, because an inflationary number is announced on the economic scene. On the other hand, upon learning of greater-than-usual political tension in the Middle East, traders may choose to buy oil futures. One thing's for certain: to be a successful commodities trader who deals in such futures, you must have the soul of a speculator. Traders must believe with all of their heart that a particular event or series of events will happen in the near term, which will change the direction of a commodity or market quickly and with enough force to create the potential for a substantial profit.

Commodity traders use what are known as *technicals* to determine market direction, and usually prefer trending markets to oscillating markets (see Chapter 5 if you'd like a short refresher). Most important, commodities traders must always be flexible enough to bail out rapidly should whatever educated guess they've made turn out to be incorrect. Otherwise, they risk taking gargantuan losses.

Private individuals can also participate directly in the futures game, but (as you can well imagine) I would certainly not recommend that any individual "retail investor" sit down at this extremely high-stakes table.

For those I still haven't scared away, here's an example of a futures trade: suppose I choose to buy *one* S&P 500 futures contract, betting that the market will go up. Let's say the S&P 500 Index is trading at 800. This means that I am controlling 800 times 500 (the numerical constant used to calculate the underlying value of one contract), which equals $400,000 of S&P stocks. Each type of commodity has its own margin per contract—and the S&P's required margin per contract is $15,500. With futures, the margin requirements are less than for owning outright stocks. In other words, the investor is allowed much more leverage. In exchange for this *exposure* (to acquaint you with another term we use on Wall Street), I'm willing to put up that initial margin of $15,500. (In reality the required margin varies from brokerage house to brokerage house.) Here's what might happen next:

▶ Should the market drop a total of 8 S&P 500 points, which is a 1% movement and not at all uncommon, I would stand to lose 8 × $500, for a total of $4,000. It's easy enough to calculate that $4,000 divided by $15,500 (my initial margin) equals a rather staggering 25.81% loss on my investment in the course of a single day.

▶ On the other hand, should the market move up a total of 8 S&P 500 points, I would make 8 × $500, or $4,000. Again, I divide $4,000 by my margin of $15,500, but this time celebrate the fact that I've made a 25.81% gain!

These scenarios show clearly that futures are most assuredly *not* for the faint of heart! Rest assured that a stock market crash would wipe out your entire savings. Should you choose to play in futures despite my advice, I can only urge that you read as many books as possible on the subject before you begin. Also, make absolutely sure to put in stop loss orders, so as to limit the potential losses you might suffer by triggering a close-out of a position before it goes too far against you.

That much said, for the record, I remain adamant in my advice: unless you want to make futures a full-time occupation, avoid this particular investment tool like the plague!

BOLDLY "VENTURE" WHERE NONE GONE BEFORE ...

Successful venture capitalists have a particular gift in that their brave, entrepreneurial spirit permits them to see things that are not there—to envision great possibilities that are invisible to everyone else.

I've always been puzzled by the concept of an intelligence quotient. Real geniuses often have totally new ways of thinking that simply can't be detected by tests. For example, recall how a brilliant man, Galileo, was imprisoned for rebelling against church doctrine when he announced that earth revolves around the sun. Happily today, such geniuses are more likely to be financially rewarded than thrown in prison. No longer subject to persecution or death for the crime of being different, such visionary men and women are finally able to profit from their ability to think new and extraordinary thoughts.

Having "vision" isn't enough, however, unless such vision is accompanied by pockets deep enough to provide funds that will turn your dream into reality. That's where the venture capital community enters the picture: these folk are willing and eager to finance the projects of those with viable dreams, and to do so in ways that often totally reshape and redefine the quality of human lives.

How many readers of this book have used Federal Express, or ever shopped at Staples? How many of you (or your kids) have used an Apple or Compaq computer? How many of you have a workstation manufactured by Sun Microsystems? How many of you have taken prescription medication manufactured by Amgen or Genentech?

GETTING IN ON THE GROUND FLOOR

You already know that Intel is a firm that today enjoys considerably more than $1 billion in annual sales, but let's not forget that a man named Sherman Fairchild financed the first company to focus on the silicon devices that would soon revolutionize the planet. Fairchild, no stranger to the computer business, was the largest individual shareholder of IBM (thanks to an inheritance from his father, one of IBM's original founders). Fairchild generously offered the engineers in his employ equity in his new firm rather than a mere salary. Fairchild Semiconductor was introduced, which provided engineer Robert Noyce with his very first taste of entrepreneurship. (He had just managed to turn $500 worth of equity in Fairchild's company into $250,000.)

Noyce and his colleague Gordon Moore resigned from Fairchild Semiconductor in 1968, and each invested $250,000 in a new company of his own. With the assistance of Arthur Rock, a venture capitalist who ultimately raised $2.5 million for them, they founded the firm we now know as Intel. Robert Noyce had invented something called an *integrated circuit,* which led to the further development of the entire semiconductor industry by making it possible to put transmitters, capacitators, and resistors on a single chip. Although this formed the basis of a computer's central nervous system, Noyce and Moore kept tackling the hypothesis, "if I only had a brain ...."

The "brain" (that is, the microprocessor) came into being the very next year. In 1969, the firm we now know as Intel shipped a microprocessor from the factory to its first satisfied customer—and the world would never be even remotely the same again. In short, that's what venture capitalists are all about, and why they're every bit as important as the geniuses behind the ideas that they financially back. Ask yourself this: what if Noyce and Moore had never met Sherman Fairchild or Arthur Rock? The truth is that we might all still be using keypunch cards to this very day!

LESSONS FROM A VENTURE CAPITALIST

After spending many years on the Street, the people I find most interesting by far are the venture capitalists. They are a creative lot, usually quite intelligent and somewhat skeptical by nature—yet always able to see the possibilities. Without further ado, allow me to introduce you to one of my favorite venture capitalists, Fran Janis.

Fran is a founding partner of Pomona Capital, which manages private equity partnerships with approximately $250 million in assets under management.

Ms. Janis is originally from an area adjacent to my old neighborhood of Jackson Heights in Queens. In the summer of 1980 after graduating from the State University of New York at Albany with a major in marketing, she took a job as a receptionist with Allen Patricof Associates. She needed cash to finance her attendance at business school that fall. Fran wasn't too concerned with a career path at the time, but Patricof was one of the earliest venture capital funds. It was an exciting summer for Fran, to say the least: Apple Computer and Genentech went public, and both were funded by Patricof. In 1980, Patricof had approximately $25 million in his fund, a rather huge sum of money for those times. (Patricof's most recent fund, in the amount of $250 million, was raised in 1995.)

One sunny summer's day, Fran was having her morning coffee in Paley Park, reading *The Wall Street Journal*. Mr. Patricof walked by and was somewhat surprised. "What are you doing reading the *Journal?*" he asked. Fran told him that she soon planned to leave the firm in order to enter business school; Patricof urged that she stay on instead. Fran declined. In 1982, after attending Northeastern and earning her MBA with a concentration in Finance, she joined Hambro International Venture Fund as an Associate. Happily, Hambro's very first fund accumulated $50 million, and by the time 1989 rolled around, she had become a full-fledged partner. By that time Hambro had raised its second fund—this time in the amount of roughly $80 million!

According to Fran, the average venture capital fund nowa-days is comprised of approximately $100 million, and diversifies among roughly 15 to 18 companies. She stresses that there are several different types of venture capital funds: Some specialize in industry sectors such as life sciences, information technology, and specialty retailing, while others diversify across a few different industries.

SEE HOW IT WORKS: THE LIFE CYCLE OF VENTURE CAPITAL

Venture capital is generally the riskiest of all equity investments, but venture funds don't normally lose money—thanks to a well-thought-out system of diversification. Still, it invariably takes a great deal of experience before one becomes truly knowledgeable about investing in startups. Although there's no way around such a long learning curve, once you understand the life cycle of venture capital you'll be a few steps ahead of the game.

1. *The seed stage.* During the time period when the entrepreneur is incubating ideas, the venture capitalist might give him or her some "seed money"—perhaps $250,000—for developing a business plan.

2. *Early-stage financing.* This step requires a full business plan and a partial management team. At this point, venture capitalists begin to raise money from institutional investors.

3. *Late stage.* The company is "up and running," so to speak, and some revenue is even beginning to come in. The entrepreneur's ideas haven't necessarily generated any profit, but at least a viable business has come into existence.

There is a considerably different risk/reward profile associated with each stage of the game. In stage one, for example, investors can either lose all of their money or make as much as 20 times or more in terms of profit on the original investment. In the second stage, investors are shooting for 10 times the original investment. In the third stage, which carries the least risk by far, venture capitalists are looking roughly to double their money over a three-year period.

The venture capital business is relatively new to the marketplace, since institutions only began to invest in it about twenty years ago. Venture funds have a life span of approximately ten years, so you might as well face up to the fact that any investment you make in a fund will be tied up for that length of time. For example, once a $50-million fund is raised, it takes a full three to four years to invest all of the money in deals.

Given the nature of the business, making accurate measurements of performance presents an obvious problem. Most venture capitalists can tell you that they don't even attempt to measure returns for the first five years—interim performance figures are very hard to come by. Losers tend to show their colors in the first few years of the fund, but hardly prove a good indicator of the fund's success over the long haul.

The venture capital deal for Federal Express required a full eight rounds of financing! Incredibly enough, Fedex experienced monthly losses of $1 million or more for the first 29 months of its existence. No wonder some of the fund's major investors dropped off in the early rounds, refusing to participate by anteing up more money for the venture! But those who stuck with this crazy entrepreneurial dream saw a $25-million investment turn into $1.2 billion by the time Federal Express eventually went public.

INVESTING IN A FUND OF FUNDS

Ms. Janis believes that patience is paramount and that those who choose to put a portion of their assets into venture capital should be invested in a fund of funds. These funds generally invest in several funds on behalf of their clients. Only a few are available to individuals. She cautions that, as a rule of thumb, institutions invest 3 to 5% of their assets in venture capital. She discourages the practice of private financing (what's known as *one-company deals*) because of the obvious lack of diversification. She advises those who insist on opting for this route to stay extremely connected to the company in question! She also notes that the so-called *postventure funds* purchase recently listed stock in venture-capital-backed companies. This route provides the benefit of these high-growth companies without the lack of liquidity that comes with investing in the private market.

Let's suppose for a moment that you get into one of the better funds, which is rather difficult these days because so many major institutions also invest in venture capital. You should expect to pay a management fee somewhere between 1-1/2 to 2%, plus a full 20% of the profits. Were you to invest $1 million, you yourself would shell out roughly $15,000 to $20,000 in management fees. Should the fund actually succeed in *making* $1 million for you (which means a full 100% profit on your original investment), the venture capitalists who run the fund would make roughly $200,000 as compared with the $800,000 minus the management fee that would filter down to you as the investor.

When it comes to selecting entrepreneurs with whom to do business, the venture capital community carefully scrutinizes a firm's management—always looking for those with a successful track record at creating something that's paid off in the past. The character traits required for success include plenty of passion, vision, and tenacity. Sanity is not a prerequisite, since some of the most successful entrepreneurs of all time have been viewed as a bit crazy!

You should also address the issue of character by performing a major "due diligence" on the company's management. Generally, entrepreneurs are people who envision a new business, change the way things are done, or carve out a new marketing niche. As Albert Einstein said, "Imagination is more important than knowledge."

Since this is a truly risky asset class, most investment committees or family offices, which manage more than $50 million for a family, allocate somewhere between 5 to 8% of their assets in venture capital.

Private Equity:"Angels" in America

Nicole Kubin is an "angel"—she invests her own capital in private deals. She started out 2-1/2 years ago and has invested in over 25 private deals among a number of industries.

Nicole has a degree from the University of Pennsylvania and spent many years analyzing corporate credit, primarily at Salomon Brothers, Inc., prior to investing her own money. Nicole wanted to enter the private equity arena, since it was something she was able to do on her own time—even while raising three children! Still, she cautions that being an "angel" is extremely time-consuming, and that success at it requires a real passion. Most of us will probably not follow in Nicole's footsteps, but many of us *are* likely to be approached by friends or acquaintances and asked to invest in a private equity deal. (Many such deals require investments of as little as $25,000.)

My first question to Nicole was this: "How do I know if I'm passing up the chance of a lifetime, or if I'm just throwing money away?" Nicole agreed with Fran's opinion that the most enticing deals usually go to the venture capital funds with institutional money at their disposal, but every so often a good opportunity is actually offered to individual investors like you and me.

The key to investing in a good deal, according to Nicole, is to perform tremendous due diligence on the deal. *Due diligence* basically means thoroughly investigating all facets of a company's operations. It's not only necessary to examine the fine print in an offering, but also look for omissions, which by definition are elements invisible to the naked eye!

Nicole's "style" isn't necessarily to score home runs, but rather to invest in deals that offer plenty of good prospects and quantifiable risks. Nicole advises potential investors to examine deals from what she calls a "banker's perspective." (Her recommendation is that one must always consider the worst-case scenario.) Should you be approached to be an "angel," Nicole urges that you ask a professional to assist you in analyzing the deal. This kind of outsourcing is important so that you can profit from the experience of the real pros at the business.

INVESTIGATE BEFORE YOU INVEST

You should look for these important qualities when trying to ascertain any particular deal's potential for success:

1. Determine whether the CEO of the firm in question is a dreamer or the "real thing" with a significant track record. Has he or she already managed to build a successful company—or at least a successful division in a large company? (As Nicole puts it, "Good managers are hard to find!")

2. Judge the caliber of the co-investors, and ascertain whether they're capable of playing a part in the deal over the long haul. Sometimes accomplishing a deal takes longer than projected, so it's important to make sure that your co-investors won't be unavailable for subsequent financings and cause the company to encounter financial pressure.

3. Be sure to examine the returns of the "public comparables," that is, you want to examine how public companies (those listed on one of the three exchanges) have been doing in that particular industry. You should expect more returns in the private equity market due to the lack of liquidity.

4. Take a good, close look at the caliber of the accounting firm that prepares the firm's financials. Keep in mind that figures are likely to be more reliable when coming from one of the larger, well-established firms. Simply ask whether the accounting firm is one of the "big six."

5. Likewise, don't forget to check out the caliber of the law firm representing the private offering.

6. Ask yourself where in the economic cycle is the firm you're considering, and where it will be three to five years hence.

7. Be sure you get clear and simple answers from the company's management. If anything about the firm's operations appears too difficult to understand, don't bother to invest.

8. Pass on the opportunity if the private equity offering is priced too high.

Should you choose to be an "angel" (that is, to invest in private equity) as a living, Nicole suggests that you become a real expert at credit (in other words, making sure there is enough to pay the bills). Chances are you'll be better off getting involved only in private equity offerings on those rare occasions when an irresistible deal comes your way. Do plenty of homework each time you make such an investment. After all, it's great to be able to nourish someone else's dreams; make sure that it doesn't become a personal financial nightmare!

Going Global: Investing in Emerging Markets

The term *emerging stock markets* refers to markets that are rapidly growing in size and sophistication in various economically developing countries around the world. In 1987, The Templeton Organization was the first to manage a mutual fund composed of emerging markets, which shows how relatively new this asset choice is as an option for the general public. Emerging markets offer tremendous potential for high rewards, but the risks are very real, as well.

We Americans take for granted a wide variety of conveniences such as televisions and VCRs, cars, telephones, bicycles, clothes, cosmetics—not to mention advanced health care—while for the citizens of countless nations around the world such items are still considered luxuries. Things change, however, and in many nations of the world people are rapidly acquiring the means and tastes for what were once luxury items. Such nations are referred to as *emerging markets* because a customer base—a market—for these luxury products is beginning to emerge.

Now that communism has almost disappeared and an ideological shift toward free market enterprise has occurred in Russia, China, Vietnam, Korea, as well as those countries comprising the former Eastern Bloc, a whole array of investment opportunities have opened up. Advancements in technology have made the ability to communicate and access information so simple that developing nations are now able to "leapfrog" ahead when building new infrastructures. After all, why should a developing country build already outdated forms of communication, when it can go directly to cellular phone technology; why not manufacture computers rather than typewriters? Advances in communication enhance the education of most citizens of emerging countries, and inspire them to strive for a better lifestyle—thereby enhancing the free market system.

Not long ago, while in Israel, I took a bus from Jerusalem through many miles of desert until we finally reached our destination at the Dead Sea. The desert is inhabited by Bedouins (a nomadic Arab tribe) who live in tents and tend sheep, much the same as they have for thousands of years. Yet, taking a peek into one of their tents, I was amazed to see a television set tuned in to CNN, proving once again that it's a small world after all!

WHERE THE EMERGING MARKETS ARE

In today's world, we're watching the boundaries between trade and commerce breaking down, individuals everywhere are becoming much more educated, and technology is expanding—all at the same time. These factors lead to a growth in economies all over the world. The following list includes some of the more popular emerging markets.

Argentina	Bangladesh	Brazil
Chile	China	Columbia
CIS*	Greece	Hong Kong
India	Indonesia	Jordan
Korea	Lebanon	Malaysia
Mexico	Oman	Pakistan
Peru	Philippines	Portugal
Poland	Singapore	Taiwan
Turkey	Venezuela	Vietnam

*Commonwealth of Independent States (the former Soviet Union).

Of late, the greatest financial interest in emerging markets has centered around China. The nation that boasts the largest population on earth has recently changed from being a closed communist society to a developing market economy. Consider this: China's GDP growth has been about 10% each year for the past four years, while the U.S. has experienced only between 3 and 4% on average over the same time period.

At present, China attracts more than one-third of all the investments in factories and plants in developing nations—approximately $42 billion in 1996 alone. In 1995, at least 40 China funds held over $2.7 billion in assets.

The potential for making money in emerging markets is tremendous, but the volatility factor is dramatically higher than with the markets of developed countries. For instance, market returns in Taiwan were up 22% in 1994, down 30.7% in 1995, and up 34.7% in 1996! Turkey was down 40% in 1994, down 10.6% in 1995, and up 133% in 1996. China (the Shenzen market) was down 38.8% in 1994, down 31.3% in 1995, and up 133.7% in 1996. It's easy to see why trying to predict upswings and downturns in emerging markets can be frustrating—to say the least. Developed nations tend to enjoy more predictable performance records: For example, compare the foregoing figures to the U.S. stock market (as represented by the S&P 500 Index), which was up 1.32% in 1994, up 37.53% in 1995, and up 22.95% in 1996.

EXAMINING GLOBAL RISK

Investing in emerging markets is decidedly *not* for the timid. Obviously, the profits made can be downright extraordinary—but timing truly is everything! Should you have been fortunate enough to invest in the right market at the right time, you may reap profits of more than 1,000% in a given five-year time frame. A case in point: between January 1987 and May 1993, the Argentinian market increased by 1,374%; Taiwan increased by 918%; and Mexico's market increased by 960%.

However, a number of additional risks above and beyond those we've already discussed vis-à-vis the U.S. market are associated with these markets.

1. *Political risks.* Government instability and/or radical shifts in national policy could occur at any time, which means that your assets could be unceremoniously seized. Furthermore, if the government of an emerging market nation decided to seize the assets of private companies, the foreign investors in those companies would have no recourse.

2. *Currency risks.* A country can also experience, without notice, a major devaluation in its currency. Likewise, foreign exchange controls might suddenly be imposed, which would make it impossible to remove capital from the country. In addition, you have exchange-rate risk, that is, the risk that the country's currency will fluctuate versus the U.S. dollar.

3. *Transactional risks.* Disputes may arise about the financial settlements of stocks offered for sale by the markets of developing nations, in large part due to the fact that their brokers aren't regulated as closely as are American brokers.

4. *Fraudulent manipulation of foreign companies.* Fraudulent manipulation is a problem anywhere you wish to invest—developed nation or not—but accounting rules tend not to be as stringent in emerging markets as in developed countries.

GETTING INTO EMERGING MARKETS

What follows are four different methods through which you can invest in emerging markets:

1. By directly investing in the stock on the actual foreign market, via a full-service brokerage firm.

2. By purchasing *American Depository Receipts* (ADRs) or *Global Depository Receipts* (GDRs), both of which are an indirect investment in the stock of any emerging market firm listed on a developed nation's market exchange. For instance, TELEVISA (the top Mexican television network) is listed in the U.S. stock market through an ADR. At the very least, you have the assurance that ADRs have met with satisfactory SEC accounting and disclosure rules for listing on the U.S. exchanges.

3. By investing in mutual funds—including those that are region-specific, country-specific, or broadly diversified in a number of different emerging markets.

4. By purchasing derivative instruments such as convertible bonds or warrants (suggested only for someone who's thoroughly familiar with the intricacies of these instruments).

Should you be interested in getting your feet wet in this somewhat risky investment arena, I suggest starting by investing in a fund. Since this market is relatively new, it's harder to do your homework. Not many emerging market mutual funds have been introduced, and it's often difficult (if not impossible) to obtain long-term performance statistics on them.

The minimum investment in an emerging market fund is approximately $1,000. A professional will be overlooking the countries and the companies. I think it is a wise decision to diversify your equity holdings outside the United States and recommend an allocation of worldwide mutual funds and a sliver of emerging markets. I would remain on the conservative side and allocate only between 5 to 8% of my holdings in emerging markets through the use of mutual funds.

So—Will You Join the Club?

I have provided you with a basic primer on the subject of hedge funds, derivatives, margin accounts, managed futures, venture capital, private equity, and emerging markets—and perhaps you've already decided whether you can stomach the risk involved. If so, welcome to the "High Rollers Club"!

If you decided to put your money in any of these investments, I would limit the total amount of these alternative investments to no more than 20 to 25% of my total portfolio—preferably as little as 15%. If you decided to invest with the hedge fund community, make sure the manager has a long-term performance record. It is prudent to examine the year-to-year as well as the month-to-month fluctuations of the manager. To avert disaster, you might want to employ the services of a consultant who has been in the business for some time.

chapter 10

CHOOSING AN INVESTMENT ADVISOR

A well-to-do friend of mine recently voiced a concern I've heard echoed thousands of times over the years. Shaking her head with dismay over an unpleasant (and extremely costly) investment deal she'd just been suckered into, this long-time friend heaved a sigh and said, "Marlene, there are a lot of extremely smart financial advisors in the world, and a great many others who are honest—but why is it all but impossible to find a combination of both traits in the same person?"

After proffering a shoulder on which my friend could cry (then offering to buy her a good stiff drink), I consoled her as best I could. "Finding an investment advisor with both intelligence and integrity is possible," I reassured her, "but—if you'll forgive the cliché—it's like looking for a needle in a haystack."

I was reminded of a story told to me not long ago by the development officer of a major university, concerning a private estate valued at $20 million in 1990. The estate was managed by a "reputable" investment advisory firm, yet was worth only $15 million by 1996 (a raging bull market).

How is it possible for a family's holdings to lose a staggering 25% of its value over the course of a six-year period, while the S&P 500 Index more than doubled during the same period? And why did the family not only permit this to happen, but raise no objection when their money managers hit them up for a wide variety of "expenses" to boot? The answer to both questions, of course, is that the family showed an incredible degree of naiveté and gullibility for not exercising better control over the estate's holdings. Catastrophic losses to the assets of the estate had somehow gone completely unnoticed until it was far too late to reverse the situation.

Why do so many investors suffer outrageous reversals of fortune, while the stock market flourishes as never before? In my own personal and professional opinion (since you asked), the answer is twofold:

1. The brokers who have dominated the industry for the past century have been paid on a transaction basis, rather than according to the quality of their performance. New issues have flooded the market in recent years, and the salespeople involved in these offerings are compensated quite handsomely for consummating the deals. Most successful brokers are excellent salespersons, which doesn't necessarily mean they have a talent for choosing stocks. The truth is that many of the initial public offerings they peddle are nothing but worthless junk, but a great many analysts on Wall Street will affix their stamps of quality to what they know is a bad deal. This, in turn, facilitates the sale of poor merchandise by the brokerage firm's employees. To be sure, occasionally a new issue pays off big-time, but the best IPOs are almost invariably offered to large institutions and wealthy private individuals, and snapped up long before smaller investors get wind of them.

2. Although it takes a great deal of intelligence to be a good stock picker, one need only "talk a good game" to be a *successful* broker. Some brokers excel at choosing stocks on behalf of their clients. But the sort of guy or gal who disturbs you with a phone call at home (sometimes as late as 9 or 10 o'clock at night) is often unable to read and comprehend a firm's financial statements and is incapable of thoroughly assessing the ability of the management team at the company's helm. It doesn't take a brain surgeon to dial number after number and say, "Good evening! Hope your family is doing well tonight" and launch into a well-prepared script. Should you hang up, these smooth talkers simply dial the next number on their list of leads. Eventually someone says yes.

Key Characteristics of Good Advisors

The investment business requires nonstop diligence on the part of people who are willing to read vast amounts of financial material.

Those who succeed by merit (that is, good performance in the stock market on behalf of their clients) not only love to read, but enjoy spending endless hours solving investment puzzles that most likely would boggle the minds of the world's best mathematicians. They would rather stay up late at night engaged in financial research and analysis than have a few drinks at the local Wall Street watering hole. The bottom line is that the hallmark qualities of an intelligent financial advisor are seldom found in a great salesperson.

I always seek out the modest types, and try my best to avoid the braggarts. I look for advisors who are willing to explain thoroughly the risk/reward ratio associated with each investment, and are able to answer any other questions I have about a particular stock or the management team of the company. Anyone with whom I deal must also be prepared to detail in full (and in advance) the various expenses levied by any mutual fund they suggest I sink money into.

For nearly two decades, I've watched with amazement as Wall Street salespeople talk faster and faster when pitching deals to their clients, in a manner that serves more to confuse than enlighten. I've often asked the sales rep to explain a particular aspect of the "merchandise" in question, once the client had written out a check and left the room. In more cases than not, I discovered that the broker lacked any real understanding of the "goods" just unloaded. Charming and personable as such sales folk may be, if they can't explain an investment vehicle in layperson's terms, one of two things is indicated: either they don't really know what they're talking about, or the client is being conned.

Unfortunately, the brokerage community typically bases salary, commissions, and year-end bonuses on the number and size of transactions rather than on the quality of advice that's provided. This is not the place to cover the subject of client abuse in the financial industry, so I'll simply emphasize that you shouldn't settle for anything less than an investment advisor with superior intelligence *and* unimpeachable integrity.

Without further ado, here's a rundown on the various types of investment professionals and what you need to know about them to select the advisor who's right for you.

The Registered Representative Helps You Make Decisions

Most commonly referred to as a stockbroker, these days a *registered representative* is also called a *financial consultant*. He or she can be found at such brokerage firms as Merrill Lynch, Smith Barney, Morgan Stanley–Dean Witter, Paine Webber, Goldman Sachs and the like as well as at regional houses and so-called bucket shops. (The latter type of operation is strictly bottom of the barrel, and is usually the place where they push penny stocks.)

The Securities and Exchange Commission makes sure that salespersons are properly registered before they sell financial products to investors. Each potential broker or trader must successfully pass a somewhat grueling six-hour examination for a Series 7 license. But this license does not guarantee that the newly registered "rep" has the ability to choose stocks, mutual funds, or other investment vehicles intelligently on behalf of his or her clients.

I've known a host of registered representatives with MBAs (from Ivy League schools, no less) who can only be described as total idiots when it comes to giving investment advice. One fellow who comes to mind bet heavily *against* technology stocks back in the late eighties. Not only did his clients want to put him on a hit list, but the darned fool lost his *own* shirt in the market as well! The sad truth is that he was always too busy networking to see that the already booming computer industry was about to explode. Happily, I never took his advice.

I know one or two wonderful brokers who are worth more than their weight in gold, to use the common phrase, and I feel that my own personal broker is worth his weight in *platinum*. The quality of his investment advice over the years has made all the difference in the world to my financial peace of mind. He knows which analysts are worth listening to, so we base investment decisions on the research of top-notch (and ethical) analysts. I'm also given the opportunity to make fixed income (bond) investments I wouldn't have known about otherwise.

WHAT A REP CAN DO FOR YOU

Like virtually all registered reps at full-service firms, my broker is able to offer the following investment advice and services to clients:

1. All sorts of cash instruments, including municipal money markets, U.S. Treasury money markets, and general money markets.

2. A wide variety of bond investments, including municipals, corporates, convertibles, governments, and high-yield, as well as preferred stocks.

3. A virtual cornucopia of mutual funds from which to choose, of both the no load and load variety. If I choose to invest in the latter, I'm comforted by the knowledge that the sales charge is going to someone with whom I've had a good working relationship over the long term.

4. A vast array of stocks, which (with the counsel of my own broker, at any rate) are backed up by some darned good research. Hopefully, your registered rep also knows which analysts excel at their jobs and demonstrate integrity when it comes to recommending stocks. (Rest assured that there are plenty of brokers who would sell their own grandmothers down the river if it meant putting a few farthings in the bank.)

5. An assortment of investment partnerships. Note that your participation in same could be either extremely profitable or fraught with danger. (Before you invest, it's advisable to seek out the opinion of an objective outsider.)

6. So-called wrap accounts, that permit you to invest money with a number of money managers by "wrapping" them all together in a single account.

Most brokers rely heavily on the opinions offered by their firm's research department, so it's wise to link up with a full-service house that needs and actively seeks out retail customers like you and me. (You'll likely get lost in the shuffle if you go with a brokerage firm that specializes in setting up huge banking deals instead.) Always keep in mind that *you're* the boss. Your registered rep relies on the commission he or she earns from each transaction you make. It doesn't hurt to start out any broker-client relationship by advising your "employee" that you'll close down your account and take your business elsewhere, the first time he or she sinks your money into a questionable proposition.

Many investment advisors in the industry love nothing more than to "hit on women" financially. Never let your guard down for a moment. Your personal broker should be willing (and able) to protect you from bad IPOs being pushed by the firm's investment bankers or stocks being touted just so the firm can get the investment banking business. Still, no power on earth can protect you from an unexpected earnings shortfall or an act of God that causes the stock of a well-established firm to drop in price.

You want to find the sort of guy or gal who's willing to spend time discussing investments with you—not just gallantly wining and dining you! If possible, find a broker who's been in the business for a substantial length of time, preferably with the same major firm.

Once again, I should emphasize that many brokers in the business are actually worth their weight in gold. These are the sort who always take the time to explain each investment thoroughly, and will assist you in determining your own personal financial objectives and the level of risk/reward ratio you're most comfortable with. What's more, he or she will never—but never—employ methods of flattery or intimidation in order to get you to fork over an investment check!

SELECTING A BROKER

When it comes time to select a broker, here's my advice:

1. If you're going to buy only mutual funds, seek out a discount broker (such as Charles Schwab) who will offer you an assortment of no load funds. Nondiscount brokers usually try to sell you funds of the load variety, so as to make the most money at your expense.

2. If you're going to invest in individual stocks and bonds, find a broker affiliated with a full-service brokerage or a regional house with a solid reputation. Again, be sure you're dealing with a firm that makes its bread and butter from retail customers like yourself.

3. Try to get a referral from a friend who's been investing in the market for a number of years. If no such referral presents itself, go shopping for a broker on your own. Meet with as many as

possible, and ask them to explain various research materials to you in layperson's terms. If they can't relay the information you need to know on a level you can understand, then by all means keep shopping!

4. Examine the firm's research materials to judge whether they are presented in a user-friendly manner. Make sure the firm follows high-quality stocks such as General Electric, Compaq Computer, Microsoft, Disney, Motorola, American Express, and so forth.

5. Try to find a broker who's been in the business for at least ten years—preferably more.

6. Pose the following as a direct question: "Are any of your firm's research analysts partial to investment banking deals?" If a potential broker levels with you and admits that some analysts will say anything to sell a banking client's stock, that's a very good indication of honesty. If the broker is able to assure you that he or she ignores the advice of this sort of analyst, you may well have found the broker of your dreams.

7. Meet potential brokers over lunch or dinner if at all possible, since it's important to establish a rapport. If they act like they're doing you a favor by taking you on as a client, then excuse yourself to the powder room and don't come back! Should they attempt to confuse or intimidate you, it's also time to call it a day.

8. Use my list of questions in Chapter 5 to test a prospective broker's knowledge of a particular stock's fundamentals. Many brokers rely solely on fundamental analysis, which is absolutely critical when it comes to choosing stocks. If the broker you're interviewing doesn't follow technical analysis, don't worry about it.

9. Be sure that you and your potential broker will be able to work together as a team by pursuing the same objectives. Should you fancy yourself as an aggressive investor, you wouldn't want to be saddled with an extremely conservative advisor like myself! On the other hand, the more conservatively minded investor will want to stick with a conservative broker who specializes in high-quality stocks.

10. Contact the National Association of Securities Dealers to make sure there are no complaints about any broker you're seriously considering.

11. Always take charge! Never give the broker complete discretion to do whatever he or she chooses with your money.

12. If you hear one lie come from the lips of a prospective broker, you're bound to hear more. Likewise, who needs to get involved with the "know-it-all" type who pretends to have all the answers? I much prefer the sort who asks for additional time to respond to a question before getting back to me. My dad always told me that all one has to do is listen. Most people will tell you everything you need to know about themselves in five minutes or less, so listening is really the best method of judging someone's character accurately.

Investment Advisors: For Those Who Want "Personal Shoppers"

In the previous section, you learned that all it really takes to be a registered rep is the ability to pass a six-hour examination. Would you believe it? A number of "broker wannabes" were recently caught paying professional test takers to pass the Series 7 exam for them! I'll grant you that *most* brokers pass the Series 7 test legitimately, yet as I've already stressed, passing doesn't necessarily prove that they can offer sound investment advice to their clients.

It's even easier for registered investment advisors to hang out a shingle and do business without any real market experience and expertise. They can take on an unlimited number of clients under the terms of the Investment Advisors Act of 1940, which continues to regulate the activities of such financial professionals. No national exam is required, but some states require advisors to pass the Series 65, a test administered by the National Association of Securities Dealers, which is, in fact, slightly less difficult than the Series 7. Should an individual ever be found guilty of committing a securities violation, he or she can no longer be licensed as an advisor. This thought is somewhat comforting, but serves as no guarantee that a duly licensed investment advisor can perform well in the market-place for the likes of you and me!

These days, there's no shortage of folks who brag endlessly about how they beat the market, and not all of them hold professional positions in the financial industry. Don't be surprised to learn that a barber has written a book about how he "made a killing" on Wall Street, or that a 16-year-old "whiz kid" managed to beat the S&P. The stock market performed so well in 1996 that a few investors' personal portfolios actually outdid the S&P 500 Index; the question is, were these investors smart enough to do the proper homework, or did they merely get lucky?

I beat the market significantly with my own stock portfolio in 1996, because I bet heavily on the appreciation of Intel. Such outstanding "winners" in the marketplace don't always present themselves, however. Any investor may beat the market on a fluke in a particular year, but the same investor may take a brutal beating the next.

What does a registered investment advisor do? Well, some of them act as financial consultants by offering advice to clients about which money managers should handle their assets. Other advisors specialize in choosing mutual funds for their customers (preferably of the no load variety). Truly professional investment advisors have massive databases and extensive performance statistics at their ready disposal, and can access an astonishing amount of information about the thousands of money managers in the industry. Registered investment advisors serve as "personal shoppers," by recommending a mixture of investment styles and a workable system of diversification to protect their clients' assets.

These financial professionals normally work with clients of significant wealth, so they are able to deal "in bulk." Don't forget that many of the best money managers in the business require high investment minimums. Should you decide to employ a registered investment advisor, you can diversify your assets more fully among various money managers who engage in the actual process of selecting stocks, bonds, or a mixture of both. These so-called wrap accounts are offered by many stockbrokers, but a registered investment advisor usually knows a large number of managers from whom to choose.

Some of my own personal assets are presently entrusted to two money managers with long and distinguished track records of superior performance in the marketplace, yet each requires an account minimum of more than my entire net worth. It would therefore be impossible for me to open up an individual account with either of them, were it not for the services of a "personal shopper" who's able to combine my assets with the wealth of other investors. This enables relatively small investors to play in a much higher stakes game. I should caution you, however, that a high minimum by no means guarantees high performance on the manager's part.

What can you expect to pay a registered investment advisor who does your shopping for you? Such financial consultants normally charge approximately from 0.5 to 1% of the assets they "run" for their clients. For some investors, this fee is well worth paying since their investment advisors scan the entire global marketplace for them. Also, advisors who hold no allegiance to any one brokerage house and its products tend to be much more objective when it comes to making investment choices.

SELECTING AN INVESTMENT ADVISOR

Unfortunately many advisors are unscrupulous or simply inept. When choosing your "personal shopper," here's what to look for:

1. Make sure that they recommend a wide variety of money managers from which to choose. For the record, money managers are also registered investment advisors, and you don't necessarily need to employ a personal financial consultant to recommend money managers for you.

2. Ask whether the managers they do business with meet AIMR standards. (We cover those standards in the following section of this chapter.)

3. Reach a mutual understanding as to your personal risk tolerance, and be confident that they are listening to your needs.

4. Decide which style(s) of investing you can best live with, and let your registered investment advisors find the best money managers to suit your personal risk tolerance. If you can't stand volatility, you shouldn't invest in emerging markets or aggres-

sive growth funds. On the other hand, if you want growth, you shouldn't sink most of your money in the bond market.

5. After your personal shoppers have made a selection of money managers for you, do some homework on your own. Examine the performance records of the managers in question, and make sure the investments that make up their portfolios are the sort you wish to participate in.

6. Make sure you understand the fee structure involved, before signing with any registered investment advisors. Again, a normal range of fees is between 0.5 and 1% of the assets you have under their management.

If you open an account with a registered investment advisor who's been in the business for some time and has a demonstrable track record of performance, you should be dealing with a person you can trust, who will take the time required to assess your personal level of risk tolerance. From the outset of your professional relationship with such an advisor, you need to be perfectly honest and frank about your own needs and goals for future financial security—which demands that you first be completely honest with yourself!

Should you have no real tolerance for risk, I recommend that you keep your assets in cash or intermediate fixed income—that is, bonds that mature in less than seven years. However, if you *are* able to stomach some element of risk in the hope of achieving more significant returns in the long run, then make certain that your investment advisor will work with you in adhering to a risk level with which you are comfortable.

Shop Around for Money Managers

We've already discussed the fact that registered investment advisors (also known as financial consultants) serve as personal shoppers by aligning you as an individual investor with one or more money managers. Should you prefer to do your *own* shopping, however, it stands to reason that you'll be able to avoid the additional charges involved in having someone select money managers on your behalf.

Happily, you, as an individual investor, can easily approach many excellent money managers—assuming that you are able to participate at the appropriate minimum. These managers will then proceed to buy stocks and bonds on your behalf, although you'll have very little to say about the investments they select for you. To be perfectly frank, money managers are "in the driver's seat" when it comes to making decisions for their investors, so you'll have to content yourself with sitting on the passenger's side!

In Chapter 8, we covered the various investment styles used by portfolio managers in the mutual fund industry. These include growth versus value, small-cap versus large-cap, and so forth. Fortunately, the terminology and investment styles employed by money managers are precisely the same as for mutual funds, so you won't need to memorize a whole new set of financial terms and definitions.

Remember that beating the market, or at least achieving relatively impressive performance results in any given year, is one thing, but long-term consistency is what really matters. I strongly recommend that, if you decide to do your own shopping, you do your homework: examine the returns achieved by each money manager you're considering on a year-to-year basis, and compare his or her performance to that of the S&P 500 Index. (As mentioned before, if the manager is a specialist at small-cap investments, refer to the year-to-year results for the Russell 2000 Index instead.) Don't sit back and congratulate yourself on having thoroughly completed your homework after you've managed to scrutinize the five- or ten-year average, however. Be sure to examine the returns for each individual year—again, looking for a solid record of consistency in the manager's performance.

Here's another helpful hint: Ask the money manager if his or her returns meet AIMR standards. (He or she will no doubt be impressed that you know enough to pop that question.) The Association for Investment Management and Research serves as the watchdog of professional money managers everywhere, by establishing a strict code of ethics and standards of professional conduct. For all practical purposes, the most important of these guidelines is something called the *Performance Presentation Standard*. Managers who adhere faithfully to these standards make sure that their reporting requirements are strictly topnotch. These individuals are more likely to be among the very best in the country. If a manager answers no to your question, you should not automatically disqualify him or her, but if the response is affirmative you can be assured that he or she adheres to bookkeeping standards that are higher than many others in the industry.

At this point, I should discuss the "little" matter of fees—which are often not so "little"! Most money managers charge an annual fee equal to approximately 1% of the assets you allow them to control for you in the case of equity investments, and 0.5% for fixed income (bond) investments. Again, some money managers achieve extraordinary results that warrant your paying rather high fees, while others definitely do not! Should you wish to go with one of the better-known and highly respected money managers in the marketplace, the minimum investment you'll need to make may range anywhere from $250,000 to $10 million. When analyzing money managers, it's also important to determine whether they're reporting a gross or net figure when speaking of performance. The important number is net of fees, because that indicates what you, as the investor, receive.

You're already well-acquainted with the concept of *volatility,* and with the term *standard deviation,* a measurement of volatility of a given investment portfolio. When judging money managers, it's extremely important to examine the standard deviations of their portfolios.

You may reach a better understanding of standard deviation if you assume for the moment that you're the owner of a portfolio composed of the collective incomes of a group of accountants—folk with low volatility ratings like my "steady Eddie" friend Maureen. From month to month, you could expect a consistent income from such a portfolio (except, perhaps, for a significant surge in income when tax season rolls around).

On the other hand, should your imaginary portfolio be composed of the collective incomes of itinerant actors like my extremely volatile friend Chuck, you'll never know quite how much income to expect from month to month. The bottom line is that a portfolio with a low standard deviation has much more consistent results, while one with a high standard deviation is far less predictable. The volatility factor can also be expressed as the measurement *Beta,* a measurement used to compare the volatility of a particular stock or portfolio with that of the S&P 500 Index.

As you venture into more detailed analysis of the performance of various money managers, you should also acquaint yourself with a measurement known as *Alpha*. To explain this term as simply as possible, if the Alpha associated with a given portfolio manager is greater than zero, the manager's ability to select stocks adds value to the assets of his or her investors. Conversely, if the manager's Alpha rating is less than zero, then he or she has not only failed to add value to the investors' assets, but has in fact subtracted value!

Finally, financial professionals have a measurement tool for gauging how much risk a money manager will to take in attempting to beat the market and score a high Alpha rating. This measurement is known as the *Sharpe Ratio*, named after the Nobel Prize–winning economist, William E. Sharpe. (It would take an entire chapter to explain adequately the complex formula by which the Sharpe Ratio is calculated, so I won't bore you with the details.) Suffice it to say that a money manager who earns a high Sharpe Ratio shows a greater return per unit of risk; a relatively low Sharpe Ratio indicates that the manager is achieving less return per unit of risk. Generally managers who achieve superior results without putting their investors on a "collision course" are assigned significantly higher Sharpe Ratios. To understand this concept, consider the various approaches to gaming used by black jack players in Las Vegas or Atlantic City. Some gamblers bet high stacks of chips, intent on beating the dealer big-time with each hand. Others wager a low-value chip or two at a time, in the expectation that slow and steady play may enable them to walk away from the table with a nice profit at evening's end. (Wouldn't it be nice to be a "fly on the wall" and watch a portfolio manager in action with his own money in play at a gambling casino?) So ask your potential money managers directly: "What's your Alpha?" and "What's your Sharpe Ratio?" They'll be surprised you know enough to ask. For additional information, consult publications that rank managers on an adjusted risk/reward basis. (One such publication is *Money Manager Review*, with offices in San Francisco, California.)

One final reminder: be sure that the performance records you examine apply to individual money managers, not just the portfolios they manage. The performance record of the portfolio you're looking at may belong to another manager who's moved on to even greener pastures, and who may have been replaced by a real "dud."

Always check to see whether the money manager presently in charge is the one who was responsible for the sterling track record you're examining!

What about the Advisor Next Door?

Do you recall the story I shared with you about the sound investment advice offered by my father's next-door neighbor? Dad's roofer friend was a blue-collar worker who happened to know more about picking stocks than many white-collar professionals on Wall Street at the time! I sincerely hope that my father's investment-savvy neighbor, who was as good at choosing stocks as he was repairing the roofs of houses, had enough personal savings to follow his own advice. If so, there's every chance he's now living the good life in Palm Springs (or perhaps the French Riviera) on a beachfront estate surrounded by other self-made millionaires.

You shouldn't necessarily put your full faith and confidence in every hot tip your high-living registered rep or other advisor hands you—nor should you shrug off and dismiss the financial advice of your local TV repairman or plumber. (Remember Anne Scheiber, who parlayed her $5,000 life savings and a tiny retirement stipend from the IRS into a $22 million fortune.) The average Joe or Jane is often better at doing the necessary financial homework than are egotistic Wall Street types of the know-it-all variety.

A former client of mine is a most remarkable fellow, the sort who simply loves people and treats everyone he meets with exactly the same respect. He gives out such great "vibes" that everyone he meets becomes instantly enamored of him. In fact, he probably has a wider assortment of good friends than anyone I know. I've been amazed at his ability to turn total strangers into lifelong pals at a first meeting, just by expressing a sincere interest in getting to know them on a personal level. In a world filled with braggarts, this former client is truly one in a million!

He's far too modest to permit me to use his real name, so let's just call him "Jimmy." A self-made millionaire, Jimmy became so successful at the investment game that he went into business for himself as the manager of his own hedge fund. Needless to say, Jimmy does his own homework—and then some! His personality hasn't changed one iota over the years, so he still makes scores of new friends every day. Jimmy's ability to be a good listener is without parallel.

Before Jimmy went out on his own as a hedge fund manager, he learned the business by accepting a job as an institutional research salesman at one of the more prestigious New York investment banks. Most brokers and financial consultants pursue "hot tips" from the front office of the firms that employ them, and discount all others. Jimmy paid attention to what *everyone* had to say, and carefully weighed the merit of each opinion regardless of the source. He listened to the guys and gals in the front office, back office, side office—even to the elderly shoeshine man who polished leather all day! The shoeshine man (whom we'll call "George") made a living by making rounds throughout the firm that employed Jimmy, applying plenty of spit and polish to the shoes of dozens of institutional salespeople and investment bankers each day. As always, Jimmy treated George with precisely the same respect he would any major power broker on Wall Street.

George was a lovable character to whom everyone took a "shine" in more ways than one! Consequently, George was well "tipped" for his labors, with stock "tips" as well as cash! Because Jimmy had that rarer-than-rare ability to listen to what everyone he met had to say, regardless of their station in life, he would ask George's opinion of the best deals in the marketplace that day. The moment George finished his spit-and-polish chores and moved on to the next customer, Jimmy earnestly researched whatever hot tip the shoeshine man had recommended.

Not surprisingly, the trader who sat at the desk opposite Jimmy thought his colleague was hopelessly insane! Why bother doing homework on stock tips handed you by a shoeshine man? Finally, the trader posed that very question, and Jimmy replied, "Everyone loves George," he said with a knowing smile. "The salespeople don't care if they saddle you and me with a couple of their worst ideas, but they would never forgive themselves if they gave the same bad advice to George!" You never know where you'll find the key to the gold.

CON ARTISTS AND
HOW TO AVOID THEM

There are more con artists out there than you can possibly imagine, and they're literally everywhere. That's why this is the most important chapter in the entire book. As I've said, Wall Street is abundantly populated by "grim reapers" in all-too-human form.

Most of us are unable to fathom how sheer greed and ego gratification can lead brokers to think they're "just doing their jobs" by literally robbing little old ladies of their life savings. To me, such actions are unconscionable: such people should be tarred, feathered, and run off the Street. Unscrupulous stockbrokers think, however, they're just doing what everyone else does to put millions in the bank. That's how they manage to rationalize committing every trick in the book. But it's not just older women who need to watch out for con artists. Women of all ages are targets of and, sadly, more susceptible to scams.

Are you likely to meet up with a con artist at least *once* in your lifetime? Of course, and once is all it takes to bankrupt yourself. Con artists generally display more bravado than do ethical salespeople, so it's more likely that they'll find you before you have the opportunity to find an honest John or Jane Doe to manage your money.

Finding Con Artists Where You Least Expect Them

Con artists will always be lurking in our Wall Street midst. It's the nature of a business where so much money is at stake. Remember, not all of the cons discussed here are, strictly speaking, illegal; some are only unethical. These days, they're flourishing like never before, even in the most otherwise reputable and household-name investment firms. The sad fact is that some Wall Street managers are willing to close their eyes to unethical dealings. Naturally, such bosses are "in on the take," profiting by an override on every deal consummated by their subordinates. The further tragedy is that those in top management who should be playing the role of "cops" are sometimes equally guilty of fraud and corruption—perhaps all the way to the top of a "respectable" brokerage firm.

I can't stress enough the importance of "snooping around" a bit into your potential money advisor's character and track record. (Always make sure to check out your brokers or investment advisors before they have the chance to "check out" with your cash!) Even the reputable brokerage houses miss screening out some of the rotten apples, who are just waiting to get their hands on your money. That's why your ability to judge character correctly is key. And please do not fall prey to flattery (the oldest trick in the book) or anything that smacks of intimidation—the two easiest means by which registered reps fleece their female clients. Don't be one of their victims!

There are many advisors who place their clients' money with less-than-the-best money managers in return for some sort of kickback. The acceptance of such incentive fees is a practice known in the industry as *double-dipping*. Should you have the misfortune of hiring someone like this, you'll be paying good money for an advisor who's interested only in increasing the size of his or her bank account.

For the past 18 years, I've kept my eyes wide open to what really goes on in the financial industry. Nothing upsets me more than watching salespeople try to unload worthless investment products on the basis of exclusivity. The impression many brokers give is that their clients should be honored beyond measure at the privilege of being invited to join some sort of "private club" of investors. To return to the analogy used in the previous chapter, just because there's an expensive cover charge attached to an investment doesn't mean that attending the party will prove the slightest bit worthwhile.

The best advice I can offer you is to find a broker or advisor who treats you like an intelligent human being—and take all the time you need to find one! (The time will be well spent.) Even if you're married, and you've decided to leave your investments to your husband—definitely *not* something I recommend—it's essential that you choose a broker you like and can trust. Many married women have shared horrific personal experiences with me about their visits to the Street, often to a broker or a financial planner who spoke only to their husbands.

Remember, even if the "salesperson" in question has treated your husband well in their dealings over the years, be careful that the same man or woman doesn't take advantage of you should you become widowed. Suddenly, you're alone and feeling vulnerable. That's an open invitation for the sort of "friendly neighborhood broker" who can turn into your worst nightmare! Even if your husband was a good client for decades, he could take you for the very last dime of the life insurance check you're about to receive in the mail. According to statistics, most women outlive their husbands by eight to nine years. Why not establish a new relationship with a broker of your *own* choice (whether male or female) who will treat you as an important customer, rather than a mere appendage of your husband?

Worse still is the broker who peruses the obits every morning, then preys on the recently widowed for his daily bread. Some even pose as a friend of the husband, send the widow a nice sympathy card, then show up at the funeral parlor to say a tearful farewell. The widow can say an equally tearful farewell to any money she gives him to invest on her behalf! If you think this sort of scenario doesn't happen, I respectfully suggest that you think again.

Have I scared you to death? Good! I wanted to make sure you heard the message: It's essential always to be extremely firm with your broker or financial planner. Remember, you're the boss, and the man or woman sitting across the desk from you is your employee, who should be earning his or her living by performing a service *for* you rather than *against* you! If you're not extremely careful, you could wind up with a financial advisor who could permanently destroy your financial well-being.

Your mother probably told you the same thing mine did when I was a kid: "An ounce of prevention is worth a pound of cure." It did not take long for me to find out she was right. Laws that govern securities in this country don't favor the consumer, so it is often pointless for you, as a first-time investor, to take your broker to arbitration.

Another word of advice: the brokerage firm with which you deal will always insist that you sign something known as an *arbitration clause* as part of your customer agreement. By signing same, you agree in advance that any complaint you feel obliged to make against the firm will be passed on to an arbitration panel. The upshot is that, under current legislation, the merit of your complaint will be decided by a jury of the brokerage community's peers. This is far from ideal, in my opinion at least, as the brokerage community is likely to have a built-in bias against the person filing the complaint. Even if you were eventually to win a judgment against your broker, that certainly doesn't guarantee that you'll ever see your money!

Should Congress have the wisdom to overrule such legislation, the American public would be much less susceptible to the downright acts of fraud in the financial industry. Such a legislative change would enable an investor to bring a complaint to the federal courts, rather than have the matter decided by a potentially biased arbitration panel. A change in the law may not solve the problem entirely, but it would help eliminate at least a few of those Wall Streeters who prosper at the expense of naive and helpless investors!

Protect Yourself: Be Your Own Gatekeeper

You're probably much as I was back in 1978, completely naive about how Wall Street really works. On too many occasions I put my faith in people who didn't deserve my trust. I know how hard you work at your job, and the sacrifices you've no doubt made to put a bit of your weekly paycheck aside for a rainy day. I'd love for you to be able to put those savings to better use in the stock market at perhaps double the bang for your buck. The last thing I want to happen is for you to get suckered out of every cent you have, should you happen to trust one of the "bad guys" to make money decisions for you. How I wish I could go with each of you on that first visit to an investment advisor so I could offer my personal opinion of him (or her), but I can't. However, I can teach you how to be your own "gatekeeper" or "personal body guard."

Some of this may sound simplistic, but here's the best advice I can give you:

- Don't be too trusting.

- Don't be afraid to ask questions.

- Always check references.

- Look for a brokerage firm near you with name recognition, and certainly one with checkable references.

- Refuse to write the check until you thoroughly understand all aspects of the investment being offered you. Remember, if it sounds too good to be true, it *is* to good to be true.

- Don't fall prey to a broker's flattery, and the very first time you catch your broker in a lie, find another broker. Be wary of advisors or brokers who try to impress you with tales of their wealth and connections rather than their knowledge and skills.

- Avoid brokers who purposely talk above your head. They may be attempting to throw you off balance and confuse you.

- Stay away from anyone with a reputation as a "gunslinger." Chances are he'll shoot himself in the foot at some point or other, and he just might take you for an arm or a leg as well! A gunslinger will take unnecessary risks to go for the gold.

Trust your gut. Whenever a "bad feeling" creeps over you while speaking to a money counselor over the phone or in person, simply find some pretext to end the conversation *whenever that alarm rings!* "Woman's intuition" is not really a myth. It's the special tuning device with which we're each equipped that can be used for our personal betterment. I've made my greatest mistakes when I didn't listen to my own built-in alarm system.

What's more, you should feel free to contact the Securities and Exchange Commission (at 800-SEC-0330) or the National Association of Securities Dealers (800-289-9999). Keep in mind that both organizations are staffed with folk whose salaries are paid by your tax dollar. They're there to provide information, for example, to tell you whether the dealer or registered rep you have in mind has been guilty of securities violations in the past.

Battle Scenes: How Con Artists Operate

The most experienced con artists do their best to rule the galaxy, even while new cons join that ignoble profession every day. Learn to recognize the work of a con artist.

LESSON NUMBER ONE: HOW TO FLEECE A LITTLE OLD LADY

I sometimes wonder how my mother would cope should my father die before her. But allow me to tell you about someone else's mother who's roughly 83 years old, a beautiful woman by the name of Mary Woodfield. Like millions of other women over the age of 65, she lost her spouse of many years. Mary had no experience at all with investments; her husband had always handled their financial affairs. She was particularly vulnerable after his death, left alone for the first time in her life.

What's more, she had no real family left, which made her all the more vulnerable to the telemarketers who began to phone her daily. Sadly, this interaction became a surrogate for Mary's real friends and family. When her husband died, Mary owned a three-bedroom home and had roughly $40,000 in the bank. She quickly managed to lose the $40,000 to her telemarketing "friends," and was forced to sell her home. How did they do it? Mary's new telemarketer "friends" promised riches beyond her wildest imagination! As with chain letters, Mary had only to send a check that would reserve her impending fortune. Of course, Mary never got a dime of the fortune she'd been promised. She then fell prey to *other* con artists who promised to get all of that wasted money back for her. "All you have to do is send a small check for our retainer"—you know the rest. (It's completely possible that the same telemarketers who had fleeced Mary were now posing as lawyers wanting to fight on her behalf.)

Who knows who these telemarketers were? They may have been unscrupulous advisors or they may have been thieves. In either case, the moral is the same: Never give your hard-earned money to anyone you haven't thoroughly investigated. I recently attended a conference about offering investment advice to high-net-worth individuals. One of the speakers actually said that widows care only about how much attention is paid to them. Many brokers operate on the same premise as these telemarketers. They try to get the most vulnerable to listen to them. According to this speaker, widows don't worry all that much about how well financial advisors do in terms of performance in the marketplace as long as they pay attention to them. No wonder so many Wall Street "weasels" are making a fortune.

LESSON NUMBER TWO: HOW TO FLEECE TWO SAVVY WOMEN

Speaking of *weasels,* meet the vermin who suckered two lovely women named Olga and Fannie out of house and home. Olga and Fannie, sisters, had scrimped and saved and invested whatever they could spare. They became small-time "gurus" over the years, managing to accumulate more than $1 million by investing in commercial deposits, bonds, and mutual funds. (Hetty Robinson Green would have been proud of them!)

The otherwise shrewd sisters met their Waterloo via an advertisement promising "higher yields." Here's how *Securities Week* reported the story:

> According to sources close to the case, the sisters took … a broker's advice in 1993 to liquidate most of their personal holdings and borrow additional funds from the firm to invest in what they were told were bonds guaranteed by the federal government. What [the firm] was actually selling were interest-only and principal-only strips—complicated instruments used to speculate on interest rate fluctuations, according to the sisters' filing.

How did it happen? In 1992 Olga and Fannie started down the path to financial destruction by opening something called a margin account. As I've said in Chapter 9, a margin account is something I would recommend for only the most sophisticated investor: Anyone who tries to push you into investing on margin may *not* have your best interests at heart, I assure you!

Olga and Fannie had done absolutely *everything* right in terms of investments prior to meeting a charming broker. As I've said, all it takes is one good con artist …

Enter a broker and brokerage firm straight from their worst nightmares. The broker bought loads of Fannie Mae derivatives (very risky stuff) with the sisters' hard-earned cash. He then got them into even deeper debt through the margin account he insisted they open in 1992. The particular derivative he recommended buying was a highly leveraged bet, one on which only the nation's most wealthy (or foolhardy) investors took a gamble—the future direction of interest rates. We in the industry refer to such derivatives as "toxic waste," because they're nothing short of lethal poison in most cases.

Interest rates *rose* in 1994—sadly, not the direction in which the sisters had bet. By this point Olga and Fannie not only lost their $1 million, but were hopelessly in debt, thanks to their margin account.

Complaints were eventually filed and the sisters were awarded money by a "dealer panel" set up by the National Association of Securities Dealers. Happily, Olga and Fannie were exonerated from the margin debt that had been run up for them. Sadly, however, no one knows if the sisters will ever see their savings or even a portion of it. The firm may be protected by a bankruptcy claim filed in 1994.

LESSON NUMBER THREE: HOW TO FLEECE *MILLIONS* WITH "PENNIES"

Penny stock operators work out of what are called boiler operations, where a group of men and women sit at a bank of phones and talk honest, hard-working folk like you and me out of our money. Should whatever "penny stock" they're pitching at the moment sell for 30 cents, they swear the stock will be worth 50 cents by the end of the next business day. (It will certainly hit at least the two-dollar mark by same time next week, of course.)

Guess what: The penny stock actually *does* go to 50 cents by the next business day, so you start thinking to yourself that these guys just may be on to something! What you *don't* know is that the men who control the boiler operations usually control the market for that stock. Therefore it's easy for them to manipulate the stock's price from day to day.

When the same 30-cent stock eventually climbs to $6 or $7 per share, the broker calls again, *"What are you waiting for! This stock is going straight to the moon!"* Fools that we are, we believe him. In most cases, the penny operator owned most or all of the stock when it was down at 30 cents, and he's merely selling it into an artificial market of his own creation. Once the seller has unloaded his shares for a large profit you begin to see the stock's price drifting south-ward. If you're not quick to sell, it's likely you'll be left holding the bag. The proverbial "tree primeval" that's about to come crashing down in the financial forests of Wall Street has only one sad-faced monkey left in it—and it's *you*!

How to protect yourself? Don't get suckered into such penny stock deals to begin with. Avoid the temptation as you see the stock go up.

Small stock fraud cost investors at least $6 billion a year. However, that's not the only loss investors might face. Unfortunately, what is legal, sometimes is still unethical. Many of the major brokerage hous-es bring out initial public offerings that are extremely questionable, and they sell extreme hype that is not substantiated. Initial public offerings can be a great chance to get into a very exciting new com-pany. But all too often, many of the IPO's stock certificates will be used for wallpaper the very next year. Many times, the original own-ers of the company are looking to hype their company and make a quick buck by selling ownership to the public. After the deal is done, management is basking in the sun, hoping that Wall Street's analysts are talking up the stock. Eventually, they sell their shares through a secondary, or in many cases they hedge by using derivative transac-tions. Since Wall Street deals in projections, no one can be blamed for inaccurately predicting future earnings, but in many cases, the analyst is more concerned with the investment banking fee rather than the investor.

In a March 1997 article in the pages of *Worth* magazine, Peter Lynch reported that many initial public offerings haven't reaped the sort of financial rewards that have accompanied the stock market rally in recent years. The way he puts it, "From the class of 1995, 37 percent, or 202 of the companies are selling below their IPO price. From the class of 1996, 33 percent, or 285, now trade below their offering price." The point Mr. Lynch makes is that investors in today's market can buy many of the same stocks at lower prices than the original purchasers paid for them and find some bargains. Why should this be the case?

My personal guess is that there were a few "lukewarm" issues that virtually all of the big institutions took a pass on, and that these IPOs were then offered to small individual investors who eagerly took a chance on them. The salespeople involved no doubt made their smaller clients feel privileged to "luck into" the chance to buy an IPO. Yes, there are a few bargains, but most of those stocks will never see their initial offering price again.

I simply can't place enough emphasis on the following warning: Unless you're one of the "big boys" (or "big girls") and have hundreds of thousands, if not millions, of dollars in a brokerage account, please be extremely cautious whenever you're offered a chance to invest in an IPO. Ask yourself (as well as your broker) why the deal is being offered to you rather than to one of the major mutual funds or institutional accounts. Most likely, it's because the bigger players knew full well that they were being "suckered" into a losing proposition. That's the only reason smaller investors are lucky enough (make that "unlucky" enough) to be offered a piece of the action.

The best advice I can offer you is this: whenever a penny stock operator or a broker cold calls you with an IPO, *hang up immediately!* Should the caller manage to keep you on the line long enough that you're actually *tempted* by the line he's feeding you, do the next best thing: phone the National Association of Securities Dealers and/or the Securities and Exchange Commission. Ask if there are any violations or complaints against either the brokerage house, its principals, and the broker in question. (Be warned that dishonest folk are often quite resilient and can switch firms or instantly create new firms as a home base from which to operate.)

Most solid companies are introduced to the marketplace by well-known investment banks. Occasionally, a penny stock operator comes up with a winner, but let's just say the odds are *not* in your favor.

LESSON NUMBER FOUR: HOW TO FLEECE YOUR LOVED ONES

What I call the "friends and family plan" is the most difficult of all to stomach when it comes to low-down "con artistry." When you find that you've just been "conned" by a member of your own family (or perhaps by a long-time friend), you lose much more than money. First, you lose all possiblities of a future relationship with the person who just hurt you, someone for whom you cared.

So, without further buildup, here's the sad tale of what happened to one of my own colleagues, someone I thought of as a "nice guy." Imagine my shock at seeing his story in the Sunday paper.

Nothing could have possibly made me believe that Dick would ever be involved with an investment scam—nothing short of his eventual arrest, that is. To this day, most of his colleagues join me in hoping that what happened to Dick is nothing more than some horrendous mistake.

Dick was someone we all thought of as the "social register" type. He was always impeccably dressed and seemingly well connected. Dick and his wife were also highly visible on the New York charity circuit and seemed to fit well into that particular culture as they rushed from one splendid "event" to another. He lived in a well-appointed brownstone, dabbled at collecting art and antiques, and gave of his valuable time in efforts to raise money for the Boy Scouts of America. He was even profiled in a magazine geared toward the wealthy reader. And so on, and so on ... until he was arrested and charged with fraud.

Before joining a Wall Street firm, Dick worked for a bank. Apparently, he claimed he could get investment access for a few choice friends to a special fund at the bank, promising that it would reap harvests of 18 to 20% per year in interest—about three times the prevailing risk-free rate at the time. He further claimed there would be absolutely no risk to whatever principal sum his friends and/or family cared to invest. It seemed almost too good to be true, and indeed it was.

Naturally, most of Dick's extended circle of friends and family jumped at the chance to invest in the fund. Dick managed to collect some $4 million from 30 to 50 close friends and relatives—including his in-laws! And this "special fund" managed to stay open for about ten years before Dick's scam finally caved in on him.

According to the assistant to the U.S. prosecutor pursuing the case, Dick's arrest happened after a number of complaints were made to the Securities and Exchange Commission. A few of his friends and family requested some of their money back, and were shocked when the checks they received bounced. Dick was arrested in February of 1996, then set free on $250,000 bond.

What can we learn from this tragic story? For starters, the mere fact that appearances aren't everything. But the more important lesson is: if something sounds too good to be true, it probably is. It's your responsibility to investigate investment advice—regardless of the source.

Empower Yourself by Educating Yourself

For as long as women are considered vulnerable in this society, we will continue to be victimized. Our best chance for survival is to educate and empower ourselves. If we're lucky enough to live that long, we'll all soon be honest-to-goodness "little old ladies" ourselves—women trying our very best to live out our retirement years in relative comfort. That's why the time to think of that future is *now*.

My paternal grandmother, Jeni Jupiter, happened to be blind. In that somewhat calmer and gentler era, virtually everyone in the neighborhood watched out for Grandma, who never once had to worry for her safety. Nowadays, some of the kids in that same neighborhood would not hesitate if given the chance to snatch Grandma's purse, then knock her down to the concrete sidewalk.

There's no difference whatsoever between the sort of purse-snatcher who steals from an elderly blind woman and the more sophisticated bandit who steals a widow's "purse."

How Do I Steal from You?
The Legal and Not So Legal

To summarize the chapter, investment scams usually will fall into one of these categories:

1. Small stock fraud

2. Worthless initial public offerings

3. Misappropriation of funds

4. Churning, which is buying and selling stocks only to generate commissions for the broker

5. Using extensive leverage through derivatives or margin accounts

6. Suitability, which means that the investment should be appropriate for the investor. A woman entering retirement should not be sold derivatives, highly risky investment partnerships or speculative stocks.

Want to become a rich little old lady and stay that way? The key lies in protecting yourself from all those who want to help you out of house and home. To do that, you've got to know how to assess and analyze any deal that comes your way.

LEARNING TO LIVE WITH RISK: NO GUTS, NO WEALTH!

I can't think of a better way to begin a chapter about risk taking than by quoting our twenty-sixth president, the ever rough 'n ready Theodore Roosevelt:

> It is not the critic who counts; not the man who points out how the strong man stumbles, or where the doer of deeds could have done them better. The credit belongs to the man who is actually in the arena, whose face is marred by dust and sweat and blood; who strives valiantly; who errs, and comes short again and again; because there is not effort without error and shortcoming; but who does actually strive to do the deeds; who knows the great enthusiasms, the great devotions; who spends himself in a worthy cause, who at the best knows in the end the triumphs of high achievement and at the worst, if he fails, at least fails while daring greatly, so that his place shall never be with those cold and timid souls who know neither victory nor defeat.

The word *risk* comes from the Italian word *risicare,* which means to dare. From the dawn of history, members of the human species have taken whatever risks have been required in order to survive. The time has come for women to take full responsibility not merely for surviving, but for *thriving* financially. It takes a bit of courage but each of us can dramatically change our lives for the better by learning to accept an element of calculated risk.

Lessons from a Risk Taker: Susan B. Anthony

Susan B. Anthony (1820–1906) is the only woman to be found on our nation's currency, a well-deserved recognition of her unique contribution to American history.

If I'm correct and money is a vehicle of freedom, then if it weren't for the relentless efforts of this woman, we wouldn't have had the right to vote or to acquire wealth. Anthony devoted her entire life to ensuring that women would be guaranteed equal opportunity to a good education, to own property, and to have an active voice in government.

She started her political career by petitioning for a law to prohibit the sale of alcohol because its abuse led to cruel and unjust treatment by many husbands. In the process Anthony discovered that women couldn't contribute to her cause because husbands controlled all the money. Her first victory was in securing legal rights for married women. Thanks to Miss Anthony, married women would *have* assets, not *be* assets in a husband's portfolio. She literally risked her life for us to become economically free. Without further ado, it's time for us to fulfill her mission by becoming rich.

The Pragmatic Side of Risk

Every reader of this book is no doubt acquainted with the phrase, "No pain—no gain!" Your life savings may in truth be "safer" in relatively low-interest-bearing cash investments, or safer still kept tucked under the bedroom mattress. Yet, those investment vehicles don't enable your wealth to grow very much. Once you can approach risk in a methodical fashion, you can put some of your fears aside and start building an abundance of wealth.

Taking risk is a necessary evil if you play in the investment arena. (Those who prefer not to live with financial uncertainty can stick with my suggestions for the riskless—albeit boring—investments outlined in Chapter 6.)

Before making any decision, it's important that you thoroughly understand the downside as well as upside to each investment in the marketplace, so that you can appropriately tailor a portfolio that best fits your own uniquely personal level of risk tolerance. An educated investor—much like a seasoned gambler who knows the rules of the game—is thus equipped to decide how she should stack the chips on each wager. Most women have been taught—implicitly or explicitly—to put any savings at all in the bank. This often leads us to be *overly* cautious when it comes to taking risks.

A great many women perceive investments as bearing an almost irrational quality of risk; as a result we've historically remained on the sidelines (financially speaking) by keeping most of our assets in cash. It's high time to set aside the emotional aspects of investing, and instead examine the raw data about the returns associated with each asset class.

Look at the following table, covering the years 1926–1995:

MAXIMUM AND MINIMUM VALUES OF ONE-YEAR HOLDING PERIODS

Series Annual Returns	Maximum Value Return/Year(s)	Minimum Value Return/Year(s)	Times Positive (out of 70 Years)	Times Highest Returning Asset	Standard Deviation
Large Company Stocks	53.99 1933	−43.34 1931	50	13	20.4%
Small Company Stocks	142.87 1933	−58.01 1937	49	31	34.4%
Long-Term Corporate Bonds	42.56 1982	− 8.09 1969	54	6	8.7%
Long-Term Government Bonds	40.36 1982	− 9.18 1967	51	6	9.2%
Intermediate-Term Government Bonds	29.10 1982	− 5.14 1994	63	2	5.8%
U.S. Treasury Bills	14.71 1981	− .02 1938	69	6	3.3%
Inflation	18.60 1946	−10.30 1932	60	6	

© *Source: Ibbotson Associates 1996 Yearbook,* pp. 43, 118. Computed using data from Stocks, Bonds, Bills & Inflation 1997 Yearbook,[TM] Ibbotson Associates, Chicago (annually updates work by Roger G. Ibbotson and Rex Sinquefield). Used with permission. All rights reserved.

A brief examination of this table shows that U.S. Treasury bills are the "steady Eddie" of the investment world, while the small-company stocks have been the highest performers (although accompanied by great volatility and uncertainty). Investing in them is more like enduring the highs and lows of a roller coaster ride, than merrily coasting along on the far-less-frightening painted pony of your neighborhood carousel.

THE BUILDING BLOCKS: PORTFOLIO MANAGEMENT

Assuming that you're ready to start constructing your own stock portfolio, you need to know about Modern Portfolio Theory—an academic, but very useful concept, by which you can make sure you are diversifying risk sufficiently. In brief, the goal is for you to achieve the highest potential return through the *combination* of various risk-bearing assets, the returns of which are not highly correlated.

A measurement known as *covariance* is used to quantify how assets move in relationship to one another. In simple practice, if you applied Modern Portfolio Theory to your portfolio, you could not own *only* technology stocks. Why? To save you from having a heart attack (at least figuratively) should the market suddenly decide that technology stocks were overpriced!

Modern Portfolio Theory works on the principle of diversification, with as few as eight to twelve stocks—once again, making sure that they aren't highly correlated. An investment survey known as *Value Line* recently recommended that a portfolio should consist of about 15 different stocks spread over roughly 8 different industries. (This, of course, assumes that the 15 stocks you select are of high quality. If they're not, it doesn't matter in the slightest how well you've diversified them! Your stock picks are not highly correlated, but the stocks are low caliber.)

THE BALANCING ACT

Quality is always an issue, so doing your homework is always imperative. Here are a few tips:

1. Know yourself. Then decide which types of asset classes best fit your own personal level of risk tolerance. There's no shame in being downright risk averse. Investors who just can't take the heat will probably end up burning themselves rather than patiently keeping their cool.

2. If you decide to balance your asset classes, don't feel bad about holding just a small percent of equity (stocks) until you feel more comfortable with investing money in riskier investment vehicles.

3. Should you be fortunate enough—as if by beginner's luck—to make your very first purchase or purchases as the stock market is on the upswing, by no means permit yourself to become overconfident. Remember that stocks prices fluctuate both up and down, so resist the urge to let yourself get swept away in the stampede of a bull market.

4. Be prepared to live with the worst-case scenario. Let's say, for example, that I have $50,000 that I might invest. If I can truly afford to lose only $10,000, I should assume that the market's worst historical performance scenario—a loss of 43% of its value back in the dismal 1973–74 season—will once more repeat itself. Should I be unable to live with more than a $10,000 loss, I should probably have a bit less than $20,000 in the marketplace. However unlikely it may be that the market will again experience such a dramatic downswing, it's more comforting to be prepared. It's easy to be fooled by all the sophisticated financial models that salespersons in the industry may sling at you—so always insist on breaking down the worst-case scenario in clear terms of dollars and cents.

5. If you are brave enough to do plenty of homework and select your own stocks, always look for quality—and never, ever forget to diversify!

6. Don't choose all 15 stocks and/or mutual funds for your personal portfolio at once. Instead, take your time and carefully weigh the individual merit of each investment you make. A quick side note: some mutual funds have automatic savings plans, as we discussed in Chapter 8. If you like a specific stock, you can ask the company itself if it has a dividend reinvestment plan (DRIP). If you sign up for such a plan, any dividends you earn automatically buy more shares on your behalf.

7. Don't play long shots (enough said).

8. In sizing up portfolio managers, look at their past track records of performance and risk/reward profiles, carefully analyzing where the portfolio lies in the risk/return "frontier," as follows.

MAKING CHOICES

The following graph examines how T-bills (as represented by the letter A) and the S&P 500 Index (indicated by the letter B) might perform as compared with the track record of three fictitious portfolio managers (C, D, and E) over a period of five years: Beta (as we discussed in Chapter 8) is a measurement of volatility. In this case it measures the volatility of the portfolio against the S&P 500. Which investment would you choose?

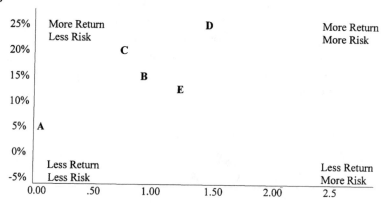

RISK RETURN ANALYSIS
FIVE-YEAR PERIOD

FIGURE 12-1.   RISK/RETURN ANALYSIS (5-YEAR PERIOD).

A = U.S. Treasury bill, 5% return, no risk
B = S&P 500 Index, approximately 15% return, and a Beta of 1.0
C = A Beta of 0.8, a 20% return, and a portfolio manager worth a look at
D = A manager with a return of 25%, but a Beta of 1.5—also worth considering for those who are comfortable with taking a risk greater than the S&P 500.
E = A manager with a 12% return, and a Beta of 1.3. I would promptly dismiss Manager E (who's providing less-than-market returns with higher risk).

The general rule of thumb, of course, is: better returns, less risk. When picking money managers, it is important to find out how they perform in returns and what risk you must live with in order to reap the benefits. Always ask for their performance and stack it against their volatility. I recently invested with a mutual fund that has a very high Beta and high returns. Because I'm prepared, I can live with the roller coaster, but I still kick myself when the portfolio takes the dive. In all cases, know your portfolio manager.

Asset Allocation: Choose Your Weapon

The subject of asset allocation is significant. However, in "fairy tale" terms, you might say we're all asking the question, "Mirror, mirror on the wall, which asset class is fairest of them all?"

By the year 2000, will the Dow Jones Industrial Average be trading at 10,000, or at 5,000? Will interest rates rest at 5% in 1998—or at 8%? Will that ugly green-eyed monster, inflation, have died out altogether? By that time, will our representatives in Congress have finally and irrevocably decided to balance the budget? Will there be a war in the Middle East that causes the price of oil to skyrocket, endangering the global economy?

Sadly, the future's not ours to see. Therefore, all that *any* of us can do is to make educated guesses about how best to diversify our assets among cash, stocks, and bonds. Recently, a number of money managers advised their investors to hold a certain amount of international equities, in order to diversify their portfolio's mix even further.

The major brokerage houses tend to prescribe a certain "mix" of assets in the marketplace, according to their overall perception of the economy at any given time. Nevertheless, such advice is nothing more than an educated guess with absolutely no guarantees. According to Murphy's law, just about anything can and *will* happen to foil the most well-thought-out and expert economic forecast.

WHAT INTEREST RATES TELL YOU

You'll no doubt recall that the prevailing interest rate serves to "orchestrate" the entire economic "symphony" of the financial marketplace. If my dad said it once, he said it a thousand times: "Always seek out the advice of those you admire most." One such individual is a man I've always admired, and a fellow who's managed to retain a sense of "humility" while both surviving and thriving for many years in the stock market: Peter Lynch, former manager of the extraordinarily successful Fidelity Magellen Fund.

In *Beating the Street*, Lynch mentions one special method by which an investor can decide when it's more appropriate to invest in bonds than in stocks. In "Peter's Principle #8," Lynch recommends this investment tactic: "When yields on long-term government bonds exceed the dividend yield of the S&P 500 by 6% or more, sell your stocks and buy bonds." As I key these words into my computer, the S&P 500 Yield is 1.87% and the 30-year government bond yield equals 6.53%. After only a few quick punches into the calculator, I learn that 6.53% minus 1.87% equals 4.66%. Therefore, according to Peter's Principle #8, stocks presently remain a more attractive investment than bonds.

WHAT PAST PERFORMANCE TELLS YOU

All types of models project economic growth, corporate profits, interest rates, and inflation. Using these data, various investment committees (who oversee the assets of institutions) try their darndest to make recommendations regarding the best method of asset allocation. The task is not easy, I assure you! At best, each investment committee makes an educated guess about probable outcomes based on past history, and casts future predictions about the overall economy and individual corporate profits.

Lessons to be learned from past performance *are* important. The Vanguard Group is a major mutual fund complex. Take a look at the Vanguard Group's recommendations for asset allocation based on an investor's age, and how it would have fared over the time span from 1926–1994:

Retirement (Your Age)	College Savings (Child's Age)	Recommended Asset Allocation	Historic Returns
20–49	0–10	Growth 80% Stocks 20% Bonds	+9.5%
50–59		Moderate Growth 60% Stocks 40% Bonds	+8.5%
60–74	11–14	Conservative Growth 40% Stocks 40% Bonds 20% Cash Reserves	+7.3%
75+		Income 20% Stocks 60% Bonds 20% Cash Reserves	+6.0%

Source: *The Vanguard Investment Planner,* 1995.

Are You Ready to Risk It?

For the sake of this exercise, let's suppose that each reader of this book has decided to start making investments in the marketplace. The first step is to check out the standard asset allocation philosophy at this point in time. We find that the experts at virtually all major investment firms are currently recommending an asset allocation of 50% in stocks, 30% in bonds, and 20% in cash. These "experts" may very well be 100% right, but even so that's *not* the single most important factor when it comes to deciding how we should allocate our money. Of *paramount* importance is the individual investor's own totally honest assessment of her *own* individual level of risk tolerance. An investor who misjudges that key factor, as noted earlier, will probably end up selling off much of her portfolio at the most inopportune time. Making investments then becomes nothing more than a high-stakes game of "chicken," with significant losses whenever the market turns even slightly in an unfavorable direction.

If you're resolutely risk averse, it's no crime to restrict yourself to totally "safe" investments for the rest of your life! However, if you *are* able to accept some risks for potentially greater rewards, you would probably be wise to start with small risks and eventually work into some of the less safe methods of asset allocation. If you want to hold 90% of your savings in cash and only 10% in stocks until you feel safer about risking your money—that's certainly your privilege! What follows is an objective look at a number of different methods of asset allocation, and how they've fared in the past. Particular attention is paid to the size of loss (where applicable), and to exactly how many times such investments have proved to be losers over the 68-year period in question.

INVESTMENT RISK: 1926–1994

Your Asset Allocation	Number of Years with a Loss	Average Loss	Two-Year Loss in 1973–1974 Bear Market	Worst Annual Loss (1931)
Growth	1 in every 4 (19 out of 69)	−10%	−30%	−36%
20% Bonds				
80% Stocks				
Moderate	1 in every 4 (16 out of 69)	−8%	−22%	−28%
40% Bonds				
60% Stocks				
Conservative	1 in every 5 (15 out of 69)	−5%	−12%	−19%
20% Cash				
40% Bonds				
40% Stocks				
Income	1 in every 6 (12 out of 69)	−3%	−3%	−12%
20% Cash				
60% Bonds				
20% Stocks				
Stocks (S&P 500 Index)	Bonds (Long-term U.S. government)	Cash Reserves (U.S. T-bills)		

Source: Vanguard Investment Planner, 1995.

Although I worked on Wall Street as a derivatives salesperson, I was quite risk averse with my own money. My dad, having survived the Depression, was always unflaggingly risk averse, and I followed suit. I hated losing money, and hence was handicapped by an almost irrationally low risk-tolerance level. I spent roughly 18 years of my career trying to hedge the risks of portfolios rather than being an active participant in the market. (I was like the security guard hired to make sure that nothing terribly violent happened to any of my clients attending the "party.") For every penny I earned that had risk attached, I paid a high price in emotional pain and torture.

Eventually, as I acquired more market knowledge and savoir-faire, I became more comfortable with allocating my assets to include the sort of volatile technology stocks that can fluctuate wildly in either direction. I also started to make venture capital investments. But I certainly didn't start out buying the Intels and Microsofts of the world! In fact, every time I bought a volatile stock, I discovered that I couldn't take the heat. Invariably, the moment the price of the stock moved against me, I sold out at a loss.

I had a difficult time learning how to handle any sort of risk at all. Fate taught me that valuable lesson. I fell madly in love with a very handsome and charming man. Johnny could "pull the trigger" (buy a stock) every time someone mentioned one that looked appealing; I was the complete opposite! I could tolerate only a little in the way of risk—but certainly did a lot of homework—while Johnny took tremendous risks without even opening the textbook, so to speak. After six months with Johnny, I was left with a broken heart (that's the bad news). The goods news is that Johnny was the catalyst who actually helped me take risks in the marketplace. Thanks to my exposure to risk I began to move my assets from safe Treasury bills into balanced mutual funds, intermediate corporate bonds, and eventually to stocks like Intel, Cisco, and Microsoft.

Most women probably need a training course in how to tolerate risk. When I was a freshman in college, I took a course in child psychology. In that course, we focused on a study of differences in behavior between male and female toddlers. The researchers placed each two-year-old child into an individual plastic cubicle—as cruel as that sounds in retrospect! The behavior of the children remains etched in my mind. Each little boy tried to get out, banging against every side and trying to push the clear plastic walls down—anything to escape! On the other hand, each little girl sat in the middle of the box and began to cry.

The study was examining whether this behavior was genetically or environmentally determined. Regardless, being helpless is something that none of us can afford to live with. To achieve the goals we set for ourselves, we must exercise our rights and follow our dreams—simply because life itself entails risk.

The fact is, risk is quantifiable. The investment process is much like learning to drive: you don't go 60 miles per hour until you're a competent driver! Learning to invest is much the same. Not all of us can win the Indy 500—most of us don't even want to try—but most of us do learn to drive at normal speeds.

YOUR MONEY *AND* YOUR LIFE

My parents' marriage has survived quite nicely for the past 43 years, which is probably why I still believe in the sanctity of marriage and hope someday to say confidently "I do"—to the right guy, of course! I've always considered myself fortunate to have been brought up in a home where my parents truly loved each other.

Before You Say "I Do" … Love and Money

Unfortunately, few marriages of my own generation stand the test of time. As I'm sure you know, roughly fifty percent of all marriages have ended in divorce over the course of the last 20 years. This is not what the "blushing bride" (or groom, for that matter) wants to think about walking down the aisle, but these are nevertheless the cold, hard facts! That's why it's truly necessary for a man and a woman to plan pragmatically on the real possibility of spending their lives "without" each other—while at the same time hoping for the best and pledging "till death do us part."

I myself believe that raising children and tending to a home is a tremendously difficult and time-consuming job. I salute motherhood, but at the same time I know full well how many of us need to work not just for intellectual stimulation or luxuries, but simply to make ends meet. Still, those of us who choose to be full-time mothers may be left quite vulnerable financially (if not downright penniless) in the aftermath of a divorce. Should we wish to return to the work force later in life, our earnings potential is probably slim.

In order to obtain an expert opinion of a woman's rights in the event of divorce, I spent a few hours with Allan J. Berke, one of the top matrimonial attorneys in New York. Allan has seen firsthand an endless stream of unnecessary pain and trauma inflicted—on both spouses and their offspring as well—as brutal divorce scenarios work themselves out. That's why Allan recommends that no couple even contemplate marriage without a fully worked-out agreement in the event of divorce! Since matrimonial laws vary from state to state, you must do your own research. For New York and many other states, the following will hold.

THE MARRIAGE CONTRACT: STARTING OFF SMALL

Allan believes that *before* the wedding, when both parties are in a rational state, prospective spouses should execute a *marriage contract*, an organized plan by which they agree on each and every issue that might result should the marriage crumble. (Regardless of the fact that you and your intended are head-over-heels in love, keep in mind that "Things change!") This contract should thoroughly address issues such as the division of assets and liabilities, as well as custody of the children—not to mention the family pets! Marriage contracts are quite affordable and should perhaps be thought of as "insurance policies" with a small, one-time cost! At the time of this writing, a marriage contract should cost no more than $1,000. All it takes is for you and your future spouse to meet with an attorney and engage in a friendly planning session.

A marriage contract works best for individuals who come into the marriage on a more or less equal financial footing. Again, it's only necessary to retain the services of a single attorney to work out the details of such a contract. On the other hand, the only way for a "monied" spouse, whether man or woman, to protect his or her assets completely in the event of a divorce is by means of a *prenuptial agreement*. As Allan puts it, the money is primary, the gender irrelevant. From a legal standpoint, the court's primary concern is that the prenuptial agreement was prepared in such a way that both parties enjoyed an equal bargaining position. That's a major difference between a marriage contract and a prenuptial—the latter requires the services of two separate attorneys, one representing each party in the marriage.

THE PRENUPTIAL: FOR THOSE WITH MORE TO LOSE

A prenuptial agreement serves to protect the monied spouse from being taken to the cleaners. While it could be either, most commonly this means the man. More typically, the wife is being left. It is important, therefore, to guarantee some degree of financial security for yourself, especially if you've given up your earning power in order to raise children and run a household. Should your marriage end, you need to have funds set aside that will enable you to maintain the lifestyle to which you've been accustomed, and perhaps to further your education and prepare your reentry into the work force.

Here are the steps Allan suggests you take to ensure an equitable prenuptial agreement:

1. Hire a specialist rather than a generalist. Consult a good matrimonial attorney (ideally, a member of The American Academy of Matrimonial Attorneys) who strictly limits his or her practice to matrimonial law. It's absolutely essential that both parties to the agreement have competent legal counsel.

2. Keep in mind that no prenuptial agreement is valid without an "adequate disclosure of assets." Simply, you must tell it like it is.

3. For an agreement to be upheld in a court of law, it must be "fair and reasonable," and mustn't appear one-sided in any way.

Allan adds that a prenuptial agreement should be renegotiated every five years, in order to take into account changes that may have occurred in either spouse's financial affairs. He notes that the average fee for a prenuptial agreement is $7,500—but far more important than the price-tag of your counsel is the degree of personal confidence and trust you can place in the client-attorney relationship. The average retainer for a litigator for divorce proceedings is about $10,000, and the average divorce takes at least one year.

Allan stresses that the law regards what each party brings into the marriage as "separate property." Consequently, if you are the monied spouse, it's extremely important *not* to comingle "separate property" with "marital assets." To illustrate this point, Allan relayed a fascinating story about a male heir of a Fortune 500 company who kept his stock in an account at one of the larger brokerage firms. His wife of only a few years suddenly decided to go back to school, so he arranged for her to have a checking account tied into his hitherto "separate" brokerage account. While this act was meant only to make his wife's expenditures more convenient, it soon proved to have disastrous consequences. When the marriage came to an abrupt end, the husband discovered that the checking account had effectively comingled what would otherwise have remained his own separate assets. As a result of this joint brokerage account, his "ex" would soon wind up owning a sizable portion of the family wealth. The bottom line: once you comingle "marital" and "separate" funds, you take on the legal obligation of disproving the court's assumption that the property is in fact "joint." This legal principle is officially known as *the fruits of the poisonous tree doctrine.*

The degree to which "separate" property appreciates in worth is subject to a determination of whether such growth in value is "passive" or "active" in nature. What's referred to as *passive appreciation* happens, for example, when either spouse owns a tract of land that increases in worth because a private individual, business concern, or government entity wants to build on that land. Such appreciation remains separate.

Active appreciation occurs, for example, if you successfully increase the worth of your assets by investing in the market—either by doing your own homework or with the assistance of a money manager, or if you profit from renovating a piece of property and reselling it. Your spouse will be entitled to such appreciation of your assets, *unless* stipulated otherwise in a prenuptial agreement.

Marital assets, meaning the property accumulated after the wedding vows have been exchanged, fall under something known as the *Equitable Distribution Statute.* The result of this statute is that a nonmonied spouse becomes entitled to up to 50% of such marital assets—tax free, no less! The actual amount that may be awarded is usually subject to the length of the marriage and a number of other variables. Most of us think a 50/50 division is fair, because the concept of an equal partnership is fundamental to the way we think of marriage—at least in the nineties.

THE CHILDREN

We've thus far neglected to mention the most important "assets" of all, which of course are a couple's offspring. It goes without saying that a strong marriage contract or prenuptial agreement will make an eventual divorce proceeding much smoother for everyone involved—including the children. For the record, Allan notes that a child's mother is granted custody in roughly 80% of all instances.

THE ATTORNEY

Divorce is a reality, one that often takes on surreal if not downright nightmarish proportions! Berke (himself a matrimonial attorney of the "good guy" variety) points out that many divorce lawyers do their best to create major battles between the parties, simply to rack up larger fees.

He strongly urges any party to a marriage contract or prenuptial agreement to acquire the services of the very best matrimonial attorney available. Allan emphasizes that it's not justice that prevails, but rather the sheer *power* wielded by your lawyer. By all means, consult with as many attorneys as possible before selecting one and extending a retainer.

Here's a fascinating fact for prospective brides to keep in mind: Berke points out that your husband is automatically disqualified from using each and every attorney with whom you have a consultation. (The converse is equally true, of course.) It's not at all uncommon for the husband and/or wife to interview as many attorneys as possible for that reason alone. Particularly if you're a married woman with high net worth, it's important to speak to the best attorney in town *before* your husband does!

Again, as Allan puts it so well, "Justice is not necessarily the deciding issue." The best way to ensure the most amicable divorce possible (while still hoping for a lifetime of marital bliss) is to come to a full agreement about this worst-case scenario in advance. Doing so could save both you and your spouse a small fortune in legal fees—not to mention what could be many years of heartache. In the event you find yourself moaning about the fact that "love is blind," having a fair and equitable marriage contract or prenuptial agreement firmly in place at least offers some rays of light at the end of the tunnel!

Buy or Rent: There's No Place Like Home

In the eighties, buying real estate in New York City was definitely the "in" thing to do. Everywhere I went, people kept asking, "Marlene, why do you still rent instead of own?" Despite my peers' unbridled enthusiasm for real estate, I continued to resist. At the time, one-bedroom apartments in New York were selling at roughly $125,000 to $175,000. The properties up for sale never seemed to be "special" in any way, and the monthly maintenance charges that came with them were far too high for my liking.

I kept hearing the question, "How could you not avail yourself of the mortgage-interest tax deduction?" Still, I steadfastly kept on renting because the basic mathematical equation attached to buying a condo or coop always seemed out of whack. Most of my friends who purchased New York City apartments moved to the suburbs for one reason or another within three years or so—often because they needed more space due to marriage and kids. More often than not, they ended up taking substantial losses on the Manhattan homes they'd purchased. (So much for the theory that real estate prices *always* go up.) The moral of the story is clear: Just because everyone else is in the mood to buy a home, doesn't mean that you should follow the pack!

Buying a home (whether an apartment or house) should be a lifestyle decision rather than a financial one. The price of real estate, just like the price of stocks, fluctuates—and it's a mistake to assume that the value of a home will continually rise. The fact is that real estate has increased in value only at a rate of approximately 3% per year over the long haul, which barely beats the green-eyed monster, inflation.

I can't stress enough how important it is to take a mid-term view when contemplating the purchase of a home. Be confident that you really want to live in that home for a considerable amount of time, because the costs associated with making the purchase are high—approximately 5 to 10%. Even if the property actually appreciates significantly in value, the transaction costs alone can wipe out whatever gain you might have stood to make.

The point is that you should never buy into the myth that you'll always make money buying real estate. Making the right decision requires a good deal of homework, so it's essential to acquaint yourself with the language of real estate—and the math associated with making a purchase. Let's begin by examining the three types of real estate from which to choose:

1. *Condominiums.* The purchase of a "condo" grants the purchaser a title to the living space. Unless the condo is paid for completely in cash, which is extremely rare, the purchaser arranges for an independent mortgage loan. The purchaser is charged monthly maintenance costs, which cover a pro-rata share of maintaining whatever common areas are shared by all the building's tenants (the lobby area and security guards' salaries, hallways, gardens, parking lots, and so forth). Such services are contracted for and managed by what's known as a *homeowners' association.* A prospective buyer is advised to obtain a copy of the association's articles of incorporation, bylaws, conditions, restrictions, and house regulations.

2. *Cooperatives.* A purchaser of a "coop" actually purchases shares in the corporation that owns the building. A single mortgage loan is taken out by the corporation, which means that if any given shareholder is unable to pay (or for whatever reason fails to pay) his or her share, the other shareholders must make up the difference. Not surprisingly, anyone seeking to purchase a cooperative must be approved by a specified majority of the shareholders.

3. *Single-family homes.* Otherwise known as "the American dream," owning a private residence is what most individuals or families aspire to. A homeowner needs only to comply with local zoning codes and maintain the integral structure of the house. Before purchasing a house, it's absolutely essential for most of us to hire an engineer to thoroughly assess its sturdiness and anticipate any repairs that might be needed, both present and future.

Now that you know the options, the first step is to analyze which purchase makes the most sense to you. (But don't let anyone dissuade you from continuing to rent your home or apartment if the disadvantages of purchasing a home outweigh the benefits.)

ADDING UP THE COSTS

Should you decide to "take the plunge" and purchase a home, it's essential to anticipate what the various expenses will amount to. You should never place yourself in financial jeopardy, so it's important to be realistic rather than let yourself be swept away. Why be realistic? If, for any reason you are not able to meet your mortgage payments or taxes, you risk forfeiting your home.

No matter which purchase option you choose, your monthly housing costs will be the following: (1) your mortgage payment, which is made up of both principal and interest; (2) the amount of property taxes you must pay—which varies not only from state to state, but from county to county; (3) your monthly insurance total, which normally includes homeowners' insurance and private mortgage insurance; and (4) monthly maintenance costs, which are generally applicable to condos, co-ops and homes in "gated" communities or communities with homeowners' associations. As a single family homeowner, you should also figure the maintenance and utilities services that you must contract on your own such as heat, hot water, electricity, garbage pickup, and so forth.

The types of insurance include *homeowner's insurance,* which covers destruction to your home or its contents, and *private mortgage insurance,* which is a policy guaranteeing that the insurance issuer will continue to make payments on the mortgage should you be unable to do so. Whoever is issuing the mortgage is, in effect, making you pay for insurance to cover the potentiality that you will default on payments.

According to most mortgage brokers, the total of items 1 through 4 should not be greater than 28% of your gross monthly income. In other words, if you make $60,000 per year, you should not place yourself in the position of paying more than $1,400 per month in the total expenses associated with the purchase of your home. Using a $60,000 per year income as our example, here's how the equation works out mathematically:

Monthly Payment Cap = Annual Gross Income × 28%, divided by 12
= $60,000 × .28 ÷ 12
= $1,400

Should you owe money to others—amounts you must pay on an automobile loan or credit cards, for example—it's important to add up your monthly debt plus housing costs. The general rule of thumb is that this total shouldn't exceed 36% of your gross monthly income.

These formulas are what most lenders use to prequalify a prospective purchaser for a mortgage. Put simply, a *mortgage* is nothing more or less than the loan one takes out in order to purchase a home. It's collateralized by the home itself—a fact that should not be taken lightly. Failure to make timely mortgage payments may very well result in the loss of your home, which is why it behooves you to purchase only what you know you can afford.

Most lenders require a down payment between 10 and 20% of the value of the property. You can also look forward to (or, rather, dread) paying a number of significant closing costs, which normally vary anywhere between 5 and 10% of the total purchase price. These *closing costs* include actually buying the title to the home, as well as a number of charges associated with its financing. Any prospective homeowner soon learns that he or she will have a number of folk "on the payroll," so to speak—including various attorneys, appraisers, and engineers. Chances are that the bank or lending institution you deal with will also hit you up with the costs associated with checking out your credit. In short, you must be prepared to shell out a significant amount of money to cover each and every expense that's tied into the actual purchase of the home.

Speaking of closings costs … one substantial portion of same is something known as *points,* a one-time-only expense that represents what your bank or other lending institution charges for having made the loan. Invariably, one point equals 1% of the entire loan but lenders offer a wide range of both interest rates and points. Generally, a loan with the higher points has the lower interest rate. A loan with lower points generally involves a higher interest rate. Don't worry, you don't need a Ph.D. in math to calculate the costs of buying a home and keeping up with the monthly expenses of owning it. Uncle Sam requires all qualified lenders to spell out fully for you the annual percentage rate (APR) associated with the mortgage, including the interest rate, the points, and the applicable private mortgage insurance.

One point on a 30-year loan at an 8% interest rate would make for an annual percentage rate of 8.11, whereas two points would cause the APR to increase to 8.21%. When calculated over a period of 30 years, you'll find that these innocuous-seeming single-digit percentages add up to a sizable amount on top of the original principal you paid for your home. That's why, when shopping around for a loan, it's absolutely key to ask what the APR will be, because this information enables you to make an intelligent financial comparison between the various mortgage loans being offered by a host of lenders.

FINDING A LENDER

"Where do I go to obtain my mortgage?" you ask. A homeowner's mortgage can be obtained through a wide variety of sources, including (to start with the most obvious) mortgage companies, banks, credit unions, and state or local housing agencies. In Chapter 7, you already became acquainted with the government agencies commonly known as "Freddie Mac" and "Fannie Mae," each of which lends money to first-time purchasers of homes. Each of these lending institutions is able to offer two types of mortgages—"fixed-rate" and "adjustable."

FIXED- VERSUS ADJUSTABLE-RATE MORTGAGES

Fixed-rate mortgages are generally of two types: 15-year and 30-year. As the name implies, a fixed-rate mortgage means that the interest rate will remain the same over the entire life of the mortgage. On the other hand, the interest rate for an adjustable-rate mortgage is subject to change, and fluctuates according to the interest rate prevailing in the economy. Should you be fortunate enough to purchase a home in a relatively low-interest-rate environment, it's generally wise to lock in a fixed-rate mortgage. Keep in mind that, should interest rates decline further by any substantial amount, you can always *refinance* the mortgage—that is, renegotiate the interest rate so as to pay off the original loan with a lower-rate mortgage. Refinancing will have some upfront costs attached.

On the other hand, availing yourself of an adjustable-rate mortgage dramatically increases your vulnerability to high interest rates. Should presently prevailing rates be relatively moderate or low, an adjustable-rate mortgage is obviously not the best choice, since a prospective homeowner should try to avoid being vulnerable to a drastic upswing in interest rates. The advantage to an adjustable-rate mortgage is that it carries what's known as an *annual cap* (normally 2%) as well as a *lifetime cap* (roughly 6% at present) on the interest rate associated with the loan. By no means let yourself be fooled by the single-digit numbers, however! One needs only work out the math to discover that a 6% boost in the interest rate effectively increases your monthly mortgage payments by roughly *50%*!

Another facet of the adjustable-rate mortgage is that it's invariably tied into a specific index rate. The more common indices are the following:

1. *The contract rate.* This is what's known as the *domestic average interest rate* on mortgages for purchases of occupied homes.

2. *The six-month Treasury bill rate.* You're already familiar with this rate from Chapter 6, so I'll just remind you that in recent years it's tended to fluctuate from 3 to 6%.

3. *One-year constant maturity.* This refers to the average yield on Treasury bills, as adjusted to a constant maturity of one year.

No matter which way you slice it, however, financing a mortgage via an adjustable-rate loan leaves you vulnerable in the event of an interest-rate hike.

CAN YOU AFFORD YOUR DREAM HOUSE?

Suppose our newlyweds have just located a beautiful home with a white picket fence in the suburbs of San Diego—and fallen madly in love with it. Let's further assume that our fictitious couple makes a combined total of $150,000 per year. Here's how they calculate whether or not the upfront cost of this home will be affordable (you must also leave room for the maintenance costs associated with owning a home):

▶ The purchase price of the home is $200,000.

▶ The down payment is 25% of purchase price, for a total of $50,000 in cash.

▶ The amount of the mortgage loan they require is therefore $150,000.

▶ They decide on a fixed-rate mortgage. The prevailing 30-year mortgage rate is between 7-1/4 and 8-1/4%, and the couple lock in on a loan with an APR of precisely 8%.

▶ The total of all the various settlement costs will be 8% of the $200,000, which means an additional cash outlay of $16,000.

▶ The total cash the couple will need to take to the closing is therefore $66,000 (down payment plus settlement costs).

▶ The property taxes associated with the home are $5,000 per year.

▶ Insurance is $600 per year.

With the foregoing information in hand, the couple can easily calculate the total of their pretax monthly payment obligation on the mortgage, according to the following formula:

Pretax Monthly Charges =	
*Monthly Principal Plus Interest =	$1,100.65
Monthly Property Tax	= $ 416.00
Monthly Insurance	= $ 50.00
Total:	$1,566.65

To calculate how much a mortgage will run, purchase or obtain a copy of *Barron's Financial Table for Mortgages.*

We've already established that the monthly gross income of the couple in question equals $12,500. From this, we can easily deduce that $1,566.65 divided by $12,500.00 = 12.5%. The rule of thumb for most mortgage companies is that anything under 28% allows an individual to be qualified in making a purchase in accordance with their means.

After-tax costs would be calculated as well. Our fictitious couple is making $150,000 per year, so they're at a 31% federal tax level. The deductible interest can be calculated using *Barron's Financial Table for Mortgages.* In this case, it would be $11,956 for the first year of the mortgage. Accordingly, their deductible property tax would equal $5,000. The total interest and property taxes would be $16,956. Deductible tax and interest reduces income tax by $16,956 times 31%, for a total of $5,256 per year. It follows that

$5,256 divided by 12 equals $438 per month. After-tax costs equals $1,566.65 minus $438.00 for a total of $1,128.00.

The bottom line? If your financial situation is fairly healthy, it often makes sense to own. However, one must always take into consideration such factors as overall objectives, location (location, *location!*), and all other costs associated with the purchase of a home.

Overcoming the College Tuition Blues

Let's assume that life is blissful, the marriage is great, the home is beautiful—and the proverbial stork has delivered the first-born offspring. Suddenly, you are thinking 18 years into the future when your child graduates from high school.

The shocking truth is that tuition plus room and board at a private college (even at the present rate) is roughly $25,000 per year. How will any of us be able to put our daughters and sons through medical and law school?

If you are not immediately able to set up a trust fund for your child(ren), it's already time to start worrying. The average tab for four years at a private college is approximately $95,000; a public college runs about $45,000. If those figures aren't enough to give you heartburn, the cost of a private college education is projected to rise to approximately $170,000 by the year 2007, whereas public college expenses should run roughly $80,000. (Note that we haven't even begun to think about graduate school and already many of us have totally depleted our bank accounts!)

Even if your child is in the very highest percentile of his or her class, landing scholarships or grants is likely to get tougher in the future. According to the U.S. Department of Education, college enrollments are expected to increase roughly 14% by the year 2007. Don't fool yourself that financial aid will be automatically available to your offspring, either. It's time to face up to the middle-class "catch 22": most of us have too much in assets to qualify for such grants.

Naturally, you can always plan on having your child enroll in the armed forces and trust that he or she will get a good education through the ROTC. But unless you want to impose that lifestyle choice (that is, military obligation) on your youngster, it's best to devise an alternate plan just as soon as you become an expectant parent. Even if you've missed that optimum "starting gate," it remains true that the present is the point of power—and it's far better to start saving for college late than never!

COMPUTING THE COSTS

The following chart from the experts at T. Rowe Price estimates what a four-year college education (either public or private) will cost between 1997 and 2016, assuming that there's a 6% increase in tuition and other costs per year. This "Start Saving Early" chart also calculates how much to save on a monthly basis, in the expectation that such investments will generate an 8% annual return. Brace yourself for some rather staggering numbers!

Years Until Student Begins College	School Year (Fall)	Projected Four-Year Total Cost		Monthly Savings	
		Public	Private	Public	Private
1	1997	$44,743	$94,416	$3,570	$7,533
2	1998	47,428	100,081	1,817	3,834
3	1999	50,274	106,086	1,232	2,600
4	2000	53,290	112,451	939	1,982
5	2001	56,487	119,198	764	1,612
6	2002	59,877	126,350	646	1,364
7	2003	63,469	133,931	562	1,187
8	2004	67,277	141,967	499	1,053
9	2005	71,314	150,485	450	950
10	2006	75,593	159,514	410	866
11	2007	80,128	169,084	378	798
12	2008	84,936	179,229	351	740
13	2009	90,032	189,983	328	692
14	2010	95,434	201,382	308	649
15	2011	101,160	213,465	290	613
16	2012	107,230	226,273	275	580
17	2013	113,664	239,849	261	552
18	2014	120,484	254,240	249	526
19	2015	127,713	269,495	238	503
20	2016	135,375	285,665	228	482

Source: T. Rowe Price Associates, Inc.

All that remains is to take a head count (how many children do you have or plan to have), then calculate how much total savings you'll need to sock away each month in order to give them a fighting chance to learn a profession and compete in what's sure to be an ever more challenging job market. Chances are that most of us would feel some fairly big-time guilt were we to deny our children a decent education when the time comes. Yet, should that time roll around and we haven't adequately prepared for such a financial burden, putting on a face mask and robbing the nearest bank isn't a satisfactory option.

INVESTING FOR YOUR CHILD'S FUTURE

The following means of financing your child's education are considerably more legitimate.

1. *Zero coupon bonds.* As you may recall, these bonds are heavily discounted, in order that they might be redeemed at maturity for their full face value. Since their duration is high, zero coupon bonds are significantly more volatile than other bonds that pay interest on a semiannual basis. You want to make sure that you won't need to cash the bonds in before maturity, as you could suffer losses from a climb in the interest rate. You *will* be taxed annually on these bonds. The decided advantage is that you can plan on having precisely the amount you need, when you need it. Should you find yourself able to buy zero coupon bonds during a period of high interest rates, you'll find they make a truly great investment.

2. *Mutual funds.* If you decide to go this route, pick and choose carefully—and by all means diversify. Timing becomes the all-important element, inasmuch as you want to ensure that there's enough time for your mutual fund portfolio to appreciate in value. Should you have from 11 to 18 years in which to plan on financing the kids' college tuition, long-term growth portfolios would probably be the best choice—perhaps diversifying your funds between a mixture of passive and active managers. Should you have less planning time (for example, 7 to 10 years), it's better to diversify between asset classes. Fidelity Mutual Fund Complex recommends a "wealth-building" portfolio, com-

posed of 65% stocks, 30% bonds, and 5% cash. Should you have only 4 to 6 years before your first-born heads off to college, a "moderate" portfolio is what Fidelity recommends, with an asset allocation of 40% stocks, 40% bonds, and 20% cash. As that first day of college edges ever near, you want most of your investment money to be in cash, because it's usually not possible to tolerate short-term fluctuations. Here are two ways in which to open up a mutual fund earmarked for a college nest egg you can bank on:

- Retain sole ownership of the mutual fund by keeping it in your name only, rather than jointly with your child(ren).

- Open up a *custodial account,* which is known more officially as establishing an "UGMA/UTMA custodial account"—inasmuch as such accounts are governed by the terms of The Uniform Gifts/Transfers to Minors Act. The account will be registered in your child's name, who will be able to take over full custody of same at an age somewhere between 18 and 21, depending on the state. The chief advantage of a custodial account is that some of the investment earnings are altogether exempt from federal income tax, while other amounts are taxed at your child's rate rather than yours. You can transfer $10,000 per year, or $20,000 per couple, to a child's UGMA/UTMA account without paying gift taxes. For any child younger than 14, the first $650 is tax free; amounts between $651 and $1,300 are taxed at 15%; while anything above $1,300 is taxed at your own (probably much higher) rate. One more twist: should your child be over the age of 14, amounts above $650 are taxed at 15%.

A WORD OF CAUTION: If you believe that your child may receive financial aid for college tuition, it's not wise to put savings (whether mutual funds or zero coupon bonds) in the child's name. Schools tend to assess the parents' assets, and estimate a maximum of 5.65% in determining the family's contribution to the cost of college—whereas they assess the child's assets at 35% of contributions to college costs.

Many mutual funds offer special college savings accounts and plenty of free advice to those seeking loans—so give the fund you have in mind a call or pay them a visit via the World Wide Web. When the time rolls around, don't worry that your money hasn't grown quite enough to pay those impending bills: saving such a great amount of money is difficult—but even a small amount in a college fund is considerably better than nothing. What you don't have, you can always borrow!

3. *Loans.* At present there are two subsidized loans known as the *Perkins* and *Stafford* loans. The Perkins currently carries a 5% interest rate, and is given to only the most needy applicants. The Stafford carries a variable interest rate, which is capped at 8.25%. Repayment doesn't begin until six months after the student graduates. Should you manage to obtain a subsidized loan, you aren't being charged interest until the expiration of a certain grace period after graduation—which basically means that you have the use of the funds for 4-1/2 years without paying interest. If you can't get a subsidized loan, however, the interest charges keep accruing while the student is still in school. The maximum an undergraduate can borrow with a Stafford loan is $17,125. Private loans are also available to students, but the interest rates are usually higher, and there's no interest rate cap. Parents can also borrow for undergraduates under a plan known as the Parent Loan for Undergraduate Students (PLUS), which allows parents with a satisfactory credit record to borrow up to the full amount needed with an interest rate cap of 9%. Some states offer better college loan programs than others, so by all means shop around.

The 1997 tax law creates a new education IRA, essentially a new kind of savings account. The contributions are not tax deductible, but earnings accumulate tax free. Withdrawals are tax free when used for undergraduate- or graduate-level tuition. In order to qualify, a single parent must have an income below $95,000 and a couple must have an income below $150,000.

Without a doubt, putting one's children through college entails enormous expense, but for most of us a better future for our kids is the single most important investment we can make in life.

Giving Something Back:
Charitable Contributions

In 1995, Americans gave $144 billion to charities, of which 88% was from individuals. [*Source: Giving USA*] Only 5% came from corporations. Once a person has achieved a measurable degree of success in life, it's important to give something back to the needy of the world. I've chosen to support education for individuals of merit who otherwise wouldn't have the opportunity to attend a good university.

I wouldn't be able to attend my own alma mater at today's prices, yet I know what an incredible difference my college experience has made in my life. I, therefore, get tremendous gratification from giving money for the education of others. I like to think that perhaps someday one of the students who receives financial assistance from me will come up with the cure for cancer. At the very least, perhaps that student will one day donate funds to support the education of others.

I was lucky enough to sit down with Inge Reichenbach, who serves as Vice President of Alumni Affairs and Development at Cornell University. Inge spoke with me about how to stretch one's charitable dollar.

To show what charity can do, Inge told me about Ezra Cornell, who started the University in 1865 with a $500,000 gift. Ezra had only a fifth-grade education himself, yet became wealthy after developing a machine that laid cables for the predecessor of AT&T. Ezra wanted to found an institution that would combine the liberal arts with practical, job-related training. According to Inge, Ezra also literally *invented* the concept of student aid by providing opportunities to work and go to school at the same time. (Because he was a self-made man, Ezra wanted to ensure that a college education would be affordable to everyone.) One person *can* make a difference. While you may not single-handedly endow a university, it's important to know your charity, and to make sure it's in line with your own personal values. After all, it's your money!

THE PERSONAL BONUS: WHAT GIVING GIVES BACK

According to Inge, women tend to make charitable contributions in order to foster change rather than to preserve the status quo. Women are also concerned with improving the quality of life for future generations, and are more likely than men to give to causes such as education and the environment. Unlike men, who are more peer motivated, women tend to be issue oriented. Another difference between women and men when it comes to charities is that men are more likely to limit their involvement to writing out a check, while women are prone to get involved and to give actively of their time as well as their money.

Inge relayed a wonderful story about a woman who was in the class of 1918 at Cornell's Law School, who couldn't find employment after graduation except as a secretary. Her boss advised her to invest in a stock known as IBM, so she took her measly paycheck and did so. Here's the punch line: when she died not long ago, she bequeathed $20 million to Cornell, enough to build a whole new wing at the law school.

She was wonderful to leave such a legacy, but in a sense she could have also given the students of Cornell some joy through meeting her and getting to know their benefactress while she was *alive*. Why not become closely involved with your favorite charity or charities in order to give of yourself as well as your funds? The institutions to which we give can give something back to us as well. Inge's advice is that we should allow ourselves to enjoy the great satisfaction that comes with giving to a worthy cause.

On that note, I can only say that my donations to charities over the years have brought me a host of wonderful new friends and business acquaintances, an incredible exchange of ideas with like-minded people, and an overall warm "fuzzy" feeling of satisfaction and contentment.

THE FINANCIAL BONUS: TAX BENEFITS OF GIVING WISELY

Charitable gifts are tax deductible for those who itemize. To take a tax deduction, the organization must be qualified as charitable by the IRS under Code Section 501. If you give more than $250, you must keep a copy of the receipt in order to take the deduction.

Should you donate clothes, furniture or other goods, you can deduct the current market value. Again, if the amount is greater than $250, you need to get a receipt from the charity. If your charitable donations of clothing, furniture, or other household items are greater than $500, you need to fill out a special tax form (8283).

Under the right circumstances, appreciated assets are also deductible. For instance, if you buy a stock and it goes up in value, you can give that stock to a charitable organization, and reap tax benefits. Let's say that I want to make a $10,000 gift to a qualified charity. I could either write a check for $10,000 or donate 100 shares of XYZ Company, which is presently trading at $100. Let's assume that my cost basis for XYZ, that is, the original price I paid for the stock, is $50 per share. If I donate appreciated stock, I don't pay capital gains tax, yet I can still deduct the entire $10,000 from my tax bill.

Let's compare the results, assuming I'm in a 39% tax bracket:

▶ Were you to donate $10,000 in cash, your tax savings would be equal to $10,000 times .39 for a total of $3,900. Accordingly, the actual cost for your having made the $10,000 donation would be $10,000 minus $3,900, which works out to be $6,100.

▶ Were you to donate stock, on the other hand, you would avoid the capital gains tax (which at present is 28% for assets held over one year and less than eighteen months, and 20% for assets held over eighteen months) that you would have incurred when selling the stock. Because you paid only $5,000 for the 100 shares of XYZ to begin with, your capital gain would be $10,000 minus $5,000, for a total of $5,000. The capital gains tax would ordinarily be $5,000 times .20, which is equal to $1,000, but by donating the stock to a legitimate charity, you won't personally be liable for paying such a tax. Nonetheless, you enjoy a nice tax deduction ($10,000 times .39 equals $3,900). And the final cost of your having donated $10,000 in appreciated assets to your favorite cause would be calculated as follows: $10,000 minus $3,900 minus $1,000 equals $5,100.

▶ All types of assets can be donated to qualified charities, but it's important to keep in mind that appreciated securities are deductible only up to 30% of the donor's adjusted gross income, cash up to 50%. Any unused deduction can be carried forward up to five additional years. A painting or a book must be donated to an institution that can demonstrate "related use"—i.e., that actually uses the book or the painting as part of its mission. Should the goods that are donated not be directly related to the purpose of the recipient charity, the tax deduction is based on a cost, rather than an appreciated cost, basis.

Should you be fortunate enough to have substantial assets to contribute to one or more charities, you will most assuredly require the services of one or more lawyers. Many types of trusts and foundations can be set up, but the processes involved are complex enough that you'll certainly need to consult with trust attorneys and accountants. Many institutions help administer the contributions according to your wishes—although such institutions often require that 50% of your contributions go to them! Should you want to make such donations to such a group anyway, it's wise to take advantage of foundation programs, since they will save you a great deal in administrative fees. These programs are known as *donor-advised funds,* and in most cases require a giving commitment of $25,000 or more. Chances are that your gift will be well managed. (For example, you can take a deduction for a gift, and have that sum of money allocated over a lengthy period of time—perhaps many years into the future—and to several different charitable organizations.) If this sounds like an option of interest to you, simply consult the folk at your favorite charity!

Three types of trusts are associated with charitable giving: charitable remainder trusts, charitable lead trusts and wealth replacement trusts. Each serves a different purpose. In each case, you need the assistance of a qualified professional. Most people don't start to think about trusts until planning where to give their money on death, sad to say. The fact is, charitable giving can greatly enhance and enrich your life—while you're still alive!

I hasten to add that one doesn't necessarily have to be rich to be involved in charitable giving. Most charities welcome with open arms all those who are willing to donate their time, even if they're unable to give from their personal finances. My advice is to give what you can. Charity will enrich your life.

Planning for Retirement

Anyone approaching the age of 40 should certainly begin planning for the future. (Ideally, you should start preparing for retirement as soon as you start your first job.) Why?

1. You can't count on social security being there for you by the time you retire.

2. Our life spans have increased, so retirement years will be considerably longer than previously estimated—which means that our savings will need to last longer, as well.

3. Most companies are no longer providing for their employees' retirements, and lifelong employment is a thing of the past.

4. With the increasing rate of divorce, you can no longer count on marital support for the course of a lifetime.

As psychologically discomforting as we may find the thought of growing old, consider the alternative! We should all plan ahead, in order to make sure to enjoy our golden years without constant financial worries. Today, the median income of American women aged 65 or older is roughly $9,500 per year. Much of that comes from the social security system, and we don't now know what the future of that system will hold.

SAVE NOW, PAY LATER: TAX INCENTIVES

We must therefore adequately provide for our own retirements. Uncle Sam has assisted by creating some tax breaks for those who avail themselves of 401(k) and 403(b) plans, IRAs, SEP-IRAs, KEOGHs, and annuities.

A considerable number of corporations still offer pension plans. (So do various government agencies.) These are known as *defined benefit plans*—that is, employer-paid retirement plans. Such plans specify the payment you will receive at retirement, which is normally calculated through a formula that factors in the employee's compensation and years of service.

However, the trend these days is toward *defined contribution plans,* in which the employee bears most of the financial burden for his or her 401(k) or 403(b) plan—although the employer often makes a contribution as well. The former are offered to employees in the private sector; the latter to those who work for charitable organizations. (They are basically the same sort of plan.) In either case, the employee contributes a certain portion of his or her income each year. Some companies offer to match the amount of such contributions; other firms do not. The best news is that any funds in such savings plans are not taxable until withdrawn at retirement.

Should you earn $60,000 per year, and contribute $3,000 into your retirement plan, you will be taxed only on $57,000. (The maximum contribution you can make is $9,500.) Most employers offer a variety of investment choices by which you can diversify assets in your plan: usually a growth portfolio, a balanced portfolio, a fixed income portfolio, and money market funds for the more risk averse. Many companies offer a variety of mutual funds, including emerging markets and international funds. There may be as many as 30 different mutual funds from which to choose, so it's important that you choose wisely.

Moreover, some firms offer their own stock as an investment vehicle. You may not want to exercise this option, however, since it's "putting all one's eggs in one basket." One friend of mine put all of her life savings (approximately $80,000) in her company's stock. The firm went bankrupt, which meant she not only lost her job—but her savings as well! If you really believe in the future of the firm for which you work, then by all means invest some of your money in its stock. On the other hand, don't put yourself at too much risk should such a worst-case scenario happen to you!

Another investment vehicle many corporations offer is what's known as a *guaranteed investment contract* (GIC). This interest-bearing deposit is guaranteed by an insurance company. During the early nineties, many of these insurance companies became vulnerable due to shaky real estate investments like the Citicorp loan portfolio discussed in Chapter 8. Some actually went bankrupt, so it's a good idea to ask your human resources department about the credit rating of the insurance company that issues the GIC.

Those who are relatively young should consider the 401(k) plans for allocating the majority of the funds in a growth portfolio—unless interest rates are extremely high at the time of allocation. Most plans allow for the flexibility to switch choices. All the income, dividends, and capital gains are free from taxation, and the money you'll save will add up to a significant amount over time.

The money you contribute is yours, whereas the amount the employer contributes doesn't actually belong to you until you are *vested,* that is, until you have been with the firm for a specific length of time (usually two or more years). Should you leave the firm, you can either roll over your 401(k) into another company's plan or transfer it into an IRA direct rollover. Both Charles Schwab and

Fidelity offer wonderful plans through which you can choose from more than 500 funds—many of them of the no load variety. A small fee is usually involved, but such fees may be waived for those with IRAs of $30,000 or more.

The early withdrawal of any amount from a 401(k) means that you'll not only have to pay taxes on it, but be subject to a 10% penalty as well. Make sure that the funds you've earmarked for retirement actually remain there for you until you reach retirement age! You can begin to withdraw funds at the age of 59-1/2 without penalty. One final word of advice: never borrow against your 401(k) plan. You can't afford to jeopardize your savings. If you can't afford to make a purchase without dipping into your retirement savings, then by all means wait until you can.

Individual retirement accounts (more commonly known as IRAs) are another vehicle for accumulating tax-free savings. However, if you also have a 401(k) plan, the IRA generally loses its tax deductibility. You can contribute $2,000 per year if you hold a job, and—as of January 1, 1997—nonworking spouses are also eligible to contribute $2,000. Traditional IRAs are deductible if the individual makes less than $30,000 per year ($50,000 if married and filing jointly). Those income limits are to be increased to $50,000 for singles in 2005 and $80,000 for married couples filing jointly in 2007 and beyond.

Those individuals with a 401(k) who earn more than $40,000 ($60,000 for those married and filing jointly) may still contribute $2,000 per year to an IRA—but the contributions won't be deductible from your income. However, if a spouse is not an active participant in an employer-sponsored retirement plan, and the couple's adjusted gross income doesn't exceed $150,000, that participant can fully deduct the $2,000 IRA contribution.

The new tax law creates another type of IRA; the *Roth IRA*. Contributions to these accounts aren't deductible, but distributions will be tax-free if certain requirements are met. Roth IRAs are for individuals with adjusted gross income below $95,000 and for joint filers with adjusted gross income below $150,000.

Many options are available for asset allocation [cash, bonds, equity (stocks), international funds and emerging markets]. Brokerage firms, banks, and mutual funds are set up to house IRAs. It's wise to go directly to the mutual fund itself—or a discount broker—to cut out the middle man when availing oneself of a good IRA plan.

For those who are self-employed, a couple of retirement plans allow you to make larger contributions than a simple IRA.

1. A SEP-IRA (simplified employee pension) is very much like an IRA. You can contribute 15% of the first $150,000 of net earnings per year from self-employment up to a maximum of $22,500. Should you have employees, you may need to contribute for them as well.

2. Keogh is a plan for the self-employed. There are several types of Keoghs: with a defined contribution plan you can contribute up to $30,000 or 25% of compensation, whichever is less. There is also a profit sharing plan that allows you to contribute 15% of your first $150,000 in net earnings, up to a maximum of $22,500.

Both plans allow you to deduct the amount from your income, and permit it to grow tax free until you reach the age of 59-1/2. Just as with an IRA or 401(k), if you cash in on any of these plans before that age, substantial penalties apply.

One final way to stash some cash away for retirement is through an *annuity*. Suppose you have some money that won't be needed until your retirement, and it's presently invested in a mutual fund and/or Treasury bills—which means you're getting taxed on both capital gains and interest income. If you were to put this money into an annuity, any capital gains, interest income and/or dividends would not be taxed until withdrawal at age 59-1/2. Since you haven't been paying taxes in the interim, all of your money has been hard at work earning even more money for your retirement. It has lost a little bit of its desirability since the capital gain tax rate was cut. The annuity will be taxed as income so it depends on your future tax rate.

Another thing to keep in mind is that an annuity is a contract between you and an insurance company. This means that payment is directly tied to that company. If the firm fails, you risk losing the entirety of your assets. Since annuities are to be kept for many years, it's important to have confidence in the financial soundness of the insurance company with which you deal. Many mutual fund complexes offer annuities, and one can only hope that they've thoroughly investigated the insurance company that creates each contract!

To close out this section, the following three charts indicate the future value of saving different amounts of money on various schedules—assuming deferred taxation on the amounts saved:

FUTURE VALUE OF SAVING $100 PER MONTH
RATE OF RETURN*

Number of Years	4%	6%	8%	10%
10	14,725	16,388	18,295	20,484
20	26,361	46,204	58,902	75,937
30	69,405	100,452	149,036	226,049
40	118,196	199,149	349,101	632,408

*Assumes that savings are invested in a deferred retirement or annuity plan, which is not taxed until paid out.

Source: Retirement Security by David Walker (Exhibit 12-2), © 1997 John Wiley & Sons. Reprinted by permission of John Wiley & Sons, Inc.

TAX-FREE COMPOUND OF A $2,000 ANNUAL IRA CONTRIBUTION

Number of Years	4%	6%	8%	10%
5	10,833	11,276	11,735	12,212
10	24,012	26,363	28,975	31,877
20	59,556	73,574	91,529	114,557
30	112,170	158,122	226,576	329,005
40	190,051	309,534	518,135	885,230

Source: Retirement Security by David Walker (Exhibit 12-4), © 1997 John Wiley & Sons. Reprinted by permission of John Wiley & Sons, Inc.

ACCUMULATION OF $10,000 INVESTED TODAY

Number of Years	4%	6%	8%	10%
10	14,802	17,908	21,589	25,937
20	21,911	32,071	46,610	67,275
30	32,434	57,435	100,627	174,494
40	48,010	102,857	217,245	452,493

Source: Retirement Security by David Walker (Exhibit 12-19), © 1997 John Wiley & Sons. Reprinted by permission of John Wiley & Sons, Inc.

To sum up this section of the chapter, I feel compelled to remind you that, for safety's sake, you should avoid the "hot" mutual fund of the day and stick with funds that have good track records over the years. Moreover, it's important to be patient enough to survive the occasional (and inevitable) dips in the market without bailing out prematurely. Again, diversification is key.

Finally, as you can see from the foregoing three charts, it's never too early to start saving! For most of us, however, one of the major hurdles to overcome in saving money is the fact that Uncle Sam wants his share off the top.

Taxes: The Unavoidable

At a meeting of my university council, I stood next to a woman who was a vice chairwoman of a major corporation, as well as a trustee of the college, and a member of the boards of at least a dozen top-notch firms (including AT&T). Her advice to me was twofold: (1) get the money; and (2) don't do your own taxes.

I took this sage advice, called a CPA who happened to be an old friend from Jackson Heights, and left the April 15 blues to him from then on. Sure, I pay him—but, after all, it's a tax deduction!

Whether or not you hire someone to do your taxes, here's what you should know:

● Dividend and interest income are taxed as ordinary income.

● Short-term capital gains are taxed as ordinary income. Long-term capital gains are taxed at a maximum of 28% for assets held between one year and eighteen months, a maximum of 20% for assets held between 18 months and 5 years, and a maximum of 18% for assets held over 5 years.

● A couple can exclude up to $500,000 in capital gains from the sale of a home as long as it has been the primary residence of at least one spouse for two of the last five years. A single person can exclude up to $250,000 in capital gains.

● Each state has its own tax system, with New York and California being the most heavily taxed, and Florida and Texas the least.

- State taxes are deductible from federal tax.

- The average state and local tax is about 5%.

- Some states have wealth taxes, which levy an overall tax on a majority of your assets.

- Any sort of real estate entails a property tax, which is also deductible from the federal tax bite.

Always keep in mind that the government is your business partner—whether you like it or not!

Preparing a Last Will and Testament

Flashback to childhood: whenever my parents had to leave me in the care of another family member in order to take a trip, either for business or pleasure, my dad would invariably sit me down and explain where the family assets were held in the event anything should happen to them. Naturally, I would expect the worst and be totally devastated with worry until their safe return. My dad (a bit of a worrier himself) had only the best intentions but, since the family lawyer had Dad's will on file, which spelled out everything in detail, there was no real need for the two of us to have that sort of chat.

A *will* is usually a written statement which disposes of one's property after death. A *testator* is the masculine term for someone who makes out a will, while a *testatrix* is the female equivalent. The will becomes effective at such time as the testator or testatrix and the court jurisdiction accepts a written document as the final wishes of the deceased (a procedure known as *probating the will*). The testator or testatrix has the right to revoke the will at any time, however; indeed, it's recommended that wills be updated at least once every five years.

For a will to be legal, you must be at least eighteen years of age and of sound mind. The document must be signed by you, as well as by at least two credible witnesses. Wills can be kept at your lawyer's office, in a safe deposit box, or at the bank or trust company you've named as the will's executor. An *executor* or *executrix* is someone you appoint to administer your estate after your death.

Such person must be of [majority] age and may not ever have been convicted of a serious crime. Moreover, he or she must be a U.S. citizen and must *not* be a courtroom judge. (Some states impose additional restrictions.) It's important to appoint an executor or executrix who may not be construed to have a conflict of interest, such as would be the case with a business partner, for example. An executor is entitled to a commission on the estate, so it's wise to "keep it in the family" if at all possible!

Such commissions established by each state run as high as 9% for the first $20,000 of the estate, plus 3.6% of the balance. Let's suppose that an estate is worth $500,000. Here's how to calculate what an executor or executrix would make as a commission:

$$\$20,000 \times 0.09 = \$\ \ 1,800$$
$$\$480,000 \times .036 = \underline{\$17,280}$$
$$\text{TOTAL: } \$19,080$$

That's a fairly high fee merely for executing an estate, which is basically much ado about nothing. If you plan to leave your money to family members, I imagine you'd rather see such a sum go toward your grandchild(ren)'s education! As stated earlier, the services of a good attorney are essential, but a contract can probably be negotiated for a reasonable price.

I'm sure you won't be surprised to learn that your business partners in death (as in life) are the federal and state governments (not even in death do *you* part). Depending on the state in which you were residing at the time of your death, the executor or executrix of your will can expect to receive a *tax waiver*. The individual you've appointed must then move all checking and savings accounts—as well as stocks, bonds and mutual funds—into the name of your estate. Other assets, which likewise need to be placed into your estate, are life insurance policies, pension plans, union benefits, disability insurance claims, and any general partnerships.

Once the various assets are collected, they must be safeguarded with safety of principal and duly distributed to the beneficiaries. The executor must file with the courts a document called an *inventory* which lists each of the assets owned by the decedent at the time of his or her death. When all is said and done, it's time to pay good ol' Uncle Sam—as well as the state—something known as *death taxes,* which include the following:

1. Federal estate tax

2. State-imposed inheritance tax

3. State-imposed estate tax

The good news (even in death) is that, as an individual, you may transfer up to $600,000 to anyone you choose, and the entirety of an estate to a spouse (assuming he or she is a U.S. citizen), completely free of federal estate tax. You also benefit from an unlimited charitable deduction. Remember the story relayed in Chapter 4 about Anne Scheiber, the IRS employee who turned $5,000 into $22 million, then left it all to charity? Guess what? Her charitable act ensured that her "friends and colleagues" at the IRS wouldn't receive a single dime!

Once your charitable deductions have been factored in, your estate is subject to taxes if the remainder is valued at $600,000 or more. By the year 2006, the exemption will be increased to $1,000,000. After computing your estate tax, you must remember to deduct what's known as a *unified estate credit* (which is a maximum of $192,800). What follows is the unifed rate schedule, which should give you a rough idea of what your estate taxes will amount to.

Over	Up to	Tax Due
$500,000	$750,000	$155,800 + 37% of amount over $500,000
$750,000	$1,000,000	$248,300 + 39% of amount over $750,000
$1,000,000	$1,250,000	$345,800 + 41% of amount over $1,000,000
$1,250,000	$1,500,000	$448,300 + 43% of amount over $1,250,000
$1,500,000	$2,000,000	$555,800 + 45% of amount over $1,500,000
$2,000,000	$2,500,000	$780,800 + 49% of amount over $2,000,000
$2,500,000	$3,000,000	$1,025,800 + 53% of amount over $2,500,000
$3,000,000	Unlimited	$1,290,800 + 55% of amount over $3,000,000

With the help of the foregoing chart, it's easy enough to calculate what you would owe in estate taxes should, for example, your estate be worth $2 million after charitable deductions:

1. Two million dollars would be liable for $780,800 in estate taxes.

2. You could deduct the Unified Estate Tax Credit of $192,800, so your tax bill would equal $780,800 minus $192,800, for a total of $588,000.

Here's some good news: You can use a trust to reduce the estate tax as well as to bestow special provisions on family members. Again, it's essential to seek professional legal and financial advice, especially since so many types of trusts are available from which to choose.

Should you have young children, take special care to spell out your choice of guardian. Said guardian should be a family member or very good friend who has the physical and financial ability to take care of your children. The choice of guardian should be agreed to by both parents, as well as by the individual you've chosen for such a serious responsibility.

There's no way out of this world alive, sad to say, but here's hoping that each of you "live long and prosper"!

YOU CAN BE RICH, TOO!

I only wish there were "ten steps to financial success" so tried and true that all I need do was to list them and admonish you to commit them to memory. The truth is that people acquire wealth in many different ways, ranging from the slow and steady approach to the instant success that comes with choosing one singularly sensational investment.

Let Me Count the Ways ...

Consider this: Had you purchased a mere 100 shares of Intel when it was introduced to the marketplace in 1971, your $2,350 would have grown to more than $2 million by the end of 1996. A mere $2,000 investment in George Soros' Quantum Fund in 1969 would be worth more than $4 million today. A few smart cabbies in Rochester, New York, had the sense to put money into Xerox back in 1969. Chances are they leave the driving to others nowadays, comfortably settled into the back seats of stretch limousines!

I suppose I've been fortunate enough in the management of my own finances to travel in similar style, but I'm the sort of diehard spendthrift who prefers to save money by negotiating my way around the island of Manhattan by subway and cab. An added bonus is that I often get to meet the most interesting people. For example, not long ago, in a taxi after a business dinner, I engaged in casual conversation with the driver. He broke into a broad smile and became quite excited when I mentioned that I worked on Wall Street. In fact, he immediately sprang open the cab's glove compartment, which was filled to overflowing with papers related to his own stock portfolio. Before I knew it, he began reciting figures for the earnings growth and other margins for each of his holdings. My taxi driver was clearly doing his homework!

Do you recall Ann Scheiber? Think of the determination (to say nothing of "drive") it took for a 15-year-old to take a job as bookkeeper, eventually financing her way through law school. Imagine the disappointment Anne must have felt when, after finally passing the bar exam at the age of 32, she had to settle for a desk job with the IRS. As a woman (and a Jewish woman, at that) she had to endure the humiliation of being passed over each time an opportunity for promotion presented itself. According to an article by Frank Lalli in the January 1996 issue of *Money,* "Anne Scheiber ultimately concluded that she couldn't do much to change other people's prejudices, but she could do a lot to take care of herself." *She who laughs last, laughs best!* As you know, Anne turned $5,000 in savings and a small monthly retirement check into $22 million before she was through. What's even more impressive, Anne managed an average annual return of 22.2% on her investments over the course of 51 years. Compare that figure to a slightly better average return of 22.7% earned over 27 years by present-day investment genius Warren Buffett. Only time will tell whether Mr. Buffett will manage to hang onto his slim lead after the passage of another 24 years.

How did she do it? Anne Scheiber's talented broker of choice (William Fay of Merrill Lynch) is quoted as saying that she "nibbled" at various investments, usually buying only 100 shares of stock at a time. In his article in *Money,* Lalli goes on to describe a few lessons we can learn from Anne's financial strategies, which I've paraphrased for you:

1. Invest in the stock of firms that manufacture products you enjoy using, and in leading brands. Do homework on those stocks. (As an avid film lover, for example, Scheiber particularly enjoyed investing in the movie industry.)

2. Invest in stocks that demonstrate earnings growth, since a high P/E ratio is worth it if it's clear that the firm has the ability to increase profits.

3. Arrange to invest as automatically as possible (in good markets as well as bad), and keep reinvesting dividends over time.

4. Attend shareholders' meetings.

Anne frequently attended various shareholders' meetings in New York and compared her notes with those of the top analysts at her brokerage firm. Care to guess who fared better over the years? (I'll give you one clue: it wasn't Merrill Lynch!)

Savvy Tips from the Experts

I'm reminded of watching diners at an outdoor Florida restaurant not long ago, as they tossed pieces of bread from their plates to the catfish in the water. The catfish would all charge for the morsels at once, almost killing themselves (and each other) in the process. I noticed a single catfish who didn't follow the pack; instead, it searched out food in other places—and with considerably more success.

In the pages that follow, you're about to meet four highly successful portfolio managers, as well as the president of John A. Levin & Co., formerly the executive vice president of Smith Barney. I've asked each of them to "cast their bread upon the waters" by offering advice on how to choose individual stocks and mutual funds, as well as how to devise a game plan for asset allocation. The way I figure it, if these six "top guns" in the Wall Street arena can't teach average investors how to become rich, who can?

INVESTING FOR GROWTH: MAREN LINDSTROM

First, let me introduce you to a top-notch portfolio manager at the well-respected money management firm of Nicholas Applegate at its headquarters in San Diego. Maren Lindstrom's job is to run (manage) more than $4 billion in assets. Most of her investments are in firms with capitalizations anywhere between $500 million and $3 billion. For Maren Lindstrom, the name of the game is growth—and plenty of it!

To provide a bit of background: Maren lost her father when she was quite young and learned about money the hard way, by helping her widowed mom make ends meet. "I always wanted to be a money manager," she says now. Lindstrom studied economics at the University of Michigan, and received her MBA from UCLA in 1989. She began her career at Nicholas Applegate by running its $500 million convertible bond fund, and has been with the firm ever since.

I began my interview by asking Maren to offer a few tips to those who are risk averse when it comes to choosing stocks. "An interesting low-risk approach to stock investing is to use a convertible bond fund with a good track record," was her reply. "That sort of investment can provide you with roughly 80% of the upside potential of the market, accompanied by approximately 50% of the downside risk. Convertibles offer a yield via their coupons, and—unless the issuer of the bond is in financial jeopardy—convertibles retain a nice percentage of their value even when the stock market goes down."

Her advice to those who are comfortable with *some* degree of risk is to adopt what she calls *the Peter Lynch method*: once you see a product you like, take the time to research its manufacturer. She insists that one must remain objective when doing homework on a stock, and accumulate as much information as possible. "And remember that you don't buy stocks, you rent them!"

When it comes to choosing growth stocks, Maren recommends investing in firms that demonstrate accelerating growth in earnings, revenue, and cash flow. (The latter is defined as net earnings plus depreciation.) It's essential to examine the company's growth record in every respect, determine precisely what stage of the corporate cycle it's in, and evaluate the overall track record of its management. "Don't forget to take a look at the current competition," she cautions, "as well as what the barriers to entry are to would-be competitors."

To illustrate the latter point, Maren provided the following hypothetical example: suppose two different firms (Company A and Company B) are the nation's leading manufacturers of "widgets." One need only glance at the financial reports of Company A to realize that it's not just highly leveraged, but so much in debt that bankruptcy is a very real prospect. Since financial reports are publicly available to everyone, you can be sure that the management of Company B is well aware that its main competitor may soon go under. Company B may therefore be tempted to speed that day's coming by lowering its own prices, which could then be raised again (and then some) once it's cornered the widget market! Company B's eventual price increase should result in the growth of both margins and revenues, assuming that its management team is a good one.

The point Maren makes is that an investment in the stock of Company B looks like a smart move at first glance, yet there's always the "human error" factor to worry about. She warns that one must be particularly wary of managers who become overly confident once they've outpaced their competition (or virtually cornered the market, as in the case cited), as this sometimes leads to general sloppiness in running a business. Maren stresses how key a firm's management is to the growth one can expect from a stock. It's essential that the company's managers are the sort who continually try to upgrade the product or service involved, keep costs down, and keep customers happy. Whereas Maren's imaginary Company B looks like a sure-fire winner at first glance, if management isn't careful the firm may soon be forced into bankruptcy by a new competitor in the form of Company C!

It takes a good deal of courage to invest in a small firm that's just starting out, especially one with limited capital. In many cases, the company's most valuable asset may be nothing more than a brilliant idea—but who's to say where that will lead in time? Others may spot the same trend and try to cut themselves in on the action, or perhaps a few disgruntled workers will walk away from the firm and start up another business to compete with their former employer.

"Money managers study what the movers and shakers have up their sleeves at each stage of a company's life," notes Maren. "You want to find a company that knows how to manage its business at each stage. If the management team is good, the earnings will usually follow."

The important thing is not what management says, of course, but what it does. I asked Maren to cite an example. She'd recently had dinner with the chief financial officer of a company. She listened as he bragged about how incredibly well his firm was doing. When the company announced its earnings two days later, Maren discovered that his "big talk" had been nothing but talk. (Not that she had believed him.) No matter what the CEOs or CFOs of various companies tell her, she retains her objectivity and does her homework to separate fact from fiction. (I'll second that.)

Maren carefully examines all the company's financials before making each investment decision, then uses technical analysis to confirm the fundamentals. "If there's any 'red flag' raised in your mind at all about the prospects of a company," Maren advises, "then don't invest a dime of your money until the very last of those flags goes down!"

I asked Maren how many stocks a reader of this book should keep in her portfolio. She suggested that 20 should be sufficient for most investors, but added that a number of wonderful mutual funds are also available to the retail customer. "What's key is to do your homework and remain diversified," claims Maren. "And never let yourself get 'married' to a particular stock. Once you realize you've made a poor wager, don't try to rationalize your decision as you watch it go down in price. It's far better to sell quickly, and learn from your mistakes."

Maren's parting words of advice were earmarked for each of us: "Our social security checks and 401(k) plans won't suffice for a comfortable retirement," she warned, "so we really do need to put away for the future as much money as possible."

Maren and I are both self-confessed tightwads, and darned proud of it. (We both shared a laugh over the fact that Maren still has her childhood "piggy bank" filled with the coins she earned from her parents for having tidied up her room.) Perhaps we'd all be better off financially if we could rid our minds of the word's negative connotation. As Maren points out, *tightwad* is synonymous with *good money manager* because both hate to lose money!

Thanks for the great advice, Maren.

LOOKING FOR VALUE: JANE FREEMAN

Rockefeller & Co., headquartered in New York City, is a registered investment advisor with more than $4 billion under management— an outgrowth of the family office founded by John D. Rockefeller in 1882. The firm now manages money for both the Rockefeller family and other private investors.

One of many world-class portfolio managers you'll find there is a woman named Jane Freeman, who manages a total of roughly $500 million. She also serves as cochair of Rockefeller & Co.'s asset allocation committee. (In short, Jane is one busy lady!) I'm grateful that she found the time to share a few investment tips with me.

Unlike Maren Lindstrom, Jane didn't have a clue as to what she wanted to do for a living until some time after graduating from college. She studied mathematics and chemistry at Cornell, and then went on to earn her MBA in 1978.

Jane was "clueless" about the stock market, until she was hired as a summer intern in the research department of Citibank. Jane thought that trying her hand as an analyst would be a good way to check out which firms might make good employers, but soon discovered that she actually loved her job. She had no idea that it was only a matter of time before big-league CEOs and CFOs would be making presentations and trying to win her attention, rather than the other way around!

Her first job after graduation was with the well-known money management firm of Scudder, Stevens & Clark, where she served as junior oil analyst. "I didn't know a thing about oil," Jane admits, "but it was in an up-cycle and Scudder needed more people to cover the industry."

"The senior oil analyst became a wonderful mentor," she adds, "and I'll always be grateful for what he taught me about the business."

Jane eventually became portfolio manager of the much more diversified Scudder Development Fund, a job she held until joining Rockefeller & Co. in 1988.

What excites Jane most about her profession is "thoroughly researching how an industry works." She likes to monitor the day-to-day operations of a business and do lots of homework on both the quality of its products and the competition it faces from others within the same industry. Shopping for value stocks is one of Jane's specialties, so I asked her to put all modesty aside and share a success story or two with us.

"One of my favorite client picks was a firm called Computer Task Group," Jane reported. "It was a 'temp agency' of sorts that rents out computer programmers." While Jane had faith in the company's potential, it was obvious that CTG was going through some difficult financial times. It seems that CTG had a handful of major clients that began slicing the hourly rates they were willing to pay the firm's computer professionals, not a good sign for CTG's bottom line. "The stock was out of favor," she added, "but I instinctively knew that the firm was starting to turn around."

The balance sheet looked good to Jane, indicating that there was more than enough cash on hand. The firm also had a low ratio of market capitalization to revenues. (For a discussion of this concept, see Chapter 4, where it's referred to as the *price-to-sales ratio*.) Best of all, however, was Jane's impression that the management of CTG earnestly wanted to fix anything that was presently wrong with the firm. (Admittedly, Jane has an advantage over most of us. She was able to speak personally to the management team, which soon won her trust, and in time she developed a close rapport with the firm's CEO.) Deciding to "take the plunge," Jane bought the stock at $8.62 per share in 1992. There was little movement in price for the next two years, until it began a steady ascent—rising to roughly $42 per share by the end of 1996. By June of 1997, it had split two for one, trading at 33-3/4 (67-1/2 "presplit").

Another of Jane's major successes centers on La Quinta Motor Inns. The huge boom in the hotel/motel industry that lasted through the early eighties had nearly gone bust by the decade's end. La Quinta was a small-cap firm, a former "glamour stock" that had fallen on hard times. From the looks of the company's balance sheet (something we *can* study), Jane knew that La Quinta would remain in a financial bind until efforts were made to reduce costs and revitalize the company. She knew that such turnarounds usually require the intervention of a powerful outside force.

That's when a few Texas billionaires entered the picture. Representatives of the Bass family joined La Quinta's board of directors, bought a sizable amount of stock, and helped bring in new management. The Basses saw the same sort of potential for value that Jane had spotted: The "debt-adjusted market value per room" was $22,000. The barrier to entry for competitors was prohibitively high; the cost of buying already existing hotels ran close to $30,000 per room, while those who wished to *build* new hotels would have to pay approximately $45,000 to $55,000 for each unit!

Jane knew a bargain when she saw one, and bought a substantial amount of La Quinta's stock at $2.86 back in 1991. By May of 1997, La Quinta's price had increased to $22 per share, which meant that both Jane's clients and the Basses had earned roughly ten times what they had originally invested.

Investing in value stocks is much like trying to figure out the key to a mystery novel before it ends. If you can unravel the "clues" that remain invisible to others, chances are you'll be quite successful at shopping for value.

But you can't win them all. Jane was good-natured enough to admit a few of the mistakes she's made along the way, including a cellular phone stock she was sure would prove a winner. The name of the firm in question was Vanguard Cellular, which owned what Jane felt were undervalued assets. After Jane invested money in the firm, however, new competitors (including the Internet) entered the marketplace. The price of the stock never took off. "If you're betting money on the only horse in town, there's no way you can lose the race," says Jane, "unless a dozen other horses show up all of a sudden! The biggest mistake you can make is thinking that a stock is a bargain, even as you watch its fundamental value decline faster than the price."

Jane readily confesses that, on at least one occasion, she was wrong about an entire industry! The medical laboratory industry once looked good to her based on fundamental analysis. Little did she know that Medicare would soon start cutting costs, or that more employers and workers would shift over to HMO plans. Various labs across the country proceeded to cut deals with the HMOs, which meant that their profit margins decreased. To make matters worse, the media began to report that many lab tests were unnecessary, and various HMOs discouraged random testing. The result of this succession of events was a further loss of revenues for laboratories in general. As Jane notes, the medical laboratory industry is one with fixed costs, yet profits were being squeezed by decreasing revenues and lower margins. "In certain cases, the balance sheet and income statements can't tell you the whole story," notes Jane. "It's a mistake not to see whatever structural change is taking place within in a particular industry—not to mention any competition on the horizon in terms of new alternatives."

My final question to Jane concerned how she coped with risk on a daily basis after two decades of toiling in the arena of money management. While Jane admits to spending the occasional sleepless night, she insists that an investor should do sufficient homework to gain confidence in the stocks to be added to a personal portfolio. Out-of-favor stocks often provide a good potential for value, simply because other investors are running scared. "Never let your emotions get the best of you," cautions Jane, who says the upswings and downswings of the market should never paralyze you when putting together a portfolio. Most important of all is diversification.

Jane recommends opening two separate accounts. For high-quality investment research, one should be with a well-respected full-service brokerage firm. For day-to-day trading, however, she suggests that a second account be opened with a discount broker-age firm.

If the hectic pace of your lifestyle doesn't leave enough time to do your own stock research, you should rely on the best mutual fund managers in the business. Jane notes that there are plenty of good ones from which to choose, whether you have $5,000 or $50 million to invest. In addition, you should try to keep up with the financial news reported in *The Wall Street Journal, Barron's,* and *Investor's Business Daily.* If you have special interests in, or knowl-edge about, a particular industry, you might want to focus your attention toward that sector. The Internet is another excellent research tool.

"Everyone who loved you before you bought stock in XYZ today will still love you tomorrow, even if the stock takes a nose dive," Jane reminds us. "Still, it helps to cultivate sources of sup-port among your circle of family, friends, and colleagues at work. Joining an investment club is one good way to feel like you're part of a team."

Thanks for the pep talk, Jane. You're a great coach!

INVESTING FOR THE LONG TERM: JESSICA BIBLIOWICZ

Next, I'd like to introduce you to the president and chief operating officer of John A. Levin & Co., the former executive vice president of Smith Barney. A graduate of Cornell University in 1981, Jessica Bibliowicz has been a Wall Street player ever since. Like me, Jessica is actively committed to educating women about all matters finan-cial in order to provide a level playing field on which they can com-pete with men in the marketplace. In fact, we hold in common the belief that (once thoroughly educated about investments) women are capable of becoming better investors than men! The way we look at it, most men who play the stock market are out to hit "home runs," whereas women tend to be more pragmatic, taking the slow and steady approach to accumulating wealth.

"Each woman needs to assess her own financial situation in terms of where she is in the life cycle," notes Jessica. "She must carefully examine her complete financial picture, including both assets and liabilities. She needs to plan realistically for her future in the event of divorce or the death of her spouse, and be on guard against con artists who love to prey on women at such vulnerable times in their lives."

According to Jessica, the first step a woman should take toward financial security is to set aside a certain amount of money to invest on a regular basis. For example, we should all "pay ourselves" a set amount (perhaps $25 or $50) from each paycheck before we're tempted to make any discretionary expenditures. Once you're able to save enough to get started, Jessica recommends taking a systematic approach to investing by means of dollar cost averaging. She notes that the real trick is in disciplining yourself to keep investing in a stock or mutual fund—even when the market is going down! Your investment strategies should change only when your overall goals and financial needs change significantly.

"Keep your eye on a horizon of at least five to ten years," advises Jessica. "Corrections in the market can be painful at times, but any long-term decision to invest shouldn't be affected by temporary downturns." Specific investment decision must always be reviewed, but market turbulence should be tolerated in order to achieve long-term growth.

For those brave enough to choose their own stocks, mutual funds, and other investments, Jessica wholeheartedly agrees with me that knowledge is power. You simply must have a thorough understanding of each type of investment, as well as the applicable risks and returns. Next, you should realistically evaluate your own level of risk tolerance, bearing in mind that those unable to take any risk at all are seldom able to accumulate enough wealth to enjoy a comfortable retirement. Keeping the bulk of your investment dollars in low-yielding money markets may prove fairly risk free, but Bibliowicz emphasizes that your returns will barely outpace inflation. "You not only *should* take some degree of market risk," according to Jessica, "you truly *have to!*"

She recommends that we try to think of the market in fairly realistic terms, setting a goal of achieving an annualized 10% return on our money. Within the asset class of equity (stocks), it's a good idea to invest a portion of money in small-cap and international mutual funds.

Jessica notes how difficult it is to tune out the media's constant barrage of financial analysis, which is bound to include a daily dose of sensationalism. It's far too easy to get caught up in the sheer drama of it all. "Remember that you can't base buy and sell decisions on the opinions of those who appear on financial news broadcasts," she cautions, "because they certainly won't be accountable for your losses!"

If you're *not* yet ready to rely on your own judgment when it comes to choosing the right investments, Jessica stresses that you should hold out for a financial advisor you know you can trust. "It's important to have a two-way relationship with your broker, and to be able to work together as a team," she advises. "If a friend tells you about a terrific broker, it's usually a good sign. What you're looking for is quality, experience, and the sort of person to whom you can relate well."

Finally, Jessica recommends that investors stick with "brand name" mutual funds, because the firms backing them up have too much at stake to let their portfolio managers become reckless. Ideally, a fund's manager should have 20 to 25 years or more of solid experience. She also suggests that you carefully examine the top ten holdings of a fund to see if they are high-quality stocks. Finding out the turnover factor is important, as well, because it serves to indicate whether a fund's profits are primarily in the form of short-term or long-term capital gains. "A fund with low turnover and a good track record will enjoy more long-term capital gains," she reminds us, "which of course will be taxed at a much lower rate!"

As Jessica points out, however, the first step is learning how to save money on a regular basis. Why not start by putting $20 in a cookie jar the next time you cash your paycheck?

STAYING FOCUSED: KIM PURVIS AND ART SPINNER

Kim Purvis, a vice president at the New-York–based investment advisory firm of Scudder, Stevens & Clark, specializes in health care investments. Overall, Scudder manages roughly more than $125 billion in assets. Kim analyzes investments spread among pharmaceutical companies, medical devices, biotechnology, managed care, hospital management companies, nursing homes, and other health care services.

I've known Kim for quite some time. We met when we worked for five years for the same investment bank. In fact, Kim and I have a great deal in common, including the fact that we both majored in the sciences as undergraduates. Kim has a B.S. in Natural Resources from the University of Michigan. "It was a big disappointment not to be a park ranger," recalls Kim. She took a "temporary" job at the University of Michigan Hospital. Six years passed by quickly, and Kim decided to pursue a Masters Degree in Health Services Administration. After achieving that goal in 1988, she went on to earn her Masters in Business Administration two years later. By 1991, Kim was working as an equity analyst at an investment bank, with a focus on the managed care industry. She eventually worked her way to the "buy side," making the move to Scudder, Stevens & Clark in 1997. Like many women who've made finance their career, Kim says, "The last place I thought I would end up was on Wall Street!"

Her advice to women? Kim suggests that we start by trying to think like the men (and women!) in the executive suite of some of the major diversified health care companies. Pretend that your biggest focus is on gobbling up smaller firms! The driving force of an investment should be a company that produces at least one unique, high-value-added product or service. For example, if you are looking to acquire a knee-implant company, you don't want to find one that produces a generic implant. Rather, you want to search out a company with a proprietary patented product that's unique in some way.

The product is the important factor, and in these cases the management of the company is the less important factor. For small companies, the quality of innovation is primary. Since those in the executive suites are searching to acquire that way—why shouldn't all investors? Once a large company takes over a small firm, it brings its own management and distribution to the company's innovative new product or service. If you're a health care professional, you should research any service or product you find that is superior to that of the competition. If it is truly superior, a large diversified firm will make the same conclusion and pay well for that product or service!

In making her own stock picks, Kim does an enormous amount of financial research. She also carefully examines statistics relating to the health care industry. Most industry statistics are available through a variety of sources. A great many government statistics are available via the Internet. Kim likes to examine a company's five years of financial statements in order to get a full picture of how the firms that interest her are faring. She then chooses companies that she expects to outperform the industry based on sales and earnings growth.

Kim combines the macro picture of the industry with the financial specifics of various firms, then evaluates the products and/or services offered by each. She's convinced me that, if each of us is willing to do that kind of homework, it's quite possible to profit in the health care sector. By way of caution, she adds: "You want to find the story before everyone else does!" She points out that the Street is wildly optimistic about the future of many health care companies in the marketplace, which makes a stock with real potential even harder to find.

Another method of targeting good investment opportunities? Focus on companies with good products or services, but without a strong enough management team to back them up. Perhaps your research indicates that the previous managers of a firm made a long line of mistakes that provoked failure instead of success. "New management at the helm could provide a unique turnaround situation," notes Kim.

Pharmaceutical companies are a bit unique, but can also be carefully researched by individual investors.

"It's best to find a company with a drug that is a true therapeutic breakthrough," she suggests, "or that replaces an existing drug with a lot of unpleasant side effects."

It's astonishing to contemplate, but Kim points out that the average cost of developing a drug and bringing it to the market is approximately $200 million. This makes investing in biotechnology companies quite speculative, at best, since the prospect of their coming out with a real "blockbuster" drug is hampered by the tremendous costs involved. According to Kim, it's more prudent to invest in the major pharmaceutical companies. Statistics indicate that very few compounds will eventually make it to the market, and an even smaller number will be blockbuster or billion-dollar drugs. The time it normally takes to develop a new drug is from four to ten years. That's why, as an investor, it's important to determine what's "in the pipeline."

A few questions to ask as you do your own homework: How many of the company's drugs are going off patent, meaning that a cheap generic equivalent becomes quickly available? What's happening in the present round of clinical trials? How many compounds are close to becoming marketable products? Kim notes that when a drug loses its patent and it becomes "generic," the pharmaceutical company needs a new drug to replace the earnings that are lost. Pharmaceutical firms will provide information concerning when their various patents expire, as well as what they have in the "pipeline" of clinical trials at present. At the end of each phase of testing, the FDA (Food and Drug Administration) publishes the results and the companies involved issue press releases, which are also important to monitor.

Another important factor to consider is whether or not the introduction of a new drug to the marketplace will have a significant market, i.e., how much of the population wil actually need to use it. The sad truth about the drug industry is that research is so expensive that only the major pharmaceutical firms can justify finding treatments or cures for diseases that don't affect much of the population. Ever wonder why prices are so high for drugs that treat rare diseases? There's simply very little economic incentive to help fight the affliction of the relatively few, rather than the many.

Kim and I are long-tenured Wall Streeters, but we haven't forgotten our common roots in the sciences! We're both very concerned about the "human side" of the equation. It's only prudent to try to profit from industry trends as investors, but we also very much hope for a better system of health care for present and future generations. An increasingly bureaucratic system of medicine is combining with the cost-cutting trends of corporate America to the point of virtually taking over the lives of all health care professionals. Finding the cure for severe diseases is often not an industry priority, simply because of the economics involved. It's not the best of all possible worlds, to say the least. We can only take solace in the fact that a number of great strides have been made via recently introduced drug treatments, medical devices and surgical procedures that serve to enhance as well as extend life—and that's the positive "trend" we want most to continue!

Art Spinner is the managing partner of Hambro-Spinner Asset Management, and has been an investor in the technology industry since 1975. Art was a client of mine who soon became a good friend, and we were both surprised to learn that we'd attended the same elementary school in Queens. Although Art was my client, not the other way around, I'll always be grateful for the tip he gave me to buy Intel back in 1994!

Since earning his MBA from Harvard, Art has become a master at investing in the technology sector. His fund has performed at a 28.0% net annualized return since its inception, outpacing the S&P 500 Index's return (including reinvested dividends) of 24%. In 1975, Art began as a venture capitalist, focusing on technology startups.

To his credit, Art has had several "big winners" in the technology world. He was the original institutional investor in Solectron, an electronics manufacturer that went from a market capitalization of $45 million to $5 billion. Mr. Spinner was the "seed" investor and a cofounder of Komag. Originally financed at $1.25 million, the company now has a market capitalization of $900 million. It is the largest independent manufacturer of computer disks in the world.

According to Art Spinner, advanced technology has often been the byproduct of military research—with the Internet possibly its greatest achievement. As most of you know, the Internet is now used on a global basis for everything from stock market research to locating the best doctor for whatever ails you. Making airline and hotel reservations has never been simpler, and you can even shop for the best summer rentals in the real estate market. Many innovations are yet to come, according to Art.

Before leaving the subject of the Internet, Art noted that inflation is an interesting economic byproduct under siege by the computer thanks to the globalization of the marketplace. Once the consumers can order virtually anything from literally everywhere, the increase in vendors and in real-time competition may do away with that green-eyed monster for good!

Another significant discovery that evolved from military research is known as Global Positioning Systems (GPS), which was invented to help missiles locate military targets. The same chip now is used as a directional device in the Lexus automobiles that are made and sold in Japan, in the BMWs of Europe, and even at your friendly neighborhood Hertz and Avis rent-a-car dealerships.

Ronald Reagan's "star wars" defense buildup in the eighties also had an unusual byproduct, in the form of a hair removal procedure. A military engineer had accidentally shot himself with a laser, then noticed that his body hair had disappeared—painlessly, and with no infection. As "hair-brained" as it seems, a firm known as Thermolase has been handsomely profiting from this fortuitous military accident ever since.

Art points out that technology is often developed for one market and finds use in many others once the technology becomes financially feasible, that is, when prices come down to the point where the products are affordable as household appliances. "As investors, you must not just consider a single product, but all the different suppliers that will benefit from the advancing technology," insists Art. "For example, color printing is becoming more and more accessible to the consumer market—with the average user able to download in color right off the Internet."

Just like any other successful portfolio manager, Art carefully scrutinizes a company's management. "If the president drives a Ferrari with golf clubs in the back seat, I'll question his focus," reports Art. Instead, he looks for down-to-earth managers without overblown egos. He spends a great deal of time visiting companies (something most of us can't do).

For those who understand the risks, however, Art recommends investing in a mutual fund that specializes in technology. Here's what to look for: (1) the portfolio manager should be at least 40 years of age, and a "survivor" of the market crash of 1987; (2) his or her performance record should be that of at least 20% when annualized over the past five years; and (3) the mutual fund should be less volatile than its peers.

As you can see, Kim and Art, like me, are great believers in doing your homework *before* investing a dime.

Thanks for the interviews, Kim and Art. It's easy to see why you're both so successful. You really know your chosen industries inside out.

Is There a Single "Best Bet" in the Marketplace?

After nearly 20 years as a Wall Streeter, I'd have to say that the surest way to achieve financial security is through diversification, with a willingness to take a calculated risk on some of your money and invest in the trend of tomorrow. In other words, bet on the future rather than on trends that have passed or are on the way out. Unfortunately, this takes a considerable amount of hard work, patience, and an ability to ride out the ups and downs attached to uncertainty.

Although I've yet to turn 40, the world has changed a great deal since the "lemonade stand" days of my youth. My dad was a civilian who worked as an accounting and finance officer for the Fort Hamilton Army Base located in Brooklyn. Occasionally, he would bring me in to the office, where I would amuse myself by typing on a keypunch machine. It was inconceivable to me how a collection of cardboards with square holes could actually mean something intelligible to what Dad referred to as a "mainframe computer"—a metallic monster so large that it occupied an entire floor!

We would then head home for dinner with Mom, which took at least an hour to prepare without the luxury of a microwave. Naturally, my dad and I lent a hand in the kitchen by helping Mom wash the dishes and silverware by hand before retiring to the living room. As middle-class Americans in the late fifties and early sixties, we were unaware that color TVs were "on the drawing board." We did enjoy sitting in front of our small black-and-white set that offered three or four channels of prime-time programming. We would then use our state-of-the-art rotary-dial phone to touch base with friends and family before turning in.

Nowadays, children from middle-class families all across America are able to e-mail grandma and grandpa instead. Many take to school laptop computers that are infinitely smarter and more powerful than the room-sized computers of yesteryear. In fact, a good deal more information is now at their fingertips than is housed on the shelves of the most massive library in the land!

I'm reminded once again of how Hetty Robinson Green became the richest woman in the world by betting on the Industrial Revolution of her era. By all accounts, the very best investment we can make is on the Information Age, which has only just begun. A lot of smart money is betting that the best is yet to come.

So how does one become rich? It is important to be pragmatic and have a diversified approach to investments. But, there will always be another Intel, Microsoft, Xerox, IBM, Loews Theaters, Cisco, American Express, McDonalds, Disney, Coca-Cola, General Electric, J. P. Morgan, Compaq Computer, and so on and so on.

Many great investment opportunities have been right in front of my nose. For some strange reason, I thought that if I could figure it out, it must be too late. For so many years I thought that investing was like finding the needle in the haystack, that it was for those who were smarter and richer than I. The truth is that the best investments are always the most obvious. In early 1990, I saw a book about the Internet and how to make money using it. "Ha," I thought to myself, "if they are so smart, why are they writing a book telling everybody?" I could kick myself. Had I picked up that book I would have understood the power of networking stocks. I would have done some research and realized that Cisco Systems could be a real winner. I would have seen an investment of $5,000 turn into $1,000,000. The information necessary to help you become rich is not esoteric. All you need is to read a book, do some research, and have a bit of courage to risk some capital.

The market will always be turbulent, and it's easy to get frightened out of your positions. Remember that the long term is your goal. Becoming rich in the market requires three things; knowledge, patience, and courage. I am extremely confident that most of you are capable of spotting the next trend and researching it. As I've learned, the hard part is not finding the foresight or the ability, but the courage. I wish you all the courage to achieve your dreams.

chapter 15

WHEN YOU'RE RICH: INVESTING IN HORSES, ART, AND JEWELRY

Although a level playing field has yet to be established in the male-dominated world of Wall Street and American society at large, I firmly believe that every woman in America has the ability to succeed financially. We should all rejoice in the fact that knowledge is power, and that a healthy dose of empowerment is all it really takes!

It's time to heartily congratulate yourself for having come this far. Once you begin to put what you've learned to use in the marketplace, you'll discover that you know more than most men about how to achieve lifetime financial security. As you know, I'm not much of a gambler, but I'm betting that each reader of this book will be able to succeed beyond her wildest dreams.

Why Not Live It Up a Little?

With success comes responsibility. Once you've achieved your personal and professional goals and ensured the future security of family and loved ones, it's important to "give something back" to others who are less fortunate and in need of financial assistance. After that, why not "give something back" to yourself, while you're at it? Tightwad that I am, I see no reason why we shouldn't pamper ourselves a bit after many years of hard work and the attainment of financial security. Many successful women feel guilty when it comes to splurging on themselves, even after they've accumulated more wealth than can be spent in a lifetime. Why not live it up a little by investing in the hobbies and pursuits that give you the most pleasure?

Make sure to spend your money wisely, however. Those with an abundance of wealth are prime targets for the con artists of the world, so take care not to get ripped off pursuing expensive hobbies such as raising thoroughbred horses or collecting valuable antiques or jewels. Hobbies like these require every bit as much homework as successful investing in the stock and bond markets.

Off to the Races

I've very much enjoyed the sport of horse racing. In fact, on my first visit to the racetrack, my roommate and I were blessed with beginner's luck. A group of girls from my dormitory had linked up with one of the fraternities for an outing to Vernon Downs, a legendary racing track located in upstate New York. At the time, my roommate and I were both involved in less-than-idyllic dating relationships, and the "losers" we were seeing both happened to be named Mike. Much to our delight, we discovered a colt named Bye-Bye Mike in the lineup, so we convinced the rest of the group to join us in betting on a long shot.

If only we'd been as lucky in love as we were at the track that day! Sure enough, our colt effortlessly crossed the finish line in first place. The thrill of victory was even sweeter when, upon our return to Cornell, we each said "bye-bye" to our respective Mikes.

More than twenty years later, I'm still enamored of "the sport of kings," so I was thrilled to meet and get to know a major female force in the thoroughbred horse racing industry. Wilhelmina McEwan Combs was gracious enough to offer some expert advice on how anyone with a passion for horses can make investments of the four-legged variety!

Wilhelmina has been passionately involved with horses since childhood. After an extensive show jumping career in the United States and Canada, the Olympic teams of both countries offered her the opportunity to go for the gold. While the young girl had thus far enjoyed the benefits of dual citizenship, she was finally faced with choosing one nation over the other. Wilhelmina opted for American citizenship and the chance to join the U.S. Olympic Team. In a perfect illustration of Murphy's law, the Carter Administration opted to boycott the Olympics that same year!

The good news, however, is that Wilhelmina took this great disappointment in stride, and went on to enjoy a remarkable career. Throughout the early eighties, she headed the thoroughbred racing operation of Spendthrift Farm in Lexington, Kentucky. She now operates Fenwick Farm, a world-renowned training facility located in Rembert, South Carolina. The latter farm has broken yearlings for some of the world's leading trainers, including D. Wayne Lukas. "Wilhelmina gets results," says Lukas, the sort of fellow who doesn't hand out such compliments lightly. "She is a competent, professional horsewoman."

Ms. Combs is an equally competent professional when it comes to getting good financial results in the horse breeding and racing industry, and over the years has become a leading advisor and mentor to many new investors and owners. "It's been a male-dominated industry from the very beginning," she notes, "but there's plenty of room for women to get involved, too!"

Imagine my surprise when she told me that America's first female owner of a Kentucky Derby winner was none other than Elizabeth Arden, whose extraordinarily successful cosmetic empire got its start with an initial investment of less than $1,000 back in 1910. While most of us think of Arden as the queen of cosmetics, she became tantamount to royalty in the sport of kings, as well. In fact, horses were such a great passion for Arden that she had an expensive thoroughbred breeding and training operation.

Is investing in horses affordable to most of us? Probably not. It's a risky enterprise at best, as Wilhelmina is quick to point out, and you really should be very well off financially before investing. For those who can afford to take a considerable risk, however, the racing industry offers an unbeatable social life and adventure galore—especially if you're the sort who loves horses. And there's at least a fair chance that you'll be able to make some money in the process, assuming you link up with the same top-notch advisors. One point Wilhelmina stresses is that you should always buy the best quality you can afford.

"It's definitely a high-risk investment," Wilhelmina admits with complete candor, "but one that offers the sort of enjoyment to be had by actively participating in the industry." She adds how important it is to remember that you'll be investing in a four-legged animal, a living creature that eats, sleeps, and breathes. "The horses in which you invest become like members of your own family, and require the same degree of love and attention that most of us reserve for a family pet."

Racing is a year-long sport throughout the United States, England, France, and much of the rest of the world. In America, the racing year begins each January in both Florida (at Gulf Stream) and California (at Santa Ana). The Triple Crown races start in May with the Kentucky Derby, which is soon followed by the Preakness in Baltimore, and the Belmont in New York. For the same horse to win all three top races is a rare achievement indeed: in all of racing history, only eleven horses thus far have won the coveted Triple Crown. Not since a horse named Affirmed completed the Triple Crown sweep in 1978 has this amazing feat been accomplished.

Should you decide to participate actively in the horse racing industry, chances are you'll become a frequent flyer—and then some. Lexington, Kentucky is the best place to go for those who want to buy horses. (Saratoga, New York is another major meeting place for buyers and sellers.) The actual breeding of horses is centered not just in Lexington, but elsewhere throughout Kentucky. The largest horse auctions take place at the Keeneland race track throughout the summer and fall. Then, chances are you'll be off to the races in high-flying style! Race tracks are conveniently located in 40 states throughout America, but why limit yourself to domestic travel? In order to catch some of the best in international racing, be prepared to pack a flight bag for such far-off locales as Australia, Hong Kong, Russia, Dubai (near Saudi Arabia), France, England, and the rest of Europe.

Wilhelmina notes that there are some "purses" worth more than $3 million in France, Dubai, Japan, Brazil, and Australia. Should one of your horses prove a winner, travel might certainly pay.

Still, Wilhelmina emphasizes that no one should participate in the horse industry unless they're financially secure enough to make a highly speculative investment. There's simply no getting around the fact that investing in horses is both a risky and expensive proposition, albeit one with the possibility of a great financial reward. Should you wish to purchase a horse, for example, the actual cost of the animal is only the beginning of the bills involved. Your "investment" will need to be fed, sheltered, trained, transported, groomed, and insured; you can anticipate approximately $30,000 each year to maintain a racehorse, and $11,000 to maintain a non-racing horse that's used only for breeding purposes.

Foreign buyers have been very aggressive in the past decade buying America's top-end horses. As a result, the competition level here is not as high as it is abroad. Nevertheless, our purses have increased tremendously over the past several years. At Keeneland the average daily purse—the total winnings for the eight or nine daily races—has increased from $266,475 in 1993 to $452,193 in 1997. At Churchill Downs, home of the Kentucky Derby, the average purse has increased from $256,584 in 1993 to $411,597 in 1997.

Because the costs are high, Wilhelmina strongly recommends that novice investors begin by participating in "horse partnerships," whereby several investors agree to share the expenses of buying, maintaining, and racing thoroughbreds. She finds these partnerships work best when three or four wealthy individuals pool their resources to invest in the purchase and nurturing of two to four horses. (The same principle of diversification—spreading the risk—that's so important with any Wall Street portfolio applies to this industry as well.) It's essential that the partnership be put together by a professional at the horse racing game, and almost equally important that the various partners enjoy each other's company and share a bond of mutual friendship and trust.

Many of the large farms such as Lane's End are more than willing to help educate new investors about each aspect of the horse industry. Wilhelmina McEwan Combs is the perfect example of the sort of advisor you need: someone who's spent a lifetime in the business and knows just about everything there is to know about breeding, training, and racing a horse. Wilhelmina emphasizes that participating in a partnership is an expensive proposition: investors should be prepared to put up at least $100,000 to $200,000 to begin with.

Another way to invest in horses is through the purchase of "stallion shares" in a horse syndicate that's been formed for the purpose of selling stud fees. These days, most syndicates offer a total of 40 shares, which again helps investors spread their risk. Inasmuch as the entire horse racing industry revolves around bloodlines, the actual breeding process is a major business in and of itself. The best studs are paid quite handsomely. (I'm reminded once more of the song, "Nice Work If You Can Get It!") The leading sire nowadays is a horse named Mr. Prospecter. This champion thoroughbred receives a flat fee of $200,000 whenever he steps up to bat, even if he fails to impregnate the mare! In most cases, however, the mare must have a live foal in order for the stud to collect his fee.

According to Wilhelmina, mares seldom have a problem reproducing and can be expected to give birth every two to three years. It's best to start breeding them at the age of five, although they're often able to give birth to healthy foals by the time they turn three. I was surprised to learn that mares can continue to have healthy babies until they've reached the age of twenty or so, and even more astonished to learn what high prices their offspring can fetch!

I asked Wilhelmina to provide some "financials" relating to a few of the leading champions, and she whipped up the following chart. The auction price column indicates the initial price paid for the horse in question, and the earnings column represents the total of purses each has won to date. The brood mare price figure reflects the amount for which a mare was sold for breeding purposes once her racing career had ended, and the offspring column provides the total price of the foals birthed (and sold) to date.

Name of Filly	Auction Price	Earnings	Brood Mare Price	Offspring
Winning Colors	$575,000	$1,526,873	$4,100,000	$1,050,000
Some Romance	$500,000	$ 545,355	$ 875,000	$1,275,000
Mariah's Storm	$ 85,000	$ 724,895	$2,600,000	No foals yet
Serena's Song	$150,000	$3,038,348	Not yet sold	
Storm Song	$100,000	$1,020,050	Still running	
Sharp Cat	$205,000	$ 887,850	Still running	
Personal Ensign	Homebred	$1,679,880	Retained by owner	$2,458,820
Prospector's Delight	Homebred	$ 432,953	Retained by owner	$ 575,000

Wilhelmina recommends that newcomers to the business begin by purchasing fillies, which carry residual value in terms of breeding regardless of their track record. Once their racing careers have ended, fillies are sold as brood mares in order to race and/or sell the offspring.

Colt are more of a "wildcat investment," because they have no residual value unless they prove successful at the racetrack. Only the real winners will be used as sires in return for handsome stud fees. For example, Gulch, A.P. Indy, and Dixieland Band earn

$60,000 each time they successfully produce a foal. Should you wish to introduce your brood mare to any of the above, you'd need to (1) have the necessary cash, and (2) go through a "ritual mating dance" with the stud's owner—who may very well think that your brood mare isn't good enough to go out with his stud!

The following table lists the "financials" relating to a few of the most famous colts in the business today, along with the prices for which they were eventually syndicated. It's not that much different from buying stocks on Wall Street, because you're literally buying the "future earnings" of your stud of choice. Note that Thunder Gulch and Seattle Slew were both sold at auction for next to nothing at all because (as Wilhelmina puts it) they simply weren't attractive. As studs, they went on to demonstrate earning power of $8 million and $12 million respectively—rather a handsome profit for the sale of syndication rights! Here's the table in full:

Name of Horse	Auction Price	Earnings	Syndication or Selling Price
Seattle Slew	$ 17,000	$1,208,725	$12,000,000
Alysheba	$ 500,000	$6,679,242	Retained by owner
A.P. Indy	$2,900,000	$2,979,815	$10,000,000
Thunder Gulch	$ 40,000	$2,915,086	$ 8,000,000
Petitionville	$ 190,000	$ 811,905	$ 2,000,000
Timber County	$ 500,000	$1,560,000	$12,000,000
Hennessey	$ 500,000	$ 580,400	$ 6,000,000
Skip Away	$ 40,000	$3,985,360	Still Running
Cigar	Homebred	$9,999,815	$25,000,000
Grindstone	Homebred	$1,224,410	$ 4,000,000
Secretariat	Homebred	$1,316,808	$ 6,080,000
Affirmed	Homebred	$2,393,818	$14,000,000
Silver Charm	$ 16,500	$1,632,300	Still Running

No real proof exists that a stallion will be able to reproduce at the time of syndication, which is why it's customary to buy insurance policies to guard against infertility as well as mortality. After being syndicated for a whopping $25 million, for example, Cigar proved to be infertile. Not to worry: the syndicate was insured by Lloyds of London (one of the major insurers in the horse industry). Infertility is rare, however, and a good stud is usually bred twice a day.

It's quite normal for a sire to produce 60 or more foals a year. A good farm carefully regulates the breeding process in order to preserve the length of the sire's career. Taking a tour of the breeding stalls at Lane's End, I was surprised to see how elaborately equipped they are. One tends to forget at times that horses are fragile animals that can be hurt by the rejection of a mate! It seems that a priceless stud risks serious injury should the mare he's matched with reject him as a mate, and give him a good swift kick or two to make her point.

Before drawing this section to a close, I should note that horse racing offers an elaborate social life. People from all over the world (and all occupations) are drawn together by their common love of horses. That's why investing in the racing industry is an ideal way to meet a broad spectrum of fascinating people—from industry captains to movie stars—and get invited to some great parties. Because horse racing takes place year-round, it's one world-class extravaganza that never stops.

Collecting Art for Fun (and Profit)

A young woman by the name of Jacqueline Cable, co-owner of the New York firm of Cable & Knight, has been in the business of advising private collectors of art, antiques, and jewelry for more than a decade. According to Jacqueline, "There are so many different areas in which to invest, there's something of interest to just about everyone."

Are you interested in the prospect of collecting rare books? How about musical instruments? You might also consider investing in Chinese, English, or French porcelain; dolls; French and English furniture; Oriental and Persian rugs; rare coins; American folk art; toy soldiers; baseball cards; Old Master Paintings; photographs; stamps; English, French, and American silver; ceramics; paperweights; drawings; American Indian rugs; Fabergé eggs; Tiffany lamps; art nouveau glass; tea caddies; Impressionist paintings; tapestry pillows; clocks; and weather vanes—just to name a few areas of collectibles!

Jacqueline suggests reading as much as possible about the area of art and collectibles that most interests you.

To acquire even more information before purchasing art or antiques, you can check out various classes at nearby colleges, browse through the offerings of local galleries and auction houses, attend art shows, and seek out the advice of experts. Auction houses generally offer seminars as a means of educating novice collectors about the auction process, and feature lectures by specialists in a variety of fields.

INVESTING IN FURNITURE

If you've never thought of furniture as an art form, think again! Jacqueline suggests that there's "no place like home" to begin, as any room in your house can be enhanced by adding a couple of interesting pieces of furniture. She notes that antique furniture not only retains its value, but normally appreciates in time. It will often prove less expensive than the furniture most of us purchase at our local department stores. As most of you know, contemporary furniture suffers considerable *depreciation* the moment the delivery truck arrives in front of your house!

"A general antiques' pricing guide such as *Kovel's Complete Antique Price List* gives you a good idea of what you might expect to pay for specific pieces," reports Jacqueline. "It provides up-to-date reports on prices that have been paid for a wide variety of items at antique dealers and auction houses throughout the country."

Medieval and early Renaissance furniture is generally massive and cumbersome, which means collectors must really have homes with high ceilings and considerable presentation space. (Such pieces were, after all, commissioned for grand palaces!) The furniture used during these periods includes cupboards, chest on stands, bureaus, and ornately carved wedding chests known as "cassones."

The principal woods used for construction during the medieval and Renaissance periods were oak and walnut. Because relatively few collectors have homes of adequate size to house such furniture, there's usually little competition for these items at auction. "Furniture that dates back to before the eighteenth century is rare, and may require restoration and considerable care," notes Jacqueline.

According to Jacqueline, eighteenth-century furniture is generally the most sought after, and therefore brings the highest prices at auction. "The most popular furniture styles are French and Continental, followed by English and American," she noted, then proceeded to provide details about each.

French Furniture. French furniture is considered by many to be the most beautiful of all. (Perhaps that's why it's the highest priced.) The level of design achieved by the combined talents of several guilds of woodcutters, carvers, painters, and guilders is simply unsurpassed. To say that furniture was important to the French does not even state the case: would you believe that there are more than 3,000 words in the French language just to describe furniture? For example, "fauteuil" refers to open armchairs, and "bergeres" to closed armchairs.

"If collecting French furniture from the eighteenth century appeals to you," says Jacqueline, "you should get in touch with established dealers, such as Didier Aaron Inc. in New York or Partridge Fine Arts, Ltd. of London." She adds it's important to check out a number of dealers before you decide on the dealers you will work with. "You should feel a comfortable rapport with whomever you choose, as it's a partnership (much like a client/broker relationship) that may last for many years."

Serious collectors should establish a few ground rules with their dealers, in terms of the future and an eventual upgrading of their investments. "It's best to work with someone who'll be willing to buy a piece of furniture back from you, and either pay its appreciated value or apply the amount to another work you want to acquire," notes Jacqueline. "In the event of your death, your dealer should be prepared either to accept the items you've acquired for sale on a consignment basis, or assist your family in disposing of your collection. The arrangement should be put in writing."

Once you've chosen the right dealer, it's time to start shopping. The good news is that French furniture is readily available. The French aristocracy and bourgeoisie collectively owned thousands of homes, many with hundreds of rooms filled with furniture. Even in the aftermath of the French Revolution and two centuries' worth of subsequent wars (both global and otherwise), a great deal of this furniture still survives. Considering the cost of contemporary reproductions, the "real McCoy" is reasonably priced!

It's quite easy to spend a fortune on French furniture, although the sale of private estates and auctions often feature terrific buys. Once again, Jacqueline reminds us that the "serious collector" should find good dealers, whose expertise should prove invaluable!

English Furniture. Those interested in English furniture, on the other hand, may not need the services of a dealer. It's possible to find good bargains at auctions, thanks to the fact that eighteenth-century English furniture is more plentiful than that of France and America—and therefore less expensive.

The building rage of eighteenth-century England was made possible by fortunes created from British colonization. Vigorous trade produced the wealth to create thousands of grand country estates, each with scores of rooms filled with furniture. Jacqueline notes, when the auctioneers of Christie's or Sotheby's went on site to dispose of an estate in the eighteenth and nineteenth century, it was not at all unusual for the sale to last 40 days or more!

Jacqueline suggests those wishing to acquire English furniture should go straight to the source. "Why not make a shopping trip to England, even if only for a few days or a week? You'll end up spending less money than had you acquired the furniture here, even after you factor in the cost of the trip and the air freight to bring your purchase to the U.S."

Monday is considered "viewing day" in London, with at least twenty furniture sales exhibits you can view. A good place to start is Christie's in South Kensington, which features reasonably priced artwork. "From there," adds Jacqueline, "you should move on to Christie's on King Street, Phillip's, Sotheby's, and end up at Bonham's."

If you're interested in buying major items, you may want to attend the sale and do the actual bidding yourself. Otherwise, it's customary to leave what's known as an "order bid" with one of the showroom boys. These fine young lads will phone you at your hotel on the day of the sale, if your bid was sufficient to acquire the piece in question. Assuming that the auction house's accounting department has already been given your credit information (a major charge card, for example), you're all set! The auction house will be happy to recommend a number of shippers from which to choose after you've shopped around and compared rates. One good piece of news in the duty-free department: No customs charges are imposed on the shipment of antiques more than 100 years old.

A buying trip to England is recommend only for those collectors who have already done sufficient homework, however. The best way for a novice at the game to become familiar with the diversity of styles and terminology is to review carefully the photos (and accompanying descriptions) featured in various auction catalogues. By all means subscribe to auction catalogues that cover the areas of furniture that interest you the most. And don't forget to visit exhibits and attend sales. "It's best to shop around for at least a year before you seriously begin to make purchases," advised Jacqueline.

One "must" she recommends is a subscription to catalogues issued by Sotheby's and Christie's. The phone number for Christie's in New York is (212) 546-1000, and Sotheby's can be reached by dialing (212) 606-7000. The first step is to ask each auction house to mail you a brochure that features the various catalogues they offer—a catalogue of catalogues, so to speak. You can easily acquaint yourself with the terminology used to describe antique furniture, by a careful review of the pictures and descriptions featured in their catalogues.

American Furniture.   The raw, primitive quality of medieval and early Renaissance English furniture can also be found in seventeenth-century American furniture, which is commonly known as that of the "Pilgrim century." It took considerable time for changes in design to cross the ocean from Europe and take root in the new land. "You can't expect the early colonists to have the sort of elaborate furniture that one had in Europe," notes Jacqueline, "because these settlers were primarily concerned with clearing forest lands, building homes, and simply surviving!"

Moreover, the Protestant values and work ethic of the first colonists made them suspicious of excessive display. When it came time to adopt various designs from England and the rest of the Continent, cabinetmakers simplified the elements to suit local taste. "The primary influence on American furniture design comes from England," according to Jacqueline. "While the major styles correspond to the respective reigns of English monarchs, the dates may extend well after those reigns ended."

She adds that woods indigenous to America (such as maple, cherry, pine, and hickory) replaced the British preference for walnut and mahogany. For the most part, American furniture is a bit less polished, with less decorative carvings. American furniture from the eighteenth century is quite rare (with far fewer pieces that are still in fine condition), and proves considerably more expensive to collect than English furniture.

Particularly sought-after pieces include American highboys (tall chests of drawers) which were usually manufactured in Philadelphia; highboys and lowboys (dressing tables) in matched sets; American Windsor chairs and Windsor settees; kneehole chests of drawers; secretaries made in Newport (desks with a richly carved shell motif); tall clocks; and Chippendale chairs.

In closing, Jacqueline notes that "Investing in antique furniture is not just buying something for practical use. You're actually acquiring an aura of the history and the political events that made the work possible—and, in so doing—become a caretaker of living history."

Diamonds—Now, As Always, a Girl's Best Friend

With any luck, most of us will own a diamond at some point in life. That's why I turned to Joseph Knight, Jacqueline's partner in the firm of Cable & Knight, for some much-needed advice on the diamond market. "The major four gems are sapphire, ruby, emerald, and diamond," Joseph reports, "but the diamond resale market has always proven to be greatest."

According to Joseph, a potential diamond purchaser should begin by shopping around. "Look at as many diamonds as possible before selecting the one you want," he advises. The four traditional shapes are pear, marquee, round brilliant, and emerald cut. In Joseph's opinion, pears and marquees look best if more than 2.5 carats; round brilliants "start to look silly" if more than 2 carats; and emerald cuts "look great over 2 carats and really terrific over 5 carats!" He adds that, once you've chosen the sort of cut you like, you'll need to know "the four Cs of diamonds":

COLOR

White diamonds are by far the most popular, and are graded for both color and clarity. Joseph recommends staying away from stones with a color grading beyond "J." The diamond industry uses the following grading system:

D, E, F (colorless)

G, H (nearly colorless)

I, J (ranging from nearly colorless to yellow)

K–Z (ranging from yellow to light yellow)

CLARITY

What follows is another grading system by the letter, this time for clarity:

FL, IF (flawless)

VVS 1 and 2 (very, very slight inclusions)

VS 1 and 2 (very slight inclusions)

SI 1 and 2 (slightly included)

I 1, 2, and 3 (included)

The term *included* doesn't mean "count me in," but rather refers to an imperfection. According to Joseph, inclusions in diamonds with a clarity rating of between FL to S1 should be invisible to the unaided eye.

CUT

Joseph tells me that the most important thing to look for is the *make,* that is, the way in which the diamond has been cut. If properly cut, the stone will have much more glitter to it. As Joseph puts it, the diamond will "face-up" on the whiter and brighter side.

The diamond should be carefully cut in a balanced manner, to ensure that it will more intensely reflect light. The make is broken down into the table, the top of the stone; the girdle, the side edge, and the pavilion, which is the bottom of the diamond.

CARATS

Any diamond of more than one carat should be certified by the Gemological Institute of America, known as GIA for short. The certificate documents the diamond's carat, color, and clarity. It also plots out whatever inclusions exist in the diamond. As a benchmark, a "G-H/VS1 round, brilliant-cut diamond" currently retails for between $6,000 and $7,000 per carat. As you increase the carat size, the price increases disproportionately. For example, a two-carat gem sells for a per-carat price that's higher by 15 to 25%.

When purchasing a diamond, Joseph stresses how important it is to find a full-service jeweler with a good reputation. "Check with your local Better Business Bureau, or ask for recommendations from friends," he advises. "A good jeweler will spend time explaining diamond grading to you," Joseph adds. "If a jeweler is interested in showing you only what he or she has in inventory, then you should take your business somewhere else!"

"It's important to examine any diamond you're considering purchasing *before* it's been set," Joseph warns, "because inclusions can be hidden under one of the prongs of the setting." He says that any reputable jeweler will offer you a *loup* (a hand-held magnifying glass) that will enable you to examine the stone at ten times its actual size.

Joseph strongly recommends flipping the diamond over, in order to view it from the underside. "You will be able to see the cuts, which appear as geometric lines. Any inclusions appear as bubbles, black spots, clouds, and feathers. Always match the inclusions you see with whatever dots have been plotted on the GIA certificate."

He goes on to warn that you shouldn't assume that your local jeweler will give you the best price, as smaller jewelers often don't have the clout of the large jewelers and retailers. "Much the same as with your dealer of eighteenth-century furniture or art, you should work with a jeweler who's willing to work with you on an 'upgrade' basis."

After you've purchased your diamond, it's highly advisable to have it appraised elsewhere in order to verify that the gem's grading is the same as that which appears on your GIA certificate. Never do business with a jeweler who isn't willing to refund your money in full should you be dissatisfied after your purchase. "It's best to make the purchase on a credit card," notes Joseph, "because you can dispute the charge with your credit card issuer if the second appraisal doesn't match the first and the jeweler refuses to refund your money."

Joseph cautions against buying any diamond with a clarity of I. "Such gems are likely to shatter under pressure and are difficult to resell," he adds. "Remember that if the diamond isn't truly beautiful, no one else will want it, size without quality is nothing."

Always ask a jeweler if you can see at least five different stones, a courtesy most are willing to extend, even if a second viewing time must be arranged. Never buy on impulse! It's far better to ask your jeweler to hold a diamond for a set period of time, while you make up your mind. It's unlikely to be sold out from under you, unless it's a particularly large diamond or one that features a magnificent make. Above all, don't let yourself get pressured into making a purchase. "If a jeweler tries to put pressure on you to buy a stone," warns Joseph, "you should find yourself another jeweler!"

In closing, Mr. Knight recommends that any purchaser of jewelry (diamond or otherwise) should adhere to two simple rules. "First, always buy something you know you'll want to wear and enjoy, rather than for what you think it's resale value will be." Rule number two is my favorite: "Always buy the best you can afford."

If it's true that "diamonds are a girl's best friend," I reckon one can never have too many.

The Very Best "Investment" of All

While still on the subject of friends, I hope I've made a few new ones by writing this book. With any luck, the information contained in these pages will help many women get started on the path to financial freedom and security.

What's the very best investment of all? I've been asked that question countless times over the years, but my answer is always the same. "As important as it is to invest in the stock and bond markets, the real payoff comes when you invest something of yourself on behalf of others." The truth is that I'm really not the slightest bit interested in diamonds—although I reserve the right to change my mind once the right man places an engagement ring on my finger! I'm far more concerned with acquiring friends of the flesh-and-blood variety, as true friendship can't be bought at any price.

It's only natural to assume that a book entitled *Savvy Investing for Women* is chiefly concerned with helping today's woman acquire as much material wealth as possible. I steadfastly maintain my conviction that money is a vehicle of freedom. As much as I want each woman reading this book to enjoy the best of everything life has to offer, the ultimate freedom is the ability to make a real and lasting difference in the lives of others.

One of my friend's daughters recently asked her mother for seed capital to start up her new "pog" business. "Pogs" are cards that bear the likeness of various cartoon characters. Her peers were trading "pogs" in the same way that previous generations traded baseball cards. While I'm pleased that a seven-year-old already has such an enterprising nature, I'm far more impressed by the reason she decided to start up her new pog business. The home of one of her schoolmates had just been destroyed by a fire, and she's using all of her proceeds to help the young girl and her family in their time of need.

Those who are able to enrich the lives of others are richer by far. Now that women are beginning to share the power once almost exclusively held by men, we have the ability to use that power with love and compassion. Let me leave you with one final thought:

> When I despair, I remember that all through history the way of truth and love has always won. There have been tyrants and murderers, and for a time they can seem invincible, but in the end they always fall. Think of it ... always.
>
> *Mohandas "Mahatma" Ghandi*
> *(1869-1948)*

INDEX

Abnormal distribution, meaning of, 11-12
Acampora, Ralph, 112-15
Accumulated depreciation, 88
Acid test ratio, 91, 95
Active investing, 168-69
Advance/decline line, 109
Advisor, investment, choosing, 219-34
  AIMR standards, 230
  bad advice, reasons for, 219-20
  broker, selecting, 224-26
  characteristics to look for, 220-21
  money managers, 229-33
    AIMR standards, 230
    alpha factor, 232
    beta factor, 231
    fees, 231
    performance records reviewed, 232-33
    Sharpe ratio, 232
    standard deviations in portfolios, 231
  Performance Presentation Standard, 230
  registered investment advisor, 226-28
    charges of, 228
    as "personal shopper," 227
    selecting, 228-29
  registered representative, 222-24
  wrap accounts, 223, 227
Allen Patricof Associates, 209
Alpha factor, 203, 232
America Online, 160
American Academy of Matrimonial Attorneys,
  263
American Depository Receipts (ADRs), 217
American Stock Exchange, 42-43
  listings, 45
  sample, 52-53
"Angel" financing, 212-14
Annuity for retirement, 285
Anthony, Susan B., 249-50
Arbitration clause, 238
Art collection for enjoyment, 320-25
  furniture, 321-25 (see also Furniture)
Assets, 85-88
  allocation, 255-57
Association for Investment Management and
  Research (AIMR), 230

Back-end sales load, 164
Balance sheet, 77
Bank of United States, 41
Barney, Charles, 121
Barron's, 64, 112, 302
  Financial Table for Mortgages, 272
Basics, financial, for every woman, 1-17
  exports, 8-9
  Fed watchers, 5
  Federal Reserve Bank, 12-14
  fiscal policy, 6, 13
  Green, Hetty Robinson, 1-3
  gross domestic product, 7-9
  gross national product (GNP), 7
  imports, 8-9
  inflation, 11-12
  interest rate, 5-6, 12-14
  investing, 9-16
  monetary policy, 6, 13
  recession, 9
  S&P 500 index, 10
  stock market, 9-16 (*see also* Stock market)
  Treasury bill, 14
  understand fully before investing, 4-5
Bear market, 98
Beating the Street, 256
Beck, Marcia, interview with, 131-35
Berke, Allan J., 262-65
Beta factor, 176, 231
Bibliowicz, Jessica, 302-4
Blue chip, 180
Bonds, buying, 27-30, 137-58
  bond rating agencies, 143
  coupons, 139
  definition, 139
  duration, 142
  government, 142, 146-49
  indenture, 145, 151
  needs, suiting by choice of bonds, 146-58
  par, 140
  premium, 145
  Russian Imperial Bonds, disaster of, 137-38,
    151
  risks, five forms of, 139-46
    call, 145

Bonds, buying, risks *(cont.)*
  credit, 143-44
  event, 146
  interest-rate, 139-42
  liquidity, 144-45
  types, 146-58
  convertible, 156-57
  corporate, 149-52
  "fallen angels," 155-56
  federally sponsored credit agency, 149
  high-yield ("junk"), 155-56
  municipal, 152-55 (*see also* Municipal bonds)
  U.S. government, 146-49
  zero coupon, 157-58
Book value, 85, 89-90, 91, 92
Borrowability, 198
Breakouts, 106
Broker:
  calling to buy stock, 47
  choosing, 57-66 (*see also* Brokerage house)
  loan rate, 196
  questions to ask, twenty-five, 115-18
  selecting, 224-26
Brokerage house, choosing, 57-66
  churning, 65
  commissions, 65-66
  discount brokerages, 63-64
  female investment advisors, 64-65
  full-service, 57-63
    brokerage unit, 60
    derivatives, 60
    financial analysts, 62
    fixed income, 60
    high-yield bonds, 60
    investment banking division, 61
    operations of, 59-63
    red herring, 62
  on-line shopping, 64
  recommendation critical, 58
  regional brokerages, 63
  Securities Investors Protection Corp., 58
  women-run investment firms, 64-65
Bucket shops, 222
Bull market, 98, 99
Buying home, 266-73 (*see also* Real estate investment)
Buying stock, 41-56 (*see also* Shopping for stocks)

Cable, Jacqueline, 320-25
Call risk in bonds, 145
Capital appreciation, 27
Capital gains, 168
Capitalization level in mutual fund, 175
Capitalization ratio, 91, 96
Cash reserves, 27-30
Certificates of deposit (CDs), 127-28
Charitable contributions, 278-81
  charitable lead trusts, 281
  charitable remainder trusts, 281
  donor-advised funds, 281

  personal rewards from, 278-79
  tax benefits, 279-81
  wealth replacement trusts, 281
Charts, understanding, 97-118 (*see also* Technical analysis)
"Chasing the stock," 48
Checking accounts, 12-23
Children, arranging for custody of, 265
China as emerging market, 216
Schreider, Harold, 113
Churning, 65
Closing costs, 269
College tuition blues, overcoming, 273-77
  costs, computing, 274-275
  investing, 275-77
  loans, 277
  mutual funds, 275-77
  Perkins loan, 277
  Stafford loans, 277
  UGMA/UTMA custodial account, 276
  zero coupon bonds, 275
Combs, Wilhelmina McEwan, 314-20
Commissions, 65-66
Commodities traders, 205-7 (*see also* High roller stakes)
Common stock net, 89
Common stocks, 27-30
Communications, current revolution in, 36
Con artists, avoiding, 235-47
  advice, 239
  arbitration clause, 238
  case histories, 240-42
  character and track record of money advisor, checking out, 236
  double-dipping, 236
  educating yourself, 246
  "exclusivity" ploy of salespeople, 236
  flattery and intimidation, 236, 239
  IPOs, caution about, 244
  penny stock operators, 242-44
  scams, categories of, 246-47
  where they are, 235-38
  "women's intuition," 239
Condominiums, 267
Confirmation, 49
  settlement date, 49
Consumer Price Index (CPI), 29, 34
Consumer Reports, 164
Convertible bonds, 156-57
Cooperatives, 267
Corporate bonds, 149-52
  subordinated debenture, 151
Coupons, bond, 139
Covariance, 252
Credit risk in bonds, 143-44
Crises, historical, 119-20
Current ratio, 90-91, 95

Death taxes, 289-91 (*see also* Will, preparing)
Defined benefit plans, 282
Defined contribution plans, 282-83
Depreciation, accumulated, 88

Derivatives, 60, 193-95 (see also High roller stakes)
Diamonds, investing in for enjoyment, 325-28
  carats, 326-27
  clarity, 326
  color, 325-26
  cut, 326
  loop, 327
Dimensional Fund Advisors, 167
Discount brokerages, 63-64
Discount rate, Federal Reserve, 123
Diversification, 19-39, 51
  bonds, 27
  cash reserves, 27
  changing times, 36-37
  common stocks, 27
  communications, current revolution in, 36
  Consumer Price Index (CPI), 29, 34
  diversified portfolio, creating, 25-27
  expectations, Wall Street and, 30-34
  history after Revolution, role of possible bankruptcy in, 19-21
  inflation, 34
  life cycles of industries, 38
  manias, 34-35
  Murphy's Law, 16, 26
  mutual funds, 29
  national financial system as determinant of all market risk, 21
  nonsystematic risk, 34
  options, knowing, 27-30
  price/earnings ratio, 31-32
  recap. 39
  risks and rewards, 21-22
  risks in stocks, six reasons for, 39
  savings account, 22
    Federal Deposit Insurance Company (FDIC), 22
  systematic risk, 30, 33
  Treasury bills, 22
  value of, 24-25
  volatility of investments, 22-24
Dividend reinvestment plan (DRIP), 253
Dividends, 27
Divorce, 261-65
  attorney, 265
  children, 265
  marriage contract, 262
  prenuptial, 263-65 (see also Prenuptial agreement)
Dollar-cost averaging, 183
Donations, 278-81 (see also Charitable contributions)
Donor-advised funds, 281
Double-dipping, 236
Dow, Charles, 53, 98
Dow Jones Industrial Average, 53-55
  Dow Theory, 54-55, 98-99
  Industrials, 53-55
  Transportation, 54-55, 98
  Utilities, 55
Downtrendline, 102, 104

Drexel Burnham, 59
DRIP, 253
Due diligence, meaning of, 212
Duff & Phelps bond rating agency, 143
Durable goods, 7

Earnings growth, 79-83
Efficient Market Theory, 166
Emerging markets, investing in, 214-18 (see also High roller stakes)
Equitable Distribution Statute, 264
Estate taxes, 290-91
Evaluating stock investment, 90-92 (see also Winners, picking and avoiding losers)
  "hot tips," 92-96
Event risk in bonds, 146
"Exclusivity" ploy of salespeople, 236
Executor/executrix of will, 288-89
Exports, 8-9

Fairchild, Sherman, 207-8
"Fallen angels," 155
FDIC, 22,122
Fed Watchers, 5
Federal Deposit Insurance Company (FDIC), 22, 122
Federal Home Loan Mortgage Corp. ("Freddie Mac"), 131, 149
Federally sponsored credit agency bonds, 149
Federal National Mortgage Association ("Fannie Mae"), 149
Federal Reserve Bank, role of, 12-14
Federal Reserve System:
  monetary policy, 6, 12-14
  responsibility of, 6
Female investment advisors, 64-65
Fidelity, 95, 129, 181, 190, 275-76, 283-84
  Contra Fund, 162
  Magellan Fund, 162, 181, 256
Financial consultant, 222-24
Fiscal policy, 6, 13
Fitch Investor Service, 143
Fixed income, 60
Flattery by money manager, rejecting, 236, 239
Foreign exchange as concern in stock market investing, 16
401(k) plans, 283-84
Fraud as concern in stock market, 16
Freeman, Jane, 298-302
Fruits of the poisonous tree doctrine, 264
Fundamental analysis, 77, 97
  broker's reliance on, 225
Furniture investing for enjoyment, 321-25
  American, 324-25
  English, 323
  French, 322

Global Depository Receipts (GDRs), 217
Goodwill, 87
Green, Hetty Robinson, 1-3
Gross domestic product (GDP), 7-9
Gross national product (GNP), 7

Gross profit margin, 70, 73, 78
Group breakout, 113
Growth rate, 95
Growth stocks in mutual funds, 170-72, 179-80
Guaranteed investment contract (GIC), 283
Guardian for children, providing for in will, 291

Hamilton, Alexander, 19-20
Hedge funds, 197-204 (see also High roller stakes)
   types, thirteen, 200-3
Heinz, F. Augustus, 120
Hennessee Hedge Fund Advisory Group, 204
High roller stakes, 193-218
   derivatives, 60, 193-195
      broker loan rate, 196
      definition, 194
      not for individual investor, 194-95
      LEAPS, 195
      options, examining, 195
   emerging markets, 214-18
      American Depository Receipts (ADRs), 217
      China, 216
      definition, 214
      fund, investing in, 218
      Global Depository Receipts (GDRs), 217
      investment, minimum, of $1,000, 218
      methods for, 217-18
      risk, examining, 216-17
      where they are, 215-16
   hedge funds, 197-204
      alpha factor, 203
      borrowability, 198
      cautions, 197
      convertible arbitrage, 202
      distressed, 202
      emerging markets, 203
      fixed income, 203
      funds of funds, 203
      growth, 201
      leveraging, 203
      macro, 201
      manager, 199-200
      market neutral, 202
      opportunistic, 201
      returns and risk associated with, 204
      risk arbitrage, 202-3
      sector funds, 203
      short only, 201-2
      shorting a stock, 198-99
      value, 201
   LEAPS, 195, 197
   managed futures, 204-7
      commodities traders, 205-7
      exposure, 206
      stop loss orders, 206
      technicals, 205
   margin accounts, 196
      margin call, 196
      ups and downs of, 196-97
      minimum maintenance equity level, 196

private equity, 212-14
venture capital, 207-12
   due diligence on company management, 212
   entrepreneurs, selecting, 211
   example: Federal Express, 210-11
   life cycle, 209-10
   new to marketplace, 210
   one-company deals discouraged, 211
High-yield ("junk") bonds, 60, 155-56
Home, purchase of, 266-73 (see also Real estate investment)
Homeowner's insurance, 268
Horse racing industry, guidance for investing in, 314-20

Ibbotson, Roger, 175
Imports, 8-9
Income statement, 76-79
Indenture, 145, 151
Individual Retirement Accounts (IRAs), 284
Inflation, 11-12
Inheritance taxes, 290-91
Insiders, 111-15
Institutional ownership, 114
Insurance, real estate, 268
Intangible assets, 87
Interest rate, 5-6, 12-14
   risk, 139-42
Intimidation by money manager, rejecting, 236
Inventories, 86, 289
Investment Act of 1940, 197
Investment advisor, choosing, 219-34 (see also Advisor, investment, choosing)
Investment risk: 1926-1994 (table), 258
Investment tools, "worry-free," 119-35
   Beck, Marcia, interview with, 131-35
   certificates of deposit, 127-28
   checking and savings accounts, 122-23
   crises, historical, 119-20
      Barney, Charles, 121
      Heinz, F. Augustus, 120
   Federal Deposit Insurance Corp., 122
   Federal Reserve System, initiation of, 122
   liquidity, 132
   money market funds, 128-30
      Fidelity Daily Income Trust, 129
      first-tier and second-tier, 129-30
      government, 130-31
      municipal, 133
      net asset value, 129
   Morgan, J.P., influence of, 119-22
   Orange County, CA default, 134-35
   Regulation Q, 128
   Treasury bills, 124-27, 131-35
   Treasury-only money market funds, 131
   yield curves, understanding, 123-24
      discount rate, 123
Investor's Business Daily, 44-45, 84, 115, 302
IRAs, 284

Janis, Fran, 208-11
Jones, Edward, 53

"Junk" bonds, 60, 155-56

Keogh plan, 285
Knight, Joseph, 325-28
Kovel's Complete Antique Price List, 321
Kubin, Nicole, 212-14

LEAPS, 195, 197
Lender for mortgage, finding, 270-71
Leveraging, 196, 203
Liabilities, 85
Life cycles of industries, 38
Life issues, 261-91
    marriage contract, 262
Limit order, 51
Lindstrom, Maren, 295-98
Liquidity, 131
    risk in bonds, 144-45
Load funds, 162-64
Loans for child's education, 277
    Parent Loan for Undergraduate Students
        (PLUS), 277
    Perkins loan, 277
    Stafford loan, 277
Long-term capital gains, 168
Lynch, Peter, 95, 162, 191-92, 243, 256

Magellan Fund, 95, 129, 162
Major market (primary) trends, 98-99
    accumulated phase, 99, 108
    distribution phase, 99, 108
    second phase (bull market model), 99
Management fees for mutual funds, 164
Manias, 34-35
Margin accounts, 196
    margin call, 196
    ups and downs of, 196-97
Market capitalization (valuation), 93-96
Marketable securities, 86
Marriage contract, 262
    and prenuptial, difference between, 262
Medric, Cindy, 115
Milken, Michael, 155-56
Minimum maintenance equity level, 196
Mismanagement as concern in stock market
        investing, 16
Modern Portfolio Theory, 252
Monetary policy, 6, 13
Money, 294
Money Manager Review, 232
Money managers, shopping for, 229-33 (see
        also Advisor, investment, closing)
Money market funds, 128-30 (see also
        Investment tools, "worry free")
    government, 130-31
    municipal, 133
Moody's Investor Services, 143
Moore, Gordon, 208
Morgan, J.P., 119-22
Morningstar Inc., 176-77, 185
Morningstar Mutual Fund Report, 177
Mortgage insurance, 268
Mortgages, 269

fixed-rate vs. adjustable-rate, 270-71
Moving averages, plotting, 108-9
Municipal bonds, 27, 152-55
    equivalent taxable yield, 153
    general obligation (GO), 152
    insurance for, 154
    money market funds, 155
    steps before investing, 154
    tax exemption of, 153-54
    tax effects, 155
Murphy's Law, 16, 26, 100, 190, 205, 255
Mutual funds, 29, 56, 159-92
    buying, how and where, 181-90
        bond funds, 189-90
        dollar cost averaging, 183
        foreign funds, 189
        funds with excellent performance record,
            185-88
        Janus, 181-83
        programmed basis, 183
        record, studying, 184-89
        Worldwide Funds, 188-89
    capitalization, 175
    for child's education, 275-77
    diversification, 161
    handling, 191-92
    language of, 179-81
    manager's style, analyzing, 170-74
        example: Citicorp, 174
        growth, 170-72
        value, 172-74
    popularized in 1970s, 161
    price tag of, evaluating, 162-65
        back-end sales load, 164
        "load" or "no load" variety, 162-64
        management fees, 164
        12B-1 fee, 164-65
    ratings, 176-77
        bell curve system, 177
        Morningstar Inc., 176-77
    returns, 177-78
    risk, 176
        beta factor, 176
        standard deviation, 176
    style, 165-70
        active investing, 168-69
        active vs. passive, choosing, 169-70
        capital gains, short-term and long-term, 168
        Dimensional Fund Advisors, 167
        Efficient Market Theory, 166
        passive investing, 165-68
        S&P 500 Index as benchmark, 165-66
        Vanguard, 165-68
    terms, 179-81
    timing, 190-91

NASDAQ Composite, 57
National Association of Securities Dealers, 226,
        239,242, 244
    Automated Quotation System (NASDAQ), 43
NDZ-100, 57
Net profit margin, 70, 73, 78-79
Net worth, 85

Neutral trendline, 102, 105
New York Stock Exchange:
  "The Big Board," 45
  establishment of, 1
  history, 41-42
  listings, 45-47
  minimum maintenance equity level, 196
  sample, 45-47
New York Times, 44, 181
No-load funds, 162-64
Nondurable goods, 7
Nonoperating income, 79
Nonsystematic risk, 34
Noyce, Robert, 208

O'Neill, William, 45, 84
Odd lots, 44
On-line shopping, 64
Operating margin, 70, 73, 78, 83-84, 96
Oscillating trendline, 102, 205
Over-the-counter market (OTC), 43
  listings, 45
  sample, 50-51

Parent Loan for Undergraduate Students
    (PLUS), 277
Passive investing, 165-68
  Efficient Market Theory, 166
Pension plans, 282
Penny stock operators, 242-43
Perkins loan, 277
Peter Lynch Method, 296
PLUS, 277
Points, 269
Portfolio, 52
Preferred stock, 180
Prenuptial agreement, 263-65
  active appreciation, 264
  children, 265
  Equitable Distribution Statute, 264
  fruits of the poisonous tree doctrine, 264
  and marriage contract, difference between,
      262
  passive appreciation, 264
Pretax profit margin, 70
Price/earnings ratio, 31-32, 94, 95
Price-to-book ratio, 94-95
Price-to-sales ratio, 94, 105, 299-300
Primary trends, 98-99 (*see also* Major market
    [primary] trends)
Private equity investing, 212-14
Probating will, 288
Pullback, 99
Purvis, Kim, 304-7

Quantum Fund, 201

Real estate investment, 266-73
  affordability, determining, 271-73
  condominiums, 267
  cooperatives, 267
  costs, adding up, 268-70

    closing costs, 269
    insurance, 268
    mortgage, 269
    points, 269
  lender, finding, 270-71
  mortgages, fixed-rate vs. adjustable-rate,
      270-71
  single-family home, 267
Receivables, 86
Recession, 9
Red herring, 62
Regional brokerages, 63
Registered investment advisor, 226-28 (*see also*
    Advisor, investment, choosing)
Registered representative, 222-24
Regulation Q, 128
Reichenbach, Inge, 278
Relative strength, 109
Reserves, 123
Resistance, 106-7
Retained earnings, 89-90
Retirement, planning for, 281-87
  future values of money saved, 286
  reasons for, 281-82
  tax incentives, 282-87
    annuity, 285
    defined benefit plans, 282
    defined contribution plans, 282-83
    401(k) plan, 283-84
    guaranteed investment contract (GIC), 283
    IRAs, 284
    Keogh plan, 285
    pension plans, 282
    Roth IRA, 284
    SEP-IRA, 295
    stock in employee's company, 283
Return on equity, 92
Risk, learning to live with, 249-60
  Anthony, Susan B. example, 249-50
  asset allocation, 255-57
    interest rates, 256
    past performance, 256-57
  pragmatic aspect of, 250-55
    choices, 254-55
    covariance, 252
    diversification, balancing, 252-53
    Modern Portfolio Theory, 252
    one-year holding periods, maximum and
        minimum values of, 251
    risk return analysis, five-year period, 254
  tolerance level, individual, 257-60
    investment risk: 1926-1994 (table), 258
Risk in bonds, five forms of, 139-46 (*see also*
    Bonds, buying)
Risk in mutual funds, 176
  beta factor, 176
  standard deviation, 176
Rock, Arthur, 208
Roth IRA, 284
Rothschild, John, 192
Round lots, 44
Rukeyser, Louis, 112

Russell Index, 57
  2000 Index, 167, 230

S&P 500 index, 10
  as benchmark for portfolio performance,
    165-66
Sales growth, 82-83
Savings accounts, risk-free, 22, 122-23
Scams, categories of, 246-47 (see also Con
    artists, avoiding)
Scheiber, Anne, 74-75, 233, 294
Schwab, Charles, 63-64, 171, 224, 283-84
Securities and Exchange Commission, 61, 239,
    244
  money market funds, 130
  registered representative, 222-24
Securities Investors Protection Corp., 58
Self, rewarding, 313-29
  art collection, 320-25
    furniture, 321-25
  diamonds, 325-28 (see also Diamonds,
    investing in for enjoyment)
  enriching others' lives as "best investment,"
    328-29
  horse racing, investing in, 314-20
Selloff, 99
Sentiment indicators, 111-12
SEP-IRA, 285
Services as part of GDP, 7-8
Settlement date, 49
Sharpe, William E., 232
Sharpe ratio, 232
"She Brokers," 65
Shopping for stocks, 41-66
  American Stock Exchange, 42-43, 52-53
  broker and brokerage house, choosing, 57-66
  Dow Jones, 53-55 (see also Dow Jones
    Industrial Average)
  Dow Theory, 54-55
  how and where to buy a stock, 44-53
    broker, trustworthy, 47-49
    "chasing the stock," 48
    confirmation, 49
    diversification, 51
    Investor's Business Daily, 44-45
    limit order, 51
    listings, reading, 45-47
    neatness critical, 52-53
    New York Times, 44
    odd lots, 44
    portfolio, 52
    round lots of 100 shares, 44
    Wall Street Journal, 44
  indices, other, 55-57
    mutual funds, 56
    NASDAQ Composite, 57
    NDX-100, 57
    Russell Index, 57
    Standard & Poor's 500 Index, 55-56
  National Association of Securities Dealers
    Automated Quotation System, 43

New York Stock Exchange, 41-42, 45-47
  history, 41-42
  over-the-counter market, 43, 50-51
  Wall Street as first exclusive men's club, 41
  history, 41-42
Short-term capital gains, 168
Siebert, Muriel, 65
Sinquefield, Rex, 175
Soros, George, 200, 201
Spinner, Art, 307-9
Stafford loans, 277
Standard deviation, 176
Standard & Poor 500 Index, 10, 55-56
  Barra Value Index, 167
  bond rating agency, 143
Statement of cash flow, 77
Stock market, 9-16
  chart, learning to read, 45-47
  competitive forces in, 16
  concerns about, 16
  and legalized gambling, comparison to, 15
  not just for rich, 15
  requirements for investing, 15-16
Stockholders' equity, 85, 89-90, 91, 92
Stop loss orders, 206
Student Loan Marketing Association (Sallie
    Mae), 131, 149
Subordinated debenture, 151
Support, 106-7
  downside breakout, 106
Systematic risk, 30, 33

T-bills, 14, 124-27, 131-35
  as risk-free, 22
Tax waiver, 289
Taxes, 287-88
Technical analysis, beginner's guide to, 97-118
  advance/decline line, 109
  broker, what to ask, 115-18
  charts, using to depict marketplace, 100-10
    daily bar chart, 102
    intermediate-term chart, 102
    long-term chart, 102
    moving averages, plotting, 108-9
    stock movement, charting, 108
    trendlines, drawing, 102-5
  Dow Theory, 98-99
    correction phases, minor, 99
    major market (primary) trends, 98-99 (see
      also Major market [primary] trend)
    pullback, 99
    secondary trends (correction phases), 98-
      99
    selloff, 99
  evaluating indicators, 112-15
    Acampora, Ralph, 112-15
    insiders, 111-15
    institutional ownership, 114
    media as influence, 111
    moving averages, plotting, 108-9
    negative divergence, 109
    oscillating market, 109
    perception as 90% of reality, 110

Technical analysis, beginner's guide*(cont.)*
prediction of ups and downs, 110-11
questions, to ask broker, 115-18
reaction low point, 106
relative strength, 109
sentiment indicators, 111-12
support and resistance phenomenon, 106-7
downside breakout, 106
as tool, 98
trending market, 109
volatility of stocks, excellent for predicting,
100
Technicals, 205
Templeton Organization, 214
Testator/testatrix, 288
Tolerance level of individual for risk, 257-60
Tools, investment, 119-35 (*see also* Investment
tools)
Treasury bills, 14, 124-27, 131-35
as risk-free investment, 22
Treasury bonds and notes, 146-49
Treasury-only money market funds, 131-35
Trendlines, drawing, 102-5
Trust, using to reduce estate tax, 291
"Tulip mania," 34-35
12B-1 fee for mutual funds, 164-65

UGMA/UTMA custodial account, 276
Unified estate credit, 290-91
Uniform Gifts/Transfers to Minors Act, 276
Uptrendline, 102-3

Value investing, 84-90, 172-74
assets, 85-88
accumulated depreciation, 88
current, 86
goodwill, 87
intangibles, 87
inventories, 86
long-term, 87
marketable securities, 86
receivables, 86
common stock net, 89
example: Citicorp, 174
liabilities, 85, 88-89
net worth, 85
retained earnings, 89-90
stockholders' equity, 85, 89-90
Value Line, 252
Vanguard Group, 256
passive investing, 165-68
Windsor, 162
Venture capitalists, 207-12 (*see also* High roller
stakes)
Volatility of investments, 22-24

Wall Street Journal, 44, 98, 302
Wall Street Week, 112
Wealth, accumulating, 293-311
case studies of experts:
Bibliowicz, Jessica, 302-4
Freeman, Jane, 298-302

Lindstrom, Maren, 295-98
Purvis, Kim, 304-7
Spinner, Art, 307-9
diversification the answer, 309-10
Wealth replacement trusts, 281
Will, preparing, 288-91
death taxes, 289-91
definition, 288
estate taxes, 290-91
executor/executrix, 288-89
guardian for children, 291
inheritance tax, 290-91
inventory, 289
probating, 288
tax waiver, 289
testator/testatrix, 288
trust, using to reduce estate tax, 291
unified estate credit, 290-91
Wilshire 4500 Index, 166
Wilshire 5000 Index, 167
Winners, picking and avoiding losers, 67-96
assets, 85-88
balance sheet, 77
"darling" of Wall Street, 80-82
earnings growth, 79-83
evaluating, 90-92
acid test ratio, 91, 95
capitalization ratio, 91, 96
current ratio, 90-91, 95
return on equity, 92
fundamental analysis, 77
gross profit margin, 70, 73, 78
growth rate, 95
homework critical to do in advance, 74-75
"hot tips," evaluating, 92-96
income statement (Intel), 76-79
investment dollars, who gets, 75-76
liabilities, 85, 88-89
market capitalization (valuation), 93-96
net profit margin, 70, 73, 78-79
net worth, 85
nonoperating income, 79
operating profit margin, 70, 73, 78, 83-84, 96
pretax profit margin, 70
price/earnings ratio, 94, 95
price-to-book ratio, 94
price-to-sales ratio, 94, 95
sales growth, 82-83
statement of cash flow, 77
stockholders' equity, 85, 89-90, 91,92
summary, 95-96
value investing, 84-90 (*see also* Value investing)
Women-run investment firms, 64-65
Woodhull, Victoria, 65
Worth magazine, 192, 243
Wrap accounts, 223, 227

Yield curves, understanding, 123-24

Zero coupon bonds, 157-58
for child's education, 275